Out of

Welsh Experience of the Great War
1914-1918
in Poetry and Prose

Out of the Fire of Hell

Welsh Experience of the Great War

1914-1918

in Poetry and Prose

Edited by
Alan Llwyd

Gomer

Picture Acknowledgements

Imperial War Museum: title page, xiv, 54, 96, 128, 160, 206, 258, 260, 282, 287, 302, 310, 312, 315, 317; *London Illustrated News:* 2; Mair Saunders Jones:14; University of Wales, Bangor, Archives: 119; Gwynedd Archive: 229, 232; Sioned O'Connor: 278.

Published in 2008 by
Gomer Press, Llandysul, Ceredigion SA44 4JL
www.gomer.co.uk

ISBN 978 1 84323 890 4

A CIP record for this title is available from the British Library

This book is published with the financial support of the
Welsh Books Council.

Printed and bound in Wales at
Gomer Press, Llandysul, Ceredigion

'Holocaust of Youth'
(After reading Great War issues of a national newspaper)

They stare at us through badly faded print,
with horror and with hate, with haunting eyes,
some soft as dawn, and some as hard as flint.
Their names are scrolled along the page, like flies

caught on fly-paper, long before they were
chiselled as deep as wounds on patient stones;
so many names, and so much weight to bear:
the village green memorial almost groans.

And yet, it seems so strange, almost uncouth,
that this debauchery of innocents,
this ceremonial butchery of youth,
is casually found amidst advertisements

for flower shows, bazaars and garden-fêtes,
the latest Chaplin film at the flea-bitten
local Palladium, the current going rates
for secretarial work. History is written

somewhere between the tips for motorists
and the hackneyed phrases of the editorial,
where names of dead appear in endless lists
(each issue in itself a war memorial).

The library is now about to close.
We reach Armistice Day with hardly a hint
that a whole world was lost along with those
who stare at us through badly faded print.

Alan Llwyd

Contents

Acknowledgements

I wish to thank the following for their invaluable assistance in the work of collecting material for this anthology: Dr Huw Walters, Senior Library Assistant in the Department of Printed Books at the National Library of Wales, Aberystwyth; Dr Jason Walford Davies, Senior Lecturer in the School of Welsh at the University of Wales Bangor; Dr Robert Griffith Jones; Einion Thomas, Archivist at the University of Wales Bangor; Camille Rosier and Dafydd Llwyd.

I also wish to thank Ceri Wyn Jones, English language editor at Gomer Press, for his enthusiasm and assistance concerning this project, and to Gomer Press in general for undertaking to publish the anthology.

All efforts have been made to delete inconsistencies in this book, but I have left 'Welsh/Welch' in 'Royal Welsh/Welch Fusiliers' exactly as used by individual authors. Both spellings are legitimate. I also wish to state that all translations from Welsh are my own.

Most of the material that appears in this anthology is out of copyright. Every effort has been made to trace copyright holders of other material included in this book. The publishers apologise if any material has been included without permission and would be pleased to hear from anyone who has not been consulted. In some instances our correspondences were not answered, and we therefore assumed that there was no objection to our intention to include certain material in the book.

The editor and the publishers wish to thank the following: University of Wales Press and Mair Saunders Jones for permission to quote from the letters of Saunders Lewis as published in *Saunders Lewis: Letters to Margaret Gilcriest*, edited by Mair Saunders Jones, Ned Thomas and Harri Pritchard Jones (1993); Oxford University Press for permission to quote from *Wilfred Owen: Collected Letters*, edited by Harold Owen and John Bell (1967); Random House Archive and Library for permission to reproduce '1914' by Wilfred Owen; Carcanet Press Limited for permission to use 'Goliath and David' and 'Sospan Fach' by Robert Graves, also the two extracts from *Goodbye to All That* (1929) and 'First Time In' by Ivor Gurney; Sioned O'Connor for permission to include the translations of the poems and prose of A. E. Jones (Cynan); and Mrs R. Vellender for kindly allowing us to use the works of Edward Thomas, her grandfather.

Alan Llwyd

Introduction

When Britain declared war against Germany on August 4, 1914, Wales, as part of the British Empire, was immediately and automatically drawn into what was to become an enormous worldwide conflict which would last for more than four years. Before the outbreak of the Great War, Wales had little to do with militarism. There were several Welsh regiments in the British Regular Army, but even Welsh regiments such as the Royal Welsh Fusiliers were mainly composed of non-Welshmen. It has been suggested that only 10% of infantry men belonging to the Royal Welsh Fusiliers were actually Welsh. The vast majority came from England. There was, on the other hand, a stronger tradition of militarism amongst the aristocracy and the landed gentry of Wales, and Welsh regiments had many Welsh officers who came from a privileged background, for example, two writers who have been included in this anthology, Eliot Crawshay-Williams and Colwyn Philipps, both educated at Eton and both professional soldiers before the outbreak of the war; but ordinary Welsh infantrymen were comparatively scarce.

Wales had a strong Nonconformist tradition before the outbreak of the First World War, and the Welsh chapels were, understandably, much opposed to war. There was also a strong peace movement in Wales, and politicians such as the pacifist Henry Richard, the 'Apostle of Peace', were held in high esteem by the Welsh people. Also the socialist movement was quick to gain a foothold in Wales from the turn of the twentieth century onwards, especially in the industrialised South. Many Welsh socialists believed that war gave profiteers and capitalists an ideal opportunity to grow richer. Other Welshmen, especially nationalists and supporters of 'Home Rule' who were committed to preserving the Welsh language and safeguarding Welsh identity, considered militarism of any kind to be a very 'English' trait, a means of maintaining and extending the British Empire.

It is therefore incredible to this day that the Welsh responded in such large numbers to the call to arms. The population of Wales at the outbreak of the Great War was two-and-a-half million; of the 400,000 Welshmen who were between the military age of 20 and 40, it is estimated that 280,000 participated in the war. This is a staggering figure, and no wonder Lloyd George said, after the war, that 'Our brave Welsh regiments have upheld the honour and the glory of Wales on many a battlefield, and have proved that the sons of liberty can endure in the defence of their principles every trial of modern warfare.' 'Welshmen are lovers of peace,' he continued, 'but they are defenders of liberty, and so long as the hills of Wales stand out from our shining valleys, so long will the honour of our race be upheld by its hardy sons.'[1]

The military correspondent of the *Western Mail* praised Wales, on the first day of Peace, for its 'splendid recruiting record, which, according to the latest official statistics divulged by Sir Auckland Geddes [Minister of National Service], works out at 13.77 per cent of the population, as compared with 13.30 per cent, recruited in England, 13.0 in Scotland, and 3.87 in Ireland.'[2] These figures were more or less confirmed in *Wales: Its Part in the War*, published in 1919, which estimated that the manpower supplied by Wales to the Armed Services constituted 13.82 per cent of the nation's population, a record unequalled by either England, Scotland or Ireland. According to the authors of *Wales: Its Part in the War*, Ivor Nicholson and Trevor Lloyd-Williams, 'These figures speak for themselves and show how eagerly the men of Wales came forward to do battle for the cause of freedom and liberty.'[3]

Why, then, did the Welsh react so positively and so enthusiastically to the call to arms? The main factor was David Lloyd George, generally acknowledged in Wales at the time as 'the Greatest Welshman of his day', if not ever. Lloyd George was a brilliant politician and was considered a great benefactor. He never missed an opportunity to justify Britain's participation in the war or to appeal for volunteers from Wales, at political meetings and at public gatherings. The Thursday of the National Eisteddfod week, traditionally the day of the Chairing Ceremony, was also known as 'Lloyd George's Day'. He usually presided at the Thursday afternoon meeting at the Eisteddfod, thrilling and enthralling audiences with eloquence and rhetoric. At the National Eisteddfod of Bangor in 1915, he once again emphasised that the war was a just war. 'Now and again,' he said, 'in the history of the world its peoples have had to fight in order to retain those elementary rights which lift man above the beasts of the field – justice, liberty, righteousness.'[4] Like others before him, he praised the Welsh for their eagerness and readiness to support the war and join the Armed Forces:[5]

> I am proud to know Wales has flung its whole strength into the struggle for humanity. We have a great army already in the battlefield. We have a still greater army ready to support their comrades in the field. There was a time when it seemed as if the military spirit of Wales had vanished into the mists of the past . . . There was a time in the last 200 years or more when we could hardly summon the material for three regiments to the flag; to-day you have a hundred thousand men who have rallied to the flag from the hills and valleys of their native land. We have a greater army from Wales alone than Wellington commanded at Waterloo – and they are just as good men, every one of them . . . Our Welsh martial spirit was not dead. It was not even slumbering. It was simply hiding in its caves amongst the hills until the call came from above.

It was Lloyd George who was mainly responsible for establishing the 38th (Welsh) Division, known as 'Lloyd George's Army', which was to draw so many young Welshmen to the ranks, from the rural Welsh-speaking areas of North Wales as well as the industrialised South. But there were also others factors. He was supported in his views by some of the most eminent Welshmen of the day, such as the poet, critic and scholar, John Morris-Jones, who believed that Germany had committed a murderous and treacherous act by violating Belgian neutrality, and O. M. Edwards, the great educationalist, who also believed that war was justified because it defended the rights of a small nation, and because Prussian militarism had to be checked. And that was another reason why so many Welshmen volunteered for active service. Belgium was a small nation which was being bullied by a much bigger nation, a situation which the Welsh could react to with some empathy.

As Robert Graves has so rightly said in *Goodbye to All That*:[6]

> In peacetime, the regular battalions of the regiment [Royal Welsh Fusiliers], though officered mainly by Anglo-Welshmen of county families, did not contain more than about one Welsh-speaking Welshman in fifty. Most recruits came from Birmingham. The only Harlech man, besides myself, who joined the regiment at the start was a golf caddie. He had got into trouble a short time before for stealing clubs. The chapels held soldiering to be sinful, and in Merioneth the chapels had the last word. Prayers were offered for me by the chapels, not because of the physical dangers I would run in France, but because of the moral dangers threatening me at home. However, when Lloyd George became Minister of Munitions in 1915, and persuaded the chapels that war was a Crusade, we had a sudden tremendous influx of Welshmen from North Wales. They were difficult soldiers, who particularly resented having to stand still while N.C.O.'s swore at them.

Robert Graves also quotes the remarks made by one of his fellow officers, Captain Dunn, in *Goodbye to All That*: 'These Welshmen are peculiar. They won't stand being shouted at. They'll do anything if you explain the reason for it – do and die, but they have to know their reason why. The best way to make them behave is not to give them too much time to think. Work them off their feet.'[7] Others, apart from Robert Graves and his fellow officer, have testified to the reluctance of the ordinary Welsh soldier to be bullied into accepting military protocol and army procedure, such as 'G.J.' in *The Welsh Outlook*. 'The ordinary Welsh recruit,' he wrote, 'if not dealt with sympathetically, is a most difficult man to deal with,' because '[b]eing very self-conscious and easily offended he seems to carry with him a sort of shell; and when an officer or instructor is unnecessarily harsh with him he disappears into this shell. And whilst he is there nothing on earth can move him, and no more useless person lives.' But '[b]e patient with him and you have a plodder . . . a man who is always reliable.'[8]

Even if the Welsh were reluctant soldiers, it seems that they were courageous fighters. Charles Pritchard Clayton saw many similarities between French and Welsh soldiers:[9]

> In the calm self-reliance and disregard of danger, and equal disregard of external discipline in a crisis; in their impatience with what they regard as the mere formalities of soldiering the Welshmen, especially the miners of whom there are so many in the Battalion, and the French in these parts at least, seem to see eye to eye. The English Officer fails, I think, to do justice in his own mind to the Welsh miner-soldier, who has no use for the martinet officer, for clean buttons in the trenches, for arms drill and sentry-go, but who, when it comes to fighting, is absolutely imperturbable. In virtue of the very independence of spirit that makes him unhappy on the parade ground, he can be depended upon to take initiative when there is no one at hand to command.

Many of these civilian-soldiers were thinking men. They were not professional soldiers, and theirs was not to do and die unquestioningly without knowing the reason why. Many of them were cultured, articulate and educated men. Others, not so well-educated perhaps, were militant socialists. The Great War produced a vast amount of written testimony because the majority could think and write. Contrary to Captain Dunn's viewpoint in *Goodbye to All That*, that the best way to make the Welsh troops behave was 'not to give them too much time to think,' they did think. And many of them, especially officers, recorded their war experiences. It is exactly that experience that this books sets out to commemorate.

And yet, to suggest that there was no opposition to the war in Wales would be to give the wrong impression. Many did oppose the war, on religious and political grounds. The greatest Welsh poet of the period, T. Gwynn Jones, was well into his forties and not of military age, but he was very much opposed to the war on conscientious and humanitarian grounds. His was a very militant pacifism, or, as he would often say, he was 'a pacifist with the emphasis on the fist.' Other poets, such as T. H. Parry-Williams and the young D. Gwenallt Jones, who was imprisoned as a conscientious objector, were also opposed to the war; and pacifists, such as A. E. Jones (Cynan), Lewis Valentine and David Ellis (who disappeared without a trace in Salonika), joined a specially formed Welsh unit of the R.A.M.C. and served as stretcher-bearers.

Many Welshmen felt that the war was very much a conflict between the major powers, and that it was essentially England's war. Throughout the war years, many referred to it as England's war against Germany. Even the Welsh themselves, Welsh speakers and non-Welsh speakers alike, referred to the Great War as England's war. It shouldn't surprise readers that Welsh identity often got lost during these turbulent years. The fact that many writers refer to England, and 'England's war' and 'England's army' (rather than the British Army) only reflects the complex psychological implications of being part of a vast Empire. It was very much a case of 'For Wales, See England' during the war years, and the fact that the inscription on the memorial at Connah's Quay includes the words, 'What stands if freedom fall, Who Dies if England Live' (from 'For All We Have and Are', Kipling), or that the panel on the Pembroke memorial in west Wales includes the verse:

> Forget us not, O land, for which we fell.
> May it go well with England, still go well.
> Keep her bright banners without spot or stain.
> Lest we should dream that we had died in vain.

shouldn't really surprise us.[10] As the Reverend D. Tecwyn Evans, a well-known figure in Welsh religious and cultural circles at the time, said after the war: 'To some of us Wales seemed to have been almost buried under the weight of Empire and War, and we sometimes feared that she would lose her own soul amid the turmoil and the horror of the world'.[11]

*   *   *

I have included in this anthology writings and recollections by participants who were born in Wales, Welsh-speakers and non-Welsh speakers alike. I have also included writers born in England of Welsh parentage, such as Saunders Lewis, who was brought up speaking Welsh, and others of Welsh parentage, who were not Welsh-speaking.

I should draw attention to a few cases. The first is Edward Thomas. Edward Thomas has always been regarded as a Welshman. He was born of Welsh parents in Lambeth, London, on March 3, 1878. His father, Philip Henry Thomas, was born in Church Street, Tredegar. Edward Thomas's grandfather, Henry Eastaway Thomas, was born in Neath, Glamorganshire, in 1827, and was working and residing at Tredegar, Monmouthshire, by the mid-1850s. He moved with his family from Tredegar to Swindon, probably at the end of the 1870s, to work as an 'engine fitter' with the Great Railway works. His son, Philip Henry Thomas, moved from Swindon to London in 1873 after having entered the Civil Service as a 'supplementary clerk' in May 1873. In 1877, he married his second cousin, Mary Elizabeth Townsend, who had been brought up in Newport, Monmouthshire. They had six sons, of which Edward Thomas was the eldest. It is assumed that Philip Henry spoke Welsh, at least as a child.

Thomas considered himself as being 'mainly Welsh'.[12] He frequently visited friends and relatives in Wales, especially in Newport, Swansea and Pontarddulais.

He became a close friend of J. Gwili Jenkins, the poet and preacher. As Thomas himself once confessed:[13]

> Day by day grows my passion for Wales. It is like a homesickness, but stronger than any homesickness I ever felt – stronger than any passion. Wales indeed, is my soul's native land, if the soul can be said to have a *patria* – or rather, a *matria*, a home with the warm sweetness of a mother's love, and with her influence, too.

As R. George Thomas says in *Edward Thomas: A Portrait*, referring to some of Thomas's early visits to Wales:[14]

> These two Long Vacation holidays at Pontardulais in 1898 and '99 – at the home of his father's first cousin, Philip Treharne Thomas – and a subsequent holiday there with his wife and son immediately after his Oxford days, formed the hard nucleus of Edward Thomas's adult love of Wales, providing memories and perceptions that filtered through into most of his narrative-descriptive sketches as well as the first half of his book *Beautiful Wales*. The intellectual influence of Owen M. Edwards and the staunch friendship of Gwili and John Williams sustained these early impressions that, later, introduced a potent realism into his recreation of moments of insight beneath everyday experiences. The small part of Wales he knew so well continued to give him balance when he needed it in later life.

Edward Thomas has always been regarded as Welsh. Reviewing his *Poems* in *The Welsh Outlook*, 'P.H.T' noted that[15]

> In reading these poems we are all the time kept aware of the Welsh descent of the author. The scenery is most frequently that of England where he happened to be born and to have lived, but the spirit is always essentially Welsh. There is Welsh fancy, Welsh tenderness, Welsh passion, but yet with a feeling of added power that possibly came from his Devonshire pedigree.

'I am interested and attracted to him and his work, firstly, because he was a Welshman; secondly, because he was a poet; and thirdly; because he was a lover of Nature and the countryside,' Lloyd George wrote about 'this young Welsh poet' in John Moore's biography of Edward Thomas.[16]

As regards nationality and identity, Wilfred Owen has always been a borderline case. Both the Welsh and the English have tried to claim him. Owen was born in England, as was Edward Thomas, but, unlike Thomas, Owen had Welsh ancestors rather than Welsh parents, although he was very conscious of his Welsh ancestry. One of his distant ancestors, on his father's side, was Lewis Owen, Sheriff of Merionethshire in 1545-6 and again in 1954-5 and Merioneth's Member of Parliament in 1547, 1553 and 1554. According to Dominic Hibberd:[17]

It was presumably as a result of Tom's stories and the family surname that both Harold and Wilfred Owen believed themselves to be Welsh by distant descent. Wilfred shared the common Victorian view that Celts had poetry and fighting in their veins. When he was on the Hindenburg Line in 1918 he thought of 'my forefathers the agile Welshmen of the Mountains', and Harold [Owen's brother] echoes that in *Journey from Obscurity* by claiming to have heard 'the succouring cry from the mountains' at moments of danger. On the other hand, in bordertowns such as Oswestry and Shrewsbury it was socially more desirable to be English. When Wilfred was described as a Welsh poet in a 1944 radio broadcast, his sister wrote to *The Listener* to say that 'we are an English family'. 'Wilfred . . . would, I feel sure, have mildly resented the suggestion that he was Welsh.' Mary's letter, her only known public utterance, was actually written for her by Harold.

No more details are given about the 1944 radio broadcast, but we know for a fact that Dylan Thomas labelled Owen a Welsh poet in a radio broadcast on January 5, 1946. The subject of his talk was 'Welsh Poets'. According to Thomas: 'Three of the very finest – perhaps *the* very finest it will be found, in another and a quieter day – of the poets who wrote in the two Great Wars of this century were Edward Thomas, Wilfred Owen, and Alun Lewis . . . All three were Welshmen.'[18] Another Anglo-Welsh poet, Dannie Abse, included Owen in his anthology, *Twentieth-Century Anglo-Welsh Poetry*, published in 1997, and several others have also included him in 'Anglo-Welsh' anthologies.

One of the most revealing remarks ever made by Owen himself was his comment, in a letter to his mother, Susan Owen, 'that if there is any power whom the Soldiery execrate more than another it is that of our distinguished countryman,' meaning Lloyd George.[19] Owen once jotted down a list of projects to undertake sometime in the future, on which was included 'To write blank-verse plays on old Welsh themes'.[20] Owen was very conscious of his Welsh roots and background, and would not have 'mildly resented the suggestion that he was Welsh'. It must also be remembered that Owen's dead soldier in 'Futility' had his home in Wales in an earlier draft of the poem.

Owen has another particular and peculiar claim to Welshness. His so-called 'half-rhymes' or pararhymes are thoroughly Welsh in character. This kind of rhyme, in which the first and last consonants of monosyllabic words are identical and the vowels different, is known in Welsh as *proest*. This type of rhyme was commonly used by the professional court poets of the 12th and 13th centuries, and by the master poets who wrote poetry in praise of the Welsh aristocracy during the following three centuries. Many attempts have been made to trace Owen's knowledge of Welsh *proest* rhymes. Both D. S. R. Welland, in his *Wilfred Owen: a Critical Study* (1960), and Cecil Day Lewis in *The Collected Poems of*

Wilfred Owen (1965) suggest that Wilfred Owen had discovered this device for himself. That may well be, but it is difficult to dismiss as a coincidence the fact that Owen was using a type of rhyme much used by his forefathers.

T. E. Lawrence was born in Tremadog, near Porthmadog, North Wales, in 1888. His father, Thomas Chapman, was an Anglo-Irish gentleman landowner, his mother, Sarah Junner, was the illegitimate child of John Lawrence, son of Thomas Lawrence, a Lloyd's surveyor who employed Sarah's mother, Elizabeth Junner, as a servant. Elizabeth Junner was born in Scotland. Sarah Junner was born in Sunderland, County Durham. Her father, John Lawrence, was born at Chepstow in 1843; his father, Thomas, was born at Swansea in 1808, his mother, Sarah, at Chepstow in 1811. T. E. Lawrence's paternal grandparents, therefore, were Welsh. Thomas Chapman abandoned his first wife Edith for Sarah Junner, whom he had appointed as a governess to look after his four daughters. Thomas Chapman and Sarah Junner were never married. They adopted the surname Lawrence, after John Lawrence, Sarah Junner's father, and had five illegitimate sons, of whom T. E. Lawrence was the second. Having a half-Welsh, half-Scottish mother and an Anglo-Irish father, it could hardly be asserted that T. E. Lawrence was English; if anything, he was Welsh.

It seems that Lawrence was conscious of his 'Welshness' at only one phase of his life, and that was during his undergraduate days at Jesus College, Oxford. The fact that he was Welsh-born qualified him to apply for the Meyricke Exhibition in History at Jesus College, a scholarship which was awarded to him in 1907. Reading modern history at Oxford, Lawrence decided to write a thesis comparing the castles of Western Europe with castles built in the Middle East during the Crusades. He wrote to his mother from Caerphilly in April 1907:[21]

> Here I am at my last Welsh castle, and, I think, in most respects my best . . .
>
> Any person wishing to create an attraction or sensation in Wales may appear without a hat. It is always sure to draw. Yesterday for instance 49 people told me that I had no hat (I thought this was obvious?) 6 told me I belonged to the hatless brigade (there is a strong branch of it at Swansea) hundreds (I counted 254 and then stopped) asked me where my hat was; nearly as many asked me if I had lost it, and streetfuls yelled to me that I hadn't got no 'at. I keep no account of Welsh remarks, but they must have been almost as numerous as the English ones.
>
> After ten days in Wales I ought to be able to sum up all the character, habits, peculiarities, virtues, vices, and other points of the Welsh people. I am sorry I cannot do this yet. They seem to me to be rather inquisitive, more dirty, and exceedingly ugly. I am at last discovering where I got my large mouth from. It's a national peculiarity.

The comment 'I keep no account of Welsh remarks, but they must have been almost as numerous as the English ones' suggests that Lawrence understood what was being said to him in Welsh, although it is not known how much Welsh he could understand, or even speak. His reference to his 'large mouth' as 'a national peculiarity' shows clearly that Lawrence knew that he had Welsh blood in his veins.

I have made only two exceptions to this general rule of inclusion – Ivor Gurney and Robert Graves. Ivor Gurney was not a Welshman, but his experiences with the Welsh were too interesting and poignant to omit; neither was Robert Graves a Welshman, but he was living in Wales when the war broke out, he served with Welsh regiments, and he was deeply interested in Welsh culture, mythology and literature, as was his father, Alfred Perceval Graves (see note on Graves in the 'List of Authors, Index and References' section).

*   *   *

I have attempted to get as close as possible to the Great War experience as written by Welsh participants, and the material included in this book falls into three categories: testimonies either written or published during the war itself, recollections and reminiscences written after the war, especially books published at the end of the 1920s and during the 1930s, and material published after the Second World War, when some veterans decided to put their experiences on record. I have relied heavily on the first two categories, but very little on the third. I found that books written in the 1970s and 1980s lacked a certain authenticity and one could trace the influence of Graves's *Goodbye to All That* on books such as *Taffy Went to War* by Emlyn Davies, for example. The years had mellowed the experience and some books seem to have been rather factually and clinically written. One such book was *Sixty Years a Welsh Territorial* by Lord Silsoe, published in 1976. For four years, Lord Silsoe commanded the 6th Battalion of the Royal Welsh Fusiliers, to which he was gazetted in 1914. He also commanded all four companies of that battalion both in Gallipoli and in Sinai during the Great War. But, as he states in his book, he never kept a diary and had to rely almost entirely on his memory to write the book. His memoirs seemed to lack poignancy and immediacy.

By now there are conflicting attitudes towards the Great War. Some critics and historians have asserted that the 'Wilfred Owen version' of the war has been too readily accepted, and that the emphasis on the horror, the futility and the unjustified slaughter of a whole generation has distorted the true meaning and the true achievement of the war. I have tried to include all kinds of experiences, viewpoints, emotions and attitudes in this book, in an attempt to establish a fairly full picture of the Great War from a Welsh angle. As to the 'true meaning' of the war, the reader will have to make up his own mind, but, personally, I would find it difficult not to endorse the 'Owen version' of the Great War. There was, certainly, a sense of adventure amongst the young men who were driven in droves to the battlefields, and a feeling that they were taking part in a huge historic event; there was also humour, grim and grotesque as it often was. This books reflects such attitudes, but it is the tragedy and not the triumph that is likely to remain, the horror and not the honour. Wilfred Owen wasn't the only poet to challenge the old lie, 'Dulce et decorum est pro patria mori', especially as the Welsh were often confused as to exactly which 'patria' they were fighting and dying for.

Sources

[1] Quoted by the *Western Mail*'s Military Correspondent, 'What Wales Has Done: Striking Achievements in Europe and the East', *Western Mail*, November 12, 1918, p. 4.

[2] Ibid.

[3] Ivor Nicholson and Trevor Lloyd-Williams, *Wales: Its Part in the War* (London, 1919), pp. 25-6.

[4] 'His Happiest Vein: Mr. Lloyd George at Bangor', *Western Mail*, August 6, 1915, p. 5.

[5] Ibid.

[6] Robert Graves, *Goodbye to All That* (1929; 1986 reprint), p. 71.

[7] Ibid., p. 86.

[8] 'G.J.', 'Some of the Royal Welsh', *The Welsh Outlook*, vol. v, no. 52, April 1918, p. 129.

[9] C. P. Clayton, *The Hungry One* (Llandysul, 1978), p. 101.

[10] Quoted in Angela Gaffney, *Aftermath: Remembering the Great War in Wales* (Cardiff, 1998), pp. 154-5.

[11] D. Tecwyn Evans, 'The Spirit of Reform', *The Welsh Outlook*, vol. vi, no. 69, September 1919, p. 234.

[12] Edward Thomas, *The South Country* (London, 1909), p. 9.

[13] Edward Thomas, quoted in R. George Thomas, *Edward Thomas: a Portrait* (Oxford, 1985), p. 80.

[14] R. George Thomas, ibid., p. 81.

[15] 'P.H.T.', 'Poems by Edward Thomas', *The Welsh Outlook*, vol. vi, no. 61, January 1919, p. 18.

[16] David Lloyd George, Foreword, *The Life and Letters of Edward Thomas*, (John Moore, 1939, second impression 1983), no p. number.

[17] Dominic Hibberd, *Wilfred Owen: a New Biography* (London, 2002), pp. 6-7.

[18] Dylan Thomas, *Quite Early One Morning: Stories, Poems and Essays*, (London, 1954, 1971 reprint), p. 151.

[19] *Wilfred Owen: Collected Letters*, edited by Harold Owen and John Bell (London, 1967), p. 428.

[20] Ibid., p. 551.

[21] *Lawrence of Arabia: The Selected Letters*, edited by Malcolm Brown, 2007, pp. 8-9.

Chronology of the Great War

1914

June

28: Archduke Franz Ferdinand, heir to the throne of the Austro-Hungarian Empire, and his wife are assassinated at Sarajevo in Bosnia by Gavrilo Princip, an 18-year-old Bosnian Serb student linked with the Serbian nationalist society known as the 'Black Hand'.

July

5: Germany promises support to Austria-Hungary in the event of conflict between Austria-Hungary and Serbia.

23: Austria-Hungary, suspecting Serbian involvement in the assassination of Franz Ferdinand, issues ultimatum to Serbia.

24: Edward Grey proposes four-power mediation of Balkan crisis, but Serbia appeals to Russia.

25: Serbia mobilises army; Germany encourages Austria-Hungary to declare war on Serbia.

26: Austria-Hungary mobilises army on Russian Frontier.

28: Austria-Hungary declares war on Serbia.

30: Russia mobilises army.

31: Germany orders Russia to stop mobilisation of army; Germany refuses Britain's request to respect Belgian neutrality; France, Austria-Hungary and Germany mobilise armies.

August

1: Germany declares war on Russia; German-Turkish treaty signed at Constantinople.

2: Germany invades Luxembourg, and sends ultimatum to Belgium to allow passage of troops.

3: Germany declares war on France; Germany invades Belgium and France.

4: Britain declares war on Germany; President Wilson of USA declares US neutrality; (–September 4) main weight of the German Army pushes through Belgium and into France; French army unsuccessfully attacks German positions in Lorraine.

5: German Second Army reaches Liège, where it is resisted by Belgian defenders until August 16.

6: Austria-Hungary declares war on Russia; Serbia and Montenegro declare war on Germany.

8: First British troops arrive in France.

10: France declares war on Austria.

12: Britain declares war on Austria-Hungary.

20: Germans occupy Brussels.

21: British Government orders the raising of the first 'New Army' of volunteers.

23: Japan declares war on Germany.

24 (–September 7): British and Belgian troops retreat from Mons.

26 (–30): Germans crush Russians at Battle of Tannenberg in East Prussia.

28: Austria-Hungary declares war on Belgium.

30: Germans take Amiens.

September

3: Germans cross the River Marne.

5: Pact of London between France, Russia and Britain, the Allied Powers, all agreeing not to make separate peace.

5 (–10): At the Battle of the Marne, French Fifth and Ninth Armies and the British Expeditionary Force halt German advance, resulting in stalemate and trench warfare.

10 (–13): Germans retreat, stabilising their line along the River Aisne.

15 (–18): The Battle of the Aisne: Allies attack the German line. First trenches are dug.

17 (–18): The 'race to the sea': Allies and Germans try to outflank each other and the Western Front is established, stretching from the North Sea through Belgium and France to Switzerland.

27: Duala in German Cameroons surrenders to British and French.

October

1: Turkey closes the Dardanelles.

9: Antwerp surrenders to Germans.

12 (–November 22): First Battle of Ypres (Belgium) on the Western Front.

14: First Canadian troops reach England.

17 (–30): On the Western Front, battle of Yser in Belgium prevents Germans from reaching Channel ports; first units of Australian Expeditionary Force leave for France.

29: Turkey enters the war on the side of the Central Powers.

November

5: France and Britain declare war on Turkey.

23: British Navy bombards Zeebrugge.

December

8: Battle of the Falkland Islands: British naval force destroys German squadron.

17: British protectorate proclaimed in Egypt; (–29) The French attempt to break the German line at the Battle of Artois, and fail.

21: First German air raid on Britain.

25: Unofficial Christmas truce declared by soldiers along the Western Front.

1915

January

1 (–March 30): Allied offensive in Artois and Champagne on the Western Front.

3: Germans start using gas-filled shells on the Western Front.

8 (–February 5): Heavy fighting in Bassée Canal and Soissons area of France.

19: First German Zeppelin airship attack on Britain.

24: The Battle of Dogger Bank in the North Sea: the British Navy sinks the German cruiser *Blücher*.

30: First German submarine attack without warning off Le Havre, on the northern coast of France.

February

3: In the war against Turkey, a British force starts to advance along the River Tigris in Mesopotamia.

4: German U-boat attacks on Allied and neutral shipping; Germany declares the establishment of a blockade around Britain and Ireland, and declares that any foreign vessel found is a legitimate target; in Egypt, Turks are repulsed from Suez Canal; British Foreign Office announces that any vessel carrying corn to Germany will be seized.

16 (–26): French bombard German forces in Champagne, France.

19: British and French fleets bombard Turkish forts at the entrance to the Dardanelles.

March

10 (–13): The Battle of Neuve Chapelle on the Western Front: British and Indian forces capture the village of Neuve Chapelle in France.

18: British and French ships attempt to push through the Dardanelles but are repulsed by Turkish gun batteries.

21: German Zeppelin airships make bombing raid on Paris.

April

22 (–May 27): Second Battle of Ypres: a German offensive pushes the Front in Belgium forward by three miles; at Langemark near Ypres, Germans use poison gas from cylinders for the first time on April 22.

25: Allied landings on the Gallipoli Peninsula in Turkey.

May

4: Italy denounces its Triple Alliance with Germany and Austria-Hungary.

4 (–18 June): Second Battle of Artois; British troops attack German positions at Aubers Ridge (May 9-10) and Festubert (May 15-25); French suffer heavy casualties.

7: German submarine sinks the British liner *Lusitania* off the Southern coast of Ireland; 1,198 perish, including 128 US citizens.

9 (–10): Battle of Aubers Ridge on the Western Front; British attack is unsuccessful.

15 (–25): Battle of Festubert on the Western Front: unsuccessful British and Canadian offensive.

23: Italy declares war on Austria-Hungary and seizes several areas of land belonging to Austria-Hungary.

25/6: British Prime Minister Herbert Asquith forms a coalition government; D. Lloyd George appointed Minister of Munitions.

June

1: First Zeppelin airship attack on London.

August

6: Allied troops land at Suvla Bay in Gallipoli, in an attempt to open a third front.

25: Italy declares war on Turkey.

September

6: Bulgaria signs military alliances with Germany and Turkey.

23: Greek army is mobilised.

25 (–October 14): Third Battle of Artois on the Western Front. The British attack the line at Loos (–November 4), with few gains.

28: British forces, advancing along the River Tigris in Mesopotamia, capture Kut-al-Imara in Mesopotamia.

October

5: Allied troops land at Salonika in neutral Greece to aid Serbia.

6: Bulgaria enters the war on the side of the Central Powers; in Britain, Lord Derby given charge of recruitment for the army.

7 (–November 20): Austria-Hungary renews the invasion of Serbia and captures Belgrade (October 9); Serbian Army retreats to the South-West, Bulgarian troops contain allied forces in Salonika.

12: Allies declare they will assist Serbia under Bucharest treaty of 1913; Greece refuses Serbian appeal for aid under Serbo-Greek treaty of 1913.

15: Britain declares war on Bulgaria.

November

22 (–December 4): Battle of Ctesiphon: Turks force the British invaders of Mesopotamia back to Kut-al-Imara.

December

8: Turks besiege the British forces at Kut-al-Imara in Mesopotamia.

18 (–19): Allied troops withdraw from Suvla.

19: Douglas Haig succeeds John French as British commander-in-chief in France and Flanders.

28: British cabinet agrees on principle of compulsory service.

1916

January

8 (–9): Allied forces withdraw from Cape Helles on the Gallipoli Peninsula, Turkey.

27: Conference of British Labour Party votes against conscription.

February

21 (–December 18): The Battle of Verdun on the Western Front: Germans try to capture the French city of Verdun, but meet strong resistance.

April

29: Turks recapture Kut-al-Imara from the British.

May

31 (–June 1): The Battle of Jutland in the North Sea: major clash between British and German surface fleets.

June

5: British War Minister Lord Kitchener drowned when HMS *Hampshire* is sunk.

6 (–24): Allies blockade Greece; start of Arab revolt against Turks in Hejaz.

July

1 (–November 19): The Battle of the Somme on the Western Front: massive offensive by French and British troops, which gains five miles; the British Army suffers 60,000 casualties (including 20,000 dead) on the first day.

6: Lloyd George appointed War Minister, in succession to Lord Kitchener.

7 (–12): The Battle of Mametz Wood, part of the Somme Offensive; several Welsh battalions, which formed part of the 38th (Welsh) Division – Lloyd

George's 'Welsh Army' – were involved; Mametz Wood, held by the Germans, was considered a key strategic objective. The attack was led by the 16th Welsh (Cardiff City) Battalion and the 11th South Wales Borderers (2nd Gwent), soon followed by two other Welsh battalions, the 10th South Wales Borderers (1st Gwent) and the 17th Royal Welsh Fusiliers, all belonging to the 115th Infantry Brigade of the 38th (Welsh) Division. Successive assaults on July 7-8 failed to gain objective. Further attacks between July 10 and July 12 by the 113th Infantry Brigade (13th, 14th, 15th and 16th Royal Welsh Fusiliers) and the 114th Infantry Brigade (13th Welsh Regiment [2nd Rhondda], 14th Welsh Regiment [Swansea], 10th Welsh Regiment [1st Rhondda], and 15th Welsh Regiment [Carmarthen]) eventually succeeded in capturing the wood. The 38th (Welsh) Division lost 4,000 men, either killed or wounded, in the engagement.

August
17 (–September 11): Bulgarians attack the Allied enclave around Salonika.
19: Germans bombard the English coast.
27: Romania joins the Allies and declares war on Austria-Hungary.

October
16: Allies occupy Athens.

November
29: British Government takes over South Wales coalfield under Defence of the Realm Act because of strikes.

December
7: Lloyd George appointed British Prime Minister; he forms a coalition government and on December 10, a War Cabinet.

1917
February
24: British forces in Mesopotamia recapture Kut-al-Imara and then advance along the Tigris.

March
11: British forces capture Baghdad.
16: On the Western Front, German troops withdraw to the specially constructed 'Hindenburg Line' between Arras and Soissons.
17 (–18): On the Western Front, British troops capture Bapaume and Péronne.

April

6: USA declares war on Germany.

9 (−16): On the Western Front, the Battle of Arras; British troops advance four miles; 9 (−14): the Battle of Vimy Ridge: Canadians take Vimy Ridge.

16 (−May 9): On the Western Front, the Chemin des Dames or Nivelle offensive (or Second Battle of the Aisne), along the River Aisne.

18 (−19): Second Battle of Gaza in Palestine: Turks, with German support, repulse British.

June

7 (−14): On the Western Front, the Battle of Messines Ridge.

29: Edmund Allenby takes over command of British forces in Palestine; Greece declares war on the Central Powers.

July

19: Zeppelin airships attack English industrial areas.

31 (−November 10): On the Western Front, the Third Battle of Ypres (otherwise known as the Battle of Passchendaele) begins.

September

29 (−October 1): German aircraft attack London on successive nights.

November

6: On the Western Front, British and Canadian troops capture Passchendaele Ridge.

17: In Palestine, British take Jaffa from Turks.

20 (−December 7): On the Western Front, the Battle of Cambrai: a British tank force breaks the German line at Cambrai in France; British forces are then repulsed by the Germans.

December

7: USA declares war on Austria-Hungary.

9: British, led by Edmund Allenby, capture Jerusalem from the Turks.

1918

March

21 (−July 17): On the Western Front, German army launches a major spring offensive, and makes great advance towards Paris, but stopped by the Allies at the Second Battle of the Marne.

May

6: Allies break through in Albania.

18: British planes make bombing raids on Germany.

29: On the Western Front, Germans capture Reims and Soissons.

June

9 (–13): On the Western Front, German offensive near Compiègne.

July

13: Turkish offensive in Palestine checked.

15 (–17): On the Western Front, the Second Battle of the Marne: Allies halt the German advance towards Paris.

18: On the Western Front, Allied counter-offensive against Germans.

22: Allies cross the River Marne.

August

8: On the Western Front, British forces break the German line and push the Germans back towards their own border.

September

1: On the Western Front, British capture Pèronne.

4: On the Western Front, Germans retreat to Siegfried Line.

15: Allied breakthrough in Bulgaria.

22: Collapse of Turkish resistance in Palestine.

30: Bulgaria signs armistice with Allies.

October

1: British and Arab forces occupy Damascus.

30: Allies sign armistice with Turkey.

November

1: British and French forces occupy Constantinople.

3: Allies sign armistice with Austria-Hungary.

11: Armistice between Allies and Germany. War ends at 11am.

At War with
Germany

David Lloyd George in full cry

The Coming of War

The 4th of August, 1914, is one of the world's fateful dates. The decision taken on that day in the name and on behalf of the British Empire altered the destiny of Europe. It is not too much to say that it gave a different turn or direction to the advance of the human race. The trumpets of war had already sounded in the East and in the West, and colossal armies were hurrying to the slaughter. Millions of men were either on the march or strapping on their armour for the conflict, and roads and railway tracks trembled with the weight of guns and munitions and all the sinister devices and mechanisms of human destruction!

Was there any hope that the great catastrophe could be averted? There were continuous meetings of the Cabinet on Friday, Saturday and Sunday. I experienced much difficulty in attending throughout because of the Conference at the Treasury to deal with the grave financial situation into which we had been plunged by War. But I heard and took part in most of the discussion. It revealed serious differences of opinion on the subject of British intervention in a Russo-German war even although France was forced by her Russian alliance to join in. Grey never definitely put before the Cabinet the proposition that Britain should, in that event, declare war. He never expressed a clear and unequivocal opinion either way and no decision was therefore taken on that point. But it was quite clear from the course of the debate inside the Cabinet and the informal conversations which took place outside during our short adjournments that we were hopelessly divided on the subject of Britain entering the War on the issue as it had developed at that date. Had the question of defending the neutrality and integrity of Belgium been raised there would not have been a dissentient voice on that issue. Lord Morley and John Burns might conceivably have stood out. Of that I am not convinced had a decision on that point alone been reached in time as a means of circumscribing the area of war and possibly of persuading Germany of the futility of waging it at all under conditions which would have been unfavourable to her preconcerted military schemes. But such a proposal was never submitted to our judgment.

The one faint glimmer still visible in the lowering sky was in the direction of Belgium.

The dark clouds were rapidly closing up, but there was still one visible corner of blue. The Germans had signed a treaty not merely to respect, but to protect the neutrality of Belgium. Would they honour their bond? Great Britain was a party to that compact. If anyone broke its terms, Britain was bound to throw in her might against the invader. Would the faith of Prussia, strengthened by the fear of Britain, prevail? If the treaty stood, the situation might yet be saved.

The policy I urged upon my colleagues was not one merely of passive non-intervention in the struggle between Germany and Austria on the one hand and

Russia and France on the other. We were not in the position of France. She was bound by Treaty to support Russia in her quarrels with Germany. We were under no such obligation. I proposed, therefore, that we should take immediate steps to increase and strengthen our Army in numbers and equipment, so that when we judged the time had come for intervention, none of the belligerents could afford to disregard our appeal. Had Germany respected the integrity of Belgium, that policy would have been the wisest course to pursue. There would have been plenty of time for passions to exhaust their force and for the sanguine expectations of military enthusiasm to evaporate. The problem of France would have been a different one; the march of events would have been slower. France, instead of having to defend a frontier of over 500 miles, without fortresses or artificial barriers, could have concentrated all her strength on defending a frontier of 250 miles protected by formidable fortresses. An army (including reserves) of 3,000,000 men, holding entrenched positions on this narrow frontier, would have been invincible, and Germany might well have been content merely to defend her frontiers in the West, and throw her armies into Poland. There, difficulties of transport, bad roads, inadequate railways, immense distances, would have postponed decision for weeks if not for months. It took Germany over 12 months' hard fighting to conquer Poland. Even then the Russian Army was still in being and ready to resume the conflict in 1916. British intervention in the cause of peace might then have induced saner counsels. Britain was the one Power in Europe that had never yet been beaten in a European war. With her immunity from attack, with her immense fleet manned by the most skilful seamen in the world, with her enormous resources, she could be reckoned upon to wear down any Power. Had Britain been able to throw into the scale a well-equipped army of a million men to support her fleet, Germany would have hesitated before she rejected terms of peace and thus brought the British Empire into the conflict on the side of her enemies. These were the arguments I advanced in favour of non-intervention in the struggle if the neutrality of Belgium were respected.

The invasion of Belgium put an end to all these possibilities. Then our Treaty obligations were involved. On Sunday, the 2nd of August, the omens were not propitious. There were clear indications that the German forces were massing on the Belgian frontier. Germany had appealed to Belgium for permission to march through her territories to attack France. Belgian Ministers hesitated, but the answer given by Belgium's heroic King constitutes one of the most thrilling pages of history. The British Government, on hearing the news, issued an ultimatum to Germany warning her that unless by twelve o'clock on August 4th assurances were received from Germany that the neutrality of Belgium would be treated as inviolate, Britain would have no alternative but to take steps to enforce that treaty. Would Germany realise what war with Britain meant, arrest the progress of her armies, change her strategy, and perhaps consent to a parley? How much depended upon the answer to these questions! We could suspect then what it meant: we know now. There were many of us who could hardly believe that those responsible for guiding the destiny of Germany would be so fatuous as deliberately to provoke the hostility of the British Empire with its inexhaustible reserves and with its grim tenacity of purpose once it engaged in a struggle . . .

It was a day full of rumours and reports, throbbing with anxiety. Hour after hour passed, and no sign came from Germany. There were only disturbing rumours of further German movements towards the Belgian line. The evening came. Still no answer. Shortly after nine o'clock I was summoned to the Cabinet Room for an important consultation. There I found Mr Asquith, Sir Edward Grey, and Mr Haldane all looking very grave. Mr M'Kenna arrived soon afterwards. A message from the German Foreign Office to the German Embassy in London had been intercepted. It was not in cipher. It informed the German Ambassador that the British Ambassador in Berlin had asked for his passports at 7 p.m. and declared war . . .

We were therefore at a loss to know what it meant. It looked like an attempt on the part of the Germans to anticipate the hour of the declaration of war in order to effect some *coup* either against British ships or British coasts. Should this intercept be treated as the commencement of hostilities, or should we wait until we either heard officially from Germany that our conditions had been rejected, or until the hour the ultimatum had expired? We sat at the green table in the famous room where so many historic decisions had been taken in the past. It was not then a very well-lighted room, and my recollection is that the lights had not all been turned on, and in the dimness you might imagine the shades of the great British statesmen of the past taking part in a conference which meant so much to the Empire, to the building up of which they had devoted their lives – Chatham, Pitt, Fox, Castlereagh, Canning, Peel, Palmerston, Disraeli, Gladstone. In that simple, unadorned, almost dingy room they also had pondered over the problems which had perplexed their day. But never had they been confronted with so tremendous a decision as that with which British Ministers were faced in these early days of August, 1914.

And now came the terrible decision: should we unleash the savage dogs of war at once, or wait until the time limit of the ultimatum had expired, and give peace the benefit of even such a doubt as existed for at least another two hours? We had no difficulty in deciding that the Admiralty was to prepare the fleet against any sudden attack from the German flotillas and to warn our coasts against any possible designs from the same quarter. But should we declare war now, or at midnight? The ultimatum expired at midnight in Berlin. That was midnight according to Central Europe time: it meant eleven o'clock to Greenwich time. We resolved to wait until eleven. Would any message arrive from Berlin before eleven informing us of the intention of Germany to respect Belgian neutrality? If it came there was still a faint hope that something might be arranged before the marching armies crashed into each other.

As the hour approached, a deep and tense solemnity fell on the room. No one spoke. It was like awaiting the signal for the pulling of a lever which would hurl millions to their doom – with just a chance that a reprieve might arrive in time. Our eyes wandered anxiously from the clock to the door, and from the door to the clock, and little was said.

'Boom!' The deep notes of Big Ben rang out into the night, the first strokes in Britain's most fateful hour since she arose out of the deep. A shuddering silence fell upon the room. Every face was suddenly contracted in a painful intensity. 'Doom!' 'Doom!' 'Doom!' to the last stroke. The big clock echoed in our years like the hammer of destiny. What destiny? Who could tell? We had challenged the most powerful military empire the world has yet brought forth. France was too weak alone to challenge its might and Russia was ill-organised, ill-equipped. corrupt. We knew what brunt Britain would have to bear. Could she stand it? There was no doubt or hesitation in any breast. But let it be admitted without shame that a thrill of horror quickened every pulse. Did we know that before peace would be restored to Europe we should have to wade through four years of the most concentrated slaughter, mutilation, suffering, devastation, and savagery which mankind has ever witnessed? That twelve millions of the gallant youth of the nations would be slain, that another twenty millions would be mutilated? That Europe would be crushed under the weight of a colossal war debt? That only one empire would stand the shock? That the three other glittering empires of the world would have been flung to the dust, and shattered beyond repair? That revolution, famine, and anarchy would sweep over half Europe, and that their menace would scorch the rest of this hapless continent?

D. Lloyd George, *War Memoirs of David Lloyd George*, volume I (1938; originally published in six volumes, 1933-6)

1914

War broke: and now the Winter of the world
With perishing great darkness closes in.
The foul tornado, centred at Berlin,
Is over all the width of Europe whirled,
Rending the sails of progress. Rent or furled
Are all Art's ensigns. Verse wails. Now begin
Famines of thought and feeling. Love's wine's thin.
The grain of human Autumn rots, down-hurled.

For after Spring had bloomed in early Greece,
And Summer blazed her glory out with Rome,
An Autumn softly fell, a harvest home,
A slow grand age, and rich with all increase.
But now, for us, wild Winter, and the need
Of sowings for new Spring, and blood for seed.

Wilfred Owen

Calling All Reservists

On the fourth of August, 1914, I was at Blaina, Mon., having a drink in the Castle Hotel with a few of my cronies, all old soldiers and the majority of them reservists. One had took us around South Africa; there wasn't a Boer left in South Africa by the time he had finished his yarn. Next I had took them around India and Burmah, and there wasn't a Pathan or Dacoit left in the world by the time I had finished mine. Now another was taking us through North China in the Boxer Rising of 1900; and he had already got hundreds of Chinks hanging on the gas brackets when someone happened to come in with a piece of news. He said that war had broken out with Germany and that the Sergeant of Police was hanging up a notice by the post office, calling all reservists to the Colours. This caused a bit of excitement and language, but it was too late in the evening for any of us to proceed to our depots so we kept on drinking and yarning until stop-tap. By that time we were getting a little top-heavy, and an old artilleryman wound up the evening by dropping howitzer shells over the mountain and destroying a mining village in the valley beyond.

The next day I proceeded to the Regimental Depot at Wrexham, arriving there about 9 p.m. On my way to barracks I called at a pub which I used to frequent very often when I was a recruit, and found it full of Royal Welsh reservists. We hadn't seen one another for years, and the landlord had a tough job to get rid of us at stop-tap. We arrived at barracks in a jovial state and found that the barrack rooms were full, so about thirty of us had to sleep on the square that night. I was medically examined next morning, and afterwards got my equipment and kit out of stores. On the evening of the 5th a draft of reservists who had arrived early in the day had left the Depot to join the Second Battalion which was stationed at Portland. The Second was the battalion I had served with abroad and had arrived back in England about March 1914, after eighteen years absence. The First Battalion was stationed at Malta, just beginning its tour overseas. On the evening of August 7th the Depot Sergeant-Major called for ten volunteers to join the Second Battalion. Every man volunteered and I was one of the selected ten. We went by train to Dorchester, where the Battalion, which had left Portland, was now billeted in the Town Hall. Two old chums of mine, Stevens and Billy, who were Section D reservists like myself, were posted to the same platoon in A Company . . . We sailed from Southampton about 2 a.m. on August 10th, and arrived about 3 p.m. at Rouen, where we were billeted in a convent. I had never visited France before.

Frank Richards, *Old Soldiers Never Die* (1933)

The Last Evening

Round a bright isle, set in a sea of gloom,
We sat together, dining,
And spoke and laughed even as in better times
Though each one knew no other might misdoubt
The doom that marched moment by moment nigher,
Whose couriers knocked on every heart like death,
And changed all things familiar to our sight
Into strange shapes and grieving ghosts that wept.
The crimson-shaded light
Shed in the garden roses of red fire
That burned and bloomed on the decorous limes.
The hungry night that lay in wait without
Made blind, blue eyes against the silver's shining
And waked the affrighted candles with its breath
Out of their steady sleep, while round the room
The shadows crouched and crept.
Among the legions of beleaguering fears,
Still we sat on and kept them still at bay,
A little while, a little longer yet,
And wooed the hurrying moments to forget
What we remembered well,
– Till the hour struck – then desperately we sought
And found no further respite – only tears
We would not shed, and words we might not say.
We needs must know that now the time was come
Yet still against the strangling foe we fought,
And some of us were brave and some
Borrowed a bubble courage nigh to breaking,
And he that went, perforce went speedily
And stayed not for leave-taking.
But even in going, as he would dispel
The bitterness of incomplete good-byes,
He paused within the circle of dim light,
And turned to us a face, lit seemingly
Less by the lamp than by his shining eyes.
So, in the radiance of his mastered fate,
A moment stood our soldier by the gate
And laughed his long farewell –
Then passed into the silence and the night.

Elinor Jenkins

New Recruits

Wherever I went I was told that employers – 'the best firms' – were dismissing men, the younger unmarried men, in order to drive them to enlist. 'Not exactly to drive them,' said one, 'but to encourage.' Nobody complained. They suggested that the 'Government' had put the employers up to it, or that 'It don't seem hardly fair,' or 'It comes near conscription, and only those that don't care will give up good wages and leave their wives to charity'. One old man at Sheffield remarked that it used to be, 'Oh, you're too old' for a job; now it's 'You're too young'. It was added that the men's places were to be kept open for them; they were to receive part of their wages; if rejected by the doctor, they would be taken back. 'They *have* to like it,' said one man. These were not the only men who had lost their work. The jewellery-makers of Birmingham, for example, young or old, could not expect to be employed in war-time. Collieries near Newcastle that used to supply Germany were naturally idle, and many of the lads from the pits enlisted. Factories that supplied Russia were not busy either, and Russian debts looked like bad debts. Some trades were profiting by the war. Leicester was so busy making boots for the English and French armies that it had to refuse an order from the Greek army. Harness-makers had as much work as they could do at Walsall. The factories for explosives at Elswick the same. Publicans were flourishing though still ambitious; one public house at Manchester had these 'Imperial Ballads' printed on a placard:

> What plucks your courage up each day;
> What washes all your cares away?
> What word do you most often say?
> Why, Imperial!

the reference being to a drink of that name. But these successes were extraordinary. Already it was said at Newcastle that shop-assistants were serving for longer hours at reduced pay. Men in motor-car works were on short time. A photographer at Manchester had to resort to this advertisement:

> Gone to the front!
> A beautiful enlargement of any photo of our
> brave comrades may be had at a discount of
> 25 per cent.

Where relief was being given, a queue of women stood along a wall in the sun.

For the women the sun was too hot, but not for the corn, the clover-hay, the apples of this great summer, nor for the recruits sleeping out. The sun gilded and regilded the gingerbread. Everybody that could made an effort to rise to the occasion of the weather. The parks and the public gardens were thronged. The public houses overflowed, often with but a single soldier as an excuse . . .

There was really no monotony of type among these recruits, though the great majority wore dark clothes and caps, had pale faces tending to leanness, and stood somewhere about five foot seven. It was only the beginning, some thought, of a wide awakening to a sense of the danger and the responsibility. Clean and dirty – some of them, that is, straight from the factory – of all ages and features, they were pouring in. Some might be loafers, far more were workers. I heard that of one batch of two hundred and fifty at Newcastle, not one was leaving less than two pounds a week. Here and there a tanned farm labourer with lighter-coloured, often brownish, clothes, chequered the pale-faced dark company. The streets never lacked a body of them or a tail disappearing. Their tents, their squads drilling this way and that, occupied the great bare Town Moor above Newcastle. The town was like a vast fair where men were changing hands instead of cattle. The ordinary racket of tramcar and crowd was drowned by brass instruments, bagpipes, drums and tin boxes beaten by small boys, men in fifties and in hundreds rounding a corner to the tune of 'It's a long, long way to Tipperary'. Thousands stood to watch them. With crowds on the kerb-stones, with other crowds going up and down and across, with men squatting forward on the pavement, it was best to have no object but to go in and out. The recruits were the constant, not the only attraction. The newest ones marching assumed as military a stiff uprightness as possible. The older ones in uniform were slacker. Some stood at corners talking to girls; others went in and out of 'pubs' attended by civilians; more and more slouched, or staggered, or were heavy-eyed with alcohol. Everyone was talking, but the only words intelligible were 'Four o'clock winner' and 'It's a long, long way to Tipperary'. At nightfall the boys who beat the drums and tins began to carry around an effigy and to sing 'The Kaiser, the Kaiser', or

> And when we go to war
> We'll put him in a jar,
> And he'll never see his daddy any more.

Companies of recruits were still appearing. Perhaps their faces were drawn and shining with drink, fatigue, and excitement, but they remained cheerful even when a young officer with a dry, lean face and no expression said 'Good night' without expression and rode off. His was the one expressionless, dead calm face in the city, the one that seemed to have business of its own, until I crossed the river and saw the women on the door-steps of the steep slum, the children on pavement and in gutter. They were not excited by the fever in

Clayton Street and Market Street, any more than by St Mary's bells banging away high above slum and river, or by the preacher at the top of Church Street bellowing about 'the blessed blood of Jesus Christ'. In an almost empty tavern a quiet old man was treating a lad in a new uniform and giving him advice: 'Eat as much as you can, and have a contented mind.' It was a fine warm evening. But what could the great crowd do to spend its excitement? As a crowd, nothing. In a short time it was doubled. For at nine o'clock the public houses had to be emptied and shut. The burly bell of St Nicholas tolled nine over thousands with nothing to do. Those who had not taken time by the forelock and drunk as much as they would normally have done by eleven, stood about aimlessly. A man took his stand in Bigg Market and sang for money. It was not what people wanted. Several youths got together at a short distance and tried to bawl down the singer. Even that was not what people wanted. Even the temperance man was only half pleased when he reflected that what he had long agitated for in vain had been done by one stroke of the military pen. There was nothing to be done but to go to bed and wait for the morning papers.

Edward Thomas, 'Tipperary', *The Last Sheaf* (1928)

Edward Thomas

Camp Life
and
Training

Saunders Lewis

Physical, Manual Labour

Wednesday afternoon.

We are having rather a hard day.

This morning from 9 to 1 a route march, carrying timber for new huts this afternoon, and there is to be a long march tonight. And after this we have another route march tomorrow, so if we come back late I may fail to get off on time for the 5.20 boat, so don't depend on my being there, and don't wait for me. My hope is that the weather will be too threatening in the morning for an all-day march.

Knowsley Park should be a very lovely place in winter. It has two lakes; one a large one, with sloping banks covered now with brown heather and silver birch trees, and in the mists of the morning you could hardly wish for anything lovelier.

Only in our work we hurry past and through it all. I know that there is stillness and sweetness lying over it, but I cannot stay to feel and experience them. It is acknowledging beauty with the mind, but not receiving it into the heart. That part of my nature must lie dormant till we are discharged. Won't that be a happy day?

You may perhaps think I am not alive to the great questions of the war, what it means for human nature, and how it must affect our belief in goodness and Providence, and in a way you would be right. They do not come to me now with the force they have, say, for you. But I think the reason is that our life here is so objective; it is all physical, manual labour, and the whole condition of life makes reflection difficult.

That is why I suppose I am so selfish; by stifling reflection you learn merely to look forward to your own future pleasure. Do you remember you once wished (*ad lunam*) that I should have a larger sympathy with humanity? Alas, I feel I am still far from having it.

Saunders Lewis, letter to Margaret Gilcriest, January 27, 1915,
from Knowsley Park Camp, Prescot, Liverpool;
Saunders Lewis: Letters to Margaret Gilcriest,
edited by Mair Saunders Jones, Ned Thomas and Harri Pritchard Jones (1993)

Camp Life on the Eastern Front

Our daily life is very simple. All parades must be over by about 8.30am on account of the heat, so reveille is at 5.15am (it afterwards became 4.30am), parade at 6am, or 6.15am. After parade the men water the horses in the Nile, and either go straight on to a palm grove and breakfast there, or return to camp for breakfast and ride out immediately afterwards. In the palm grove horses and men remain till 4.30pm, when they return to camp for stables and tea. Under the palms during the heat of the day, stables, harness-cleaning, laying (when the guns are taken out), and sometimes lectures, are possible. A monotonous and not very busy existence; but our main object now is to keep alive and overcome our enemies, heat, flies, disease, and the other plagues of Egypt. The C.O. drew the Battery up on parade the other day and 'said a few words'. He told the men that they had probably got a pretty bad time coming; that they must not either grumble at conditions or fret because they were not in the battle-line; that everyone had to do his duty where he was told to; that in confronting the difficulties we had before us we should have to display all our soldierly qualities: steadiness, endurance, patience, and discipline; that according to our success in overcoming disease and enduring hardships, and in proportion to the smallness of our casualties, we should be able to consider ourselves a capable and efficient Battery.

So now to get to it!

Eliot Crawshay-Williams,
Leaves from an Officer's Notebook (1918)

Eager to Go to the Front

My Dear Margaret,

I am beginning this letter very late as you see, but Friday we had a night march and yesterday I went home, so that time has been filled. The night work on Friday was the most realistic piece of warfare we have yet done. We marched for almost two hours to a certain position and there we had to set up piquets and outposts to guard a retreat before an imaginary enemy. This was about 8 o'clock, and the rain began to fall heavily. To take up our position we had to cross a fairly broad stream, and there was no bridge across it, so there was nothing to do but to wade across, and so we were up to our knees in water, and an hour later, in returning, we had again to wade back.

It was pretty uncomfortable, especially in a pitch darkness and rain; but when we got back we changed at once and had hot coffee and buns for supper; so we were well cared for. But it gave us a notion of what marching in dangerous country may really be.

It seems from all accounts fairly sure that we shall not be leaving here until April. The more delay the better in one way, is it not? And yet, shall I tell you, I am now almost eager to leave and go to the front. The reason is I am very tired of barrack life here and would be glad of any change; but more than that, I feel somehow that while we are here, and still only training, that the end is terribly distant, and there must be so much to go through before it can come; whereas if we got to real work, well, there would be only one more move to look forward to then – and that the return and discharge. I don't know whether this is the right way of looking at it or not, but this episode always seems to me a digression to be got over for ourselves as quickly as may be, and for the world a worse abnormality that breaks up the whole progress of existence.

Saunders Lewis, letter to Margaret Gilcriest, March 1915,
from Knowsley Park Camp, Prescot, Liverpool;
Saunders Lewis: Letters to Margaret Gilcriest

A Night School for Soldiers

Queen's Hotel,
Newport, Mon.
June 11th, 1915.

My Dear Margaret,

I have very real need for writing to you today for I badly need help.

This is how it came about. I was put in charge of the scouts and signalling sections of our battalion; in fact I was set to form them and instruct them; and as there is a great deal of writing to do in these tasks I soon discovered that a big proportion of the men is quite illiterate, and that to read, write, and spell fluently is quite exceptional – and it made my job next to impossible.

The only thing I could think of to remedy matters was to institute a night school in the battalion, and I suggested that to the men. They seemed to take to the proposal very readily; so I said that if I could get a reasonable number of men keen on joining I should myself get a room in Newport and start classes two nights a week. This is what I am now pledged to do.

I have not yet found a room, and I am to begin next Tuesday. What I should like you to tell me is how to begin and how to teach these men. I have not drawn up any plan of campaign and I am innocent of knowing any method of teaching. As yet I have purchased no books at all, so you see this venture of mine is very precariously launched. Do send me some advice – 'on Sunday'. Remember the teaching must be of a very obvious and utilitarian kind, and don't suggest ten-shilling text-books for I shall have to rig the school out myself.

I have very little news else. My time is very full, too full to reflect at all almost. We are at work every day until 6. Then we have lectures to officers two nights a week, night work two other nights, and now these classes the remaining nights. But though there is far less leisure to read and be quiet at times than there was in my previous position, up to now I am quite contented.

Saunders Lewis, letter to Margaret Gilcriest,
Saunders Lewis: Letters to Margaret Gilcriest

Camp Duties of a Second Lieutenant

Saturday
Manchester Regiment
5th Battalion
My Room

My own dear Mother,

I quite hope for your letter tomorrow morning. I am an exile here, suddenly cut off both from the present day world, and from my own past life. I feel more in a strange land than when arriving at Bordeaux! Is is due to the complete newness of the country, the people, my dress, my duties, the dialect, the air, food, everything.

I am marooned on a Crag of Superiority in an ocean of Soldiers.

I have had chiefly *General* Duties so far, such as Supernumerary Officer to the Battalion, Company Orderly Officer (today) etc.

The generality of men are hard-handed, hard-headed miners, dogged, loutish, ugly. (But I would trust them to advance under fire and to hold their trench;) blond, coarse, ungainly, strong, 'unfatigueable', unlovely, Lancashire soldiers. Saxons to the bone.

I don't know the individuals of my platoon.

Some are overseas men who have seen fighting.

Had to assist inspection of kit, this morning.

I see a toothbrush and a box of polish missing. I demand in a terrible voice 'Where's your TOOTH-BRUSH?' and learn that the fellow has just returned from 'overseas'! 'Somewhere in France' is never heard here. *All our draughts go to Egypt*; thence to Mesopotamia. I am glad.

One of our officers at Mess has been wounded.

There is none of that Levity amongst us which prevailed in the Artists'.

The sub. has a stiffish day's work: has to do the 'Third' Physical Training (i.e. most strenuous) at 6.15, carries pack on parade & march, and has a good deal of responsibility, writing, and ceremonial to fetter him. I had the misfortune to walk down the road to some Camp Shops when the men were 'at large': and had to take *millions* of salutes.

I have nearly got together my Camp effects, Bed, chair, wash-stand, etc. all necessary here.

Shall be glad of socks as soon as you can send them. Would you include my enamel *mug*, left on my dressing table.

My servant has nothing else to do but serve, so that is satisfactory.

If I am not pleased, say with my bed, I send him to change it at the shops. He is indispensable for taking my messages & reports to the Orderly Room.

Frankly, I don't like the C.O. nor does anybody, except one major, his sole friend. But never fear, we shan't 'go out' under him.

I like my Company Commander, a Lieut., and nearly all the rest.

The doctor cured my deafness, by syringing, yesterday.

Five of us, how chosen I don't know, took the Army Exam. to qualify for Service, yesterday. There is more on Monday . . .

I am staying in this week-end, in my new chair, having no pocket money whatever . . .

My most irksome duty is acting Taskmaster while the tired fellows dig: the most pleasant is marching home over the wild country at the head of my platoon, with a flourish of trumpets, and an everlasting roll of drums.

Your own boy Wilfred x

How I miss the delightful time you gave me at home is not for me to think of now.

Wilfred Owen, letter to his mother, Susan Owen, June 19, 1916,
Wilfred Owen: Collected Letters, edited by Harold Owen and John Bell (1967)

A Sergeant-Major and a Sergeant

My diary is full of minor details with, here and there, a hint of the bigger thing that kept worrying me. Our Sergeant-Major was a revelation. He had to be seen before one could credit his existence. A gaunt guardsman, he represented the least pleasant side of the British Army. On parade he was a martinet, often foul-mouthed and insulting, and off parade he cringed and crawled for drinks to men who had more than a private soldier's pay. For weeks he addressed us as 'Gentlemen', presumably because we belonged to the 4th U.P.S. (Universities and Public Schools) or 21st Royal Fusiliers. To our amusement, he persisted in this practice till the day when we put on the King's uniform for the first time. Then he strutted up and down the ranks, yelling, 'You're gentlemen no longer; you're bloody soldiers.' Poor old Gaunty! The day was to come when we should pull the pin out of a Mills bomb, fling it on to the parapet behind us, and shriek with laughter as he raced to his dugout, imagining that he was under heavy fire. It cost the Government 7s. 6d., but it was worth it.

The old Sergeant who instructed us in musketry was known throughout the battalion as 'Howsomever'. I believe his name was Humphreys, but I cannot vouch for it. A Boer War veteran, he had little command of the King's English, though he was better versed than most soldiers in the King's Regulations. He realised very early that he was dealing with a new type of 'rooky' and that a few of the many talks he was expected to give on the rifle sufficed for its explanation. Accordingly he devoted much of the time to reminiscences of his own heroic past. Halfway through the narrative, he would notice an officer approaching, pause, pick up a rifle and proceed to lecture, prefacing each new start with the remark, 'Howsummever, this is what I'm paid to talk about.'

Poor old Humphreys! He introduced variety and humour into many a dull day and the officer who could catch him out on the rights and wrongs of a private soldier had to be a lawyer by instinct and training. We passed through the musketry course with general credit and settled down to the routine of physical drill and route marches.

Morgan Watcyn-Williams, *From Khaki to Cloth*
(1948; written before his death in 1938)

The Trumpet

Rise up, rise up,
And, as the trumpet blowing
Chases the dreams of men,
As the dawn glowing
The stars that left unlit
The land and water,
Rise up and scatter
The dew that covers
The print of last night's lovers –
Scatter it, scatter it!

While you are listening
To the clear horn,
Forget, men, everything
On this earth new-born,
Except that it is lovelier
Than any mysteries.
Open your eyes to the air
That has washed the eyes of the stars
Through all the dewy night:
Up with the light,
To the old wars;
Arise, arise!

Edward Thomas

Royal Artillery Barracks
Trowbridge

My dear Eleanor,

Thank you very much for everything. But I am so sleepy I don't know how much more I can say. Lectures nearly all day make me sleepy. It is rather difficult, too, to learn about pulleys and weights and the teaching is mostly always useless. It is only 12.30 but I hardly know what I write, now or in making notes. So it is difficult to see how I shall manage it. Partly, too, the very violent physical drill explains it, and a night partly spent in trying to keep rain out of the tent. I think I told you we had some walks on Saturday and Sunday, but all the week we are practically confined to the barracks as we work till 7.30 and can't go out unless we are in our finery, which is hardly worthwhile changing into. However you can see I have some ease, because I have written some verses suggested by the trumpet calls which go all day. They are not well done and the trumpet is cracked, but the reveille pleases me (more than it does most sleepers).

Edward Thomas, letter to Eleanor Farjeon, November 1916;
quoted in *Edward Thomas: the Last Four Years*, Eleanor Farjeon (1958)

Rain

Rain, midnight rain, nothing but the wild rain
On this bleak hut, and solitude, and me
Remembering again that I shall die
And neither hear the rain nor give it thanks
For washing me cleaner than I have been
Since I was born into this solitude.
Blessed are the dead that the rain rains upon:
But here I pray that none whom once I loved
Is dying tonight or lying still awake
Solitary, listening to the rain,
Either in pain or thus in sympathy
Helpless among the living and the dead,
Like a cold water among broken reeds,
Myriads of broken reeds all still and stiff,
Like me who have no love which this wild rain
Has not dissolved except the love of death,
If love it be for what is perfect and
Cannot, the tempest tells me, disappoint.

Edward Thomas

Arms and the Boy

Let the boy try along this bayonet-blade
How cold steel is, and keen with hunger of blood;
Blue with all malice, like a madman's flash;
And thinly drawn with famishing for flesh.

Lend him to stroke these blind, blunt bullet-leads
Which long to nuzzle in the hearts of lads,
Or give him cartridges whose fine zinc teeth,
Are sharp with sharpness of grief and death.

For his teeth seem for laughing round an apple.
There lurk no claws behind his fingers supple;
And God will grow no talons at his heels,
Nor antlers through the thickness of his curls.

Wilfred Owen

Departures

First World War recruitment poster

The House by the Highway

All night, from the quiet street
    Comes the sound, without pause or break,
Of the marching legions' feet
    To listeners lying awake.

Their faces may none descry;
    Night folds them close like a pall;
But the feet of them passing by
    Tramp on the hearts of all.

What comforting makes them strong?
    What trust and what fears have they
That march without music or song
    To death at the end of the way?

What faith in our victory?
    What hopes that beguile and bless?
What heaven-sent hilarity?
    What mirth and what weariness?

What valour from vanished years
    In the heart of youth confined?
What wellsprings of unshed tears
    For the loves they leave behind?

No sleep, my soul to befriend;
    No voice, neither answering light!
But darkness that knows no end
    And feet going by in the night.

Elinor Jenkins

The Departure Platform

At Cardiff Station on the morning of Thursday, September 17th [1914], the departure platform for London was crowded to suffocation, though the sun had risen scarcely an hour before the train steamed in. Principal E. H. Griffiths and a number of the College staff were moving up and down, shaking hands will all the men they could reach, while groups of women students were making promises to care for our comfort, promises which they kept magnificently. Many of them had walked several miles from adjoining villages, and despite a surface gaiety, were betraying signs of the strain of farewell. Some were already engaged to men who three months before had been destined for decent posts in the professional world. The long vacation had changed all that and the face of things wore a new complexion. During the next few years certain trains carried their daily freight of men returning from 'leave' and one woman called that departure platform 'The Valley of the Shadow of Death'.

A huge poster, secured from the office of a notorious journal, bearing the slogan 'Another Pill for Kaiser Bill' was fastened to the front of the engine. Amid ringing cheers and much waving of hands and handkerchiefs, the train moved off.

In my compartment were three men with whom I was billeted for many months, Stan Tanner, C. H. Watkins and L. B. or Tim Greaves, brother of J. B. Greaves who was then editor of *Cap and Gown*. Jim had not yet joined us, wisely deciding to complete his London B.Sc. in Economics before he entered the Army.

We sat looking at each other, and for a few minutes each of us was left alone with his thoughts. What the future held none of us could possibly know (as a matter of fact we all came back safely), but the past remained, beautiful and pathetic, like a broken column in a deserted garden. Life reached out to a future which was destroyed before it began, and whose connection with the present was dim and intangible. Somewhere in the days of frolic and friendship there existed a foundation for what we were doing, but not one of us could put our finger on it, for we had been brought up in a tradition that was wholly unmilitary, peaceful if not pacifist. We had been lifted clean out of our world with all its promise and hope, and life was beginning anew.

Morgan Watcyn-Williams, *From Khaki to Cloth*

Leaving for Ypres

The last days have gone by with a rush. Travelling by night, and weariness and business by day, have left no time for writing. Now I must try to collect thoughts and incidents.

I changed my mind as to the war and port of disembarkation before I left. There was one sign that the French nation was at war which soon impressed itself, and that was the number of women in mourning. Every other woman wore black. Many were cheerful, some even appeared flirtatious but they wore black. It was a town in mourning.

We stayed nearly two days in the end.

Our stay at the port of disembarkation was quite pleasant. We (that is, three of us) bathed, we walked, we had a most interesting conversation with a French sergeant, who in times of peace was a professor in the University of Alberta at Edmonton. He told us the secret of the badges of rank of French officers, the lines on the hat; he showed us over the French barracks; he explained the constitution of a French regiment, and how the reserves and territorials differed and could be distinguished; he discoursed on the possibilities of a permanent peace, on the necessity for physical training, on what training in courage and character could take the place of war (which he thought odious and uncivilised); and in the end he insisted on taking us to the hotel and giving us an 'aperitif'.

Our hotel was fairly comfortable. It had a pleasant proprietor, one very surly waiter, the largest eggs I have ever seen, and no bath. We all had to fill up most detailed particulars of ourselves on forms, and one Major caused some amusement by inserting after 'Prenom', 'une nuit'.

The inhabitants seemed to love the English. Not only do the young ladies treat them with particular effusion, but even the little children run up to shake hands, looking up with adoring eyes, and crying 'Good-night! Good-night!'

I went to see the French recruits being called up. They were a class called up before their time, but all glad to go, and looking half foolish, half proud, behind the huge bouquets of tinsel and artificial flowers with which hawkers provide them just outside the Town Hall. They can also buy badges with their 'year' on them, and small 'fit' badges. I bought a couple as souvenirs. One read, 'Bon pour le service'; the other, 'Bon pour les filles'.

This port is a great base, and the stores of every imaginable article, the clearing-house of things sent back from the battlefield, the hospital, the veterinary hospital, are all wonderful sights.

We left the D.A.Q.M.G.'s office in the evening, after a half-hour's wait for our 'bus'; we were already getting accustomed to waits. Then we buzzed down the streets to the docks, where we threaded in and out of the quays and store sheds till we came to the train.

It was dark, and the great docks, with the still and starlit sky above them, made an impressive picture. Suddenly out of the gloom a voice greeted me: 'That you, sir? I was in the 80th at Sangor!' An old N.C.O. of my battery in India, now doing the 'seating' on the train. We chat about old times over a cup of chocolate in the Y.M.C.A. coffee-shop. Then 'Good-bye and good luck!' and the train rumbles off into the dark.

Eliot Crawshay-Williams, *Leaves from an Officer's Notebook*

The Draft

The tabor-drums are rattling, and through these,
 The drum, which opens doors, now fills the air:
The bagpipes rumble like a swarm of bees,
 And fifes like songbirds warble; trumpets blare,
And cymbals tinkle; then, weighed down by packs,
 An orderly line of troops with measured pace,
Carrying their treasured burden on their backs,
 File past in step, moving with equal grace,
And rifles over their hard shoulders slung,
 Sniffing their prey from afar, as they pass by,
The weak, the strong, all different, but all young;
 Onwards they go. Knowing not where nor why,
They turn to their appointed destinies,
To France, to Egypt, Canaan, to long peace.

R. Williams Parry
(Translated from the Welsh)

Leaving for France

The night before we sailed for France was marvellous. Gone was the brooding and the apprehension, giving way to a strange exhilaration which took the queerest forms. Two brothers, delightful fellows and magnificent in their strength – namesakes of mine – challenged each other to race a hundred lengths of the hut, They set out, clad only in the skin which nature and training had toughened, while the rest of us sat on our beds and cheered them on. At last they dropped exhausted, dead beat in a dead heat.

With the morning we paraded and marched to the station singing the crazy songs of the period. 'Tipperary' vied with 'Keep the Home Fires Burning', or 'Pack up Your Troubles in Your Old Kit-bag', or 'There's a Long, Long Trail Awinding', and when the band ceased playing a mouth-organ here and there continued the melody. In an hour we reached Dover and with orderly haste boarded a troopship and put on lifebelts as a precaution against submarine attack.

It was a beautiful day, warm and bright, with scarcely a cloud in the sky and a sea which reflected its calm. But for the lifebelts and two long lean destroyers which shot ahead of our vessel and then turning each in its own length encircled us, we might easily have imagined that we were taking a pleasure cruise. As the ship ploughed its way through the water, everyone turned to take yet another look at the chalk cliffs receding in the distance. People have gushed and sentimentalised over that scene but there *is* something poignant about any leave-taking which bids fair to be one's last. No one spoke in that moment and when the silence was broken we talked of cabbages and sealing-wax and kings – in short, of anything and everything except the thought which lay uppermost in our minds.

We disembarked at Boulogne and as we marched through its streets on to the hill whence Napoleon viewed our shores, dreaming his dream of conquest, little French girls and boys yelled themselves hoarse or begged for souvenirs. One tiny chap had mastered enough English to shriek 'Ginger, you balmy' to Bowes, a red-headed man in my platoon, while the long lines rocked with laughter in which he joined as heartily as anyone.

As night came, everything grew colder and dark clouds began to pile up from the north-east. By two o'clock in the morning snow was falling heavily so that tent-ropes had to be slackened, and tempers frayed lest the canvas should tumble in upon men who lay down and could not sleep. For the vast majority of us it was our first experience of 'Sunny France'.

Morgan Watcyn-Williams, *From Khaki to Cloth*

Setting Toward France

So they went most of that day and it rained with increasing vigour until night-fall. In the middle afternoon the outer parts of the town of embarkation were reached. They halted for a brief while; adjusted puttees, straightened caps, fastened undone buttons, tightened rifle-slings and attended each one to his own bedraggled and irregular condition. The band recommenced playing; and at the attention and in excellent step they passed through the suburbs, the town's centre, and so towards the docks. The people of that town did not acclaim them, nor stop about their business – for it was late in the second year.

By some effort of a corporate will the soldierly bearing of the text books maintained itself through the town, but with a realisation of the considerable distance yet to be covered through miles of dock, their frailty reasserted itself – which slackening called for fresh effort from the Quilters and the Snells, but at this stage with a more persuasive intonation, with almost motherly concern.

Out of step and with a depressing raggedness of movement and rankling of tempers they covered another mile between dismal sheds, high and tarred. Here funnels and mastheads could be seen. Here the influence of the sea and of the tackle and ways of its people fell upon them. They revived somewhat, and for a while. Yet still these interminable ways between – these incessant halts at junctions. Once they about-turned. Embarkation officers, staff people of all kinds and people who looked as though they were in the Navy but who were not, consulted with the Battalion Commander. A few more halts, more passing of messages – a further intensifying of their fatigue. The platoons of the leading company unexpectedly wheel. The spacious shed is open at either end, windy and comfortless. Multifarious accoutrements, metal and cloth and leather sink with the perspiring bodies to the concrete floor.

Certain less fortunate men were detailed for guard, John Ball amongst them. The others lay, where they first sank down, wet with rain and sweat. They smoked; they got very cold. They were given tins of bully beef and ration biscuits for the first time, and felt like real expeditionary soldiers. Sometime between midnight and 2 a.m. they were paraded. Slowly, and with every sort of hitch, platoon upon platoon formed single file and moved toward an invisible gangway. Each separate man found his own feet stepping in the darkness on an inclined plane, the smell and taste of salt and machinery, the texture of rope, and the glimmer of shielded light about him.

So without sound of farewell or acclamation, shrouded in a dense windy darkness, they set toward France. They stood close on deck and beneath deck, each man upholstered in his life-belt. From time to time a seaman would push between them about some duty belonging to his trade.

David Jones, *In Parenthesis*, part 1 (1937)

Leaving for France

[January 28, 1917] . . . We are to move at 6.30am tomorrow. Horton and Smith and I dined together laughing at imbecile jests and at Smith's own laughing. Had to change in order to send home my soiled things. Letters. Mess accounts and cheques to tradesmen.

[January 29]. Up at 5. Very cold. Off at 6.30, men marching in frosty dark to station singing 'Pack up your troubles in your old kit-bag'. The rotten song in the still dark brought one tear. No food or tea – Freezing carriage. Southampton at 9.30 and there had to wait till dusk, walking up and down, watching ice-scattered water, gulls and dark wood, beyond, or London Scottish playing improvised Rugger, or men dancing to concertina, in a great shed between railway and water. Smith and I got off for lunch after Horton and Capt. Lushington returned from theirs. Letter to Helen from 'South Western Hotel', where sea-captains were talking of the 'Black Adder' and of 'The Black Ball Line' that used to go to Australia. Hung about till dark – the seagulls as light failed nearly all floated instead of flying – then sailed at 7. Thorburn turned up. Now I'm in 2nd officer's cabin with Capt. and Horton, the men outside laughing and joking and saying fucking. Q.W.R.s and Scottish and a Field Battery and 236 S.B., also on 'The Mona Queen'. Remember the entirely serious and decorous writing in urinal whitewash – name, address, unit and date of sailing. A tumbling crossing, but rested.

[January 30]. Arrived Havre 4am. Light of stars and windows of tall pale houses and electric arcs on quay. March through bales of cotton in sun to camp. The snow first emptying its castor of finest white. Tents. Mess full of subalterns censoring letters. Breakfast at 9.45am on arrival. Afternoon in Havre, which Thorburn likes because it is French. Mess unendurably hot and stuffy, tent unendurably cold till I got into my blankets. Slept well in fug. Snow at night.

Edward Thomas, *The Diary of Edward Thomas*
1 January – 8 April 1917 (1971)

Roads

I love roads:
The goddesses that dwell
Far along invisible
Are my favourite gods.

Roads go on
While we forget, and are
Forgotten like a star
That shoots and is gone.

On this earth 'tis sure
We men have not made
Anything that doth fade
So soon, so long endure:

The hill road wet with rain
In the sun would not gleam
Like a winding stream
If we trod it not again.

They are lonely
While we sleep, lonelier
For lack of the traveller
Who is now a dream only.

From dawn's twilight
And all the clouds like sheep
On the mountains of sleep
They wind into the night.

The next turn may reveal
Heaven: upon the crest
The close pine clump, at rest
And black, may Hell conceal.

Often footsore, never
Yet of the road I weary,
Though long and steep and dreary,
As it winds on for ever.

Helen of the roads,
The mountain ways of Wales
And the Mabinogion tales
Is one of the true gods,

Abiding in the trees,
The threes and fours so wise,
The larger companies,
That by the roadside be,

And beneath the rafter
Else uninhabited
Excepting by the dead;
And it is her laughter

At morn and night I hear
When the thrush cock sings
Bright irrelevant things,
And when the chanticleer

Calls back to their own night
Troops that make loneliness
With their light footsteps' press,
As Helen's own are light.

Now all roads lead to France
And heavy is the tread
Of the living; but the dead
Returning lightly dance:

Whatever the road bring
To me or take from me,
They keep me company
With their pattering,

Crowding the solitude
Of the loops over the downs,
Hushing the roar of towns
And their brief multitude.

Edward Thomas

35

Departure of a Troopship

Departure of a troopship new style: All day long solitary officers have been arriving at the great gates leading to the docks. There they have been questioned, and, on demonstrating their business, have been directed to the Embarkation Officer. No woman, except on special duty, is allowed inside the dock gates. Farewells must be said outside. Later in the day, say about 4pm, trains full of jubilant soldiers have run right into the quays themselves. There they have disgorged their occupants, who have piled their arms and kit in the huge sheds once devoted to more peaceful purposes, and made themselves as comfortable as circumstances permit. Some have a talk, some lie and smoke, some just lie. After the first arrival there is little excitement.

The detached officers who keep arriving first interview the Embarkation Officer. He gives them a green chit to enable them to draw two days' rations, and a note to another Embarkation Officer nearer the boat. After exchanging the green chit for a cardboard box containing about a dozen apparent dog-biscuits, a tin of milk, two small tins of pressed beef, a tin of 'Plum and Apple' jam, two little oval tobacco-like tins labelled 'Grocery Rations', and sundry mysterious paper packets, these officers proceed to the second Embarkation Officer. He is a genial old Colonel with a fire-and-brimstone manner, but a good heart.

'My senior officer,' he bellows, 'says no one must take his baggage on board yet. But,' he goes on more confidentially, but still as if condemning a criminal, 'if I were you, I should run it as near the boat as I could in a cab, and then drop it on board at my own risk, of course. Anyone taking the best cabins,' he finishes, 'is liable to be turned out if senior officers afterwards arrive.'

Then all go on board. After taking cabins (with due regard to the kind advice of our fire-eating friend), there is an hour to spend before we need finally 'join our ship'. Some spend it in driving round Southampton; some are once more 'seen off'. At last all assemble on board.

Then the men march on. First the R.E. in single file marshalled by a subaltern, and directed to their places by a capable ship's under-officer. Next the R.H.A. and R.F.A. The leading draft are a somewhat weedy lot. 'Wouldn't change 'em with my chaps,' whispers a Territorial R.H.A. Major to his neighbour. But the next lot are stronger and more disciplined-looking. I suppose it depends on the locality whence they are drawn. Then comes a third draft of artillery, and all are aboard. We are only taking about 700 men over, and our boat is small and fast. The men themselves are quiet and well-behaved; an occasional 'Tipperary' or more recent ditty is the limit of their noise-making. And none are drunk. The only man who has evinced any signs of super-cheeriness is one of the boat's officers, who asks me who the C.O. is, and, when I say, 'Colonel Bowling,' replies, 'Not my ole frien' Tom Bowling? I shall have to make the acquaintance of Colonel Bowling . . .' Then he goes off walking just a little too straight to be convincing.

There is a long wait. It is seven before we are off; and, coming up from a chop (rations are not compulsory), I am just in time to see the last wharf of the docks slide past. Fifteen years ago I saw it slide past from the deck of another trooper. But that was on a very different mission, merely taking a draft to India. Today there is a grimmer feeling in the air. And we do get some cheering, after all. The crews of the boats we pass give us our send-off, and we pass little groups of waving men till at last we creep out through the great boom. The final and most uproarious interchange of salutations is between ourselves and three girls in a boat.

As the land draws away into the twilight, I wonder for how many of these cheering lads it will be their last sight of home.

Eliot Crawshay-Williams,
Leaves from an Officer's Notebook

The End of a Leave

It was on the 5th May, 1916, that this ten days of delight was destined to end. Our last evening together we spent at some theatre; I have forgotten what we ·saw, but it is easy enough, even after this long interval of time, to remember the insidious growth of the canker of sadness, and to capture once again the struggle to turn the mind away from the morrow. Six months had passed since we sat in Winchester, on the eve of my first sailing overseas, oppressed by the same burden, and making the same effort to cast it off. Love grows rapidly in the forcing-house of war, and the dull ache of absence fosters a sensitivity and quickens response. The poets have taught us that to mortals endowed with their own delicacy of emotional structure, parting can become an agony of a death, but war, with its rude barbarian violence, had made even of us ordinary creatures, a regiment of sufferers. Common clay as we were, and far enough removed as we thought ourselves from the spun glass of the poet's imagining, we found ourselves betrayed into the very emotions they had sung. That the prose of war should prove the truth of poetry's tale of man's feeling – that it should now be easy to believe that some of those magic lines were indeed a reflection of the real thoughts of real men and women – that was an astonishing discovery. I had read a quantity of poetry, and had even tried to write it, but all with a sense of projecting my personality into an adjacent field of life. Here and now I was treading, at some remove, the very paths the poets had walked before me.

Llewelyn Wyn Griffith, *Up to Mametz* (1931)

The Send-off

Down the close, darkening lanes they sang their way
To the siding-shed,
And lined the train with faces grimly gay.

Their breasts were stuck all white with wreath and spray
As men's are, dead.

Dull porters watched them, and a casual tramp
Stood staring hard,
Sorry to miss them from the upland camp.

Then, unmoved, signals nodded, and a lamp
Winked to the guard.

So secretly, like wrongs hushed-up, they went.
They were not ours:
We never heard to which front these were sent;

Nor there if they yet mock what women meant
Who gave them flowers.

Shall they return to beatings of great bells
In wild train-loads?
A few, a few, too few for drums and yells,

May creep back, silent, to still village wells
Up half-known roads.

Wilfred Owen

Somewhere
in
France

Charles Pritchard Clayton

France, 1915
(From 'The Song is Theirs')

Grey is the sky, the rain
grey in the dawn declined from dark
sodden weary benumbed. No life
but in this round of rain and wind,
no tree and all is strange
the world halted an instant here.

    There is a drum beats in the East
and Drummer Death is strong
Not Yet his drumbeats say Not Yet
I drink not wine of youth unbittered
with herb of pain Not Yet
I have a cellar in the East
will hold your days till they be ripe.
O rest, sink deep your feet in mire
till you be customwise to earthy touch
of your unnumbered kin.
    So Death.
The column moves, the bugles flaunt the rain.

Each day a testament of dying years
a wreath of mist upon the trees
tall unregarding in the dusk and still,
so far removed from all . . .
    If this be life, to count falling hours
in youth, hoard minutes,
ape the mood of age
before a line be scribed by wisdom
on this vellum of the brow
    If this be life . . .
No stars pinking the mantled grey
no moon no stir of wind waking,
along the road a file of men
and through the hundred hearts a shrinking boldness
in-and-out, longing and fear, an eager dread.

This lightning East, this thunder sunk to earth
this pulse of what new devilment
now loud now soft, what rhythm this?

A screech uprising hell-governed in its course
through wild long octaves of alarm
until the noise puts end to noise
and all is emptiness and thirst,
what rhythm this?

　　'There is a fear of Fear
hath greater skill to halt the blood
and break the man within
than aught in armoury of war.'

Quick, summon pride
to master shrinking flesh, to man the walls
in my defence.
　　　　　　　　Were there not men
withstood this press before their lives
sank into tales of bravery?

But these are eyes regard me, search me.
I am no man but in their faith
that I am more than they . . .
so little worth their trust,
sent to-and-fro by doubt and pride . . .
so little worth.

This fear I conquered now
hath it not heirs unnumbered
waiting my fall?
These tongue-dried moments . . .

　　　　I have a salve saith Time
release from fear from stabbing awe
this anodyne.

　　　　Count all my coin
there is no price I would not pay.

　　　　Turn to thy task,
this gold unstamped with pain is dross.
Hark to the Drummer.
He is thy foe, stand to thy weapon now,
seek not so soon this balm,
there are elder brethren wait.

East to the prisonwall of trench.
The tenant of this plain beyond forbids
my gaze upon his husbandry.
This clotted waste breast-high
into the far rim of hedge,
a splintered tree a mass of spears
against what fate what unconcern?

Grey imprint on the bird-bare field
pockmarked and foul
slimed with the trail of folly blind-distraught:
a land remote, soilbordered scars.
Soiled I this land with hate?

I have no hate but of this ugliness,
no fear but that I sink below
the grey disaster spread to hide
cool pricking green and May
a gift to other eyes in other lands,
colour on cloud above the hills.

This servitude of mud
this sly recumbency beneath a threat
lurking in rat-disputed dyke,
this endless struggle with a mastery
of seeping water, husbandry of filth
and rank decay, this toil to build a grave
where once the plough made furrow . . .
Gave I my freedom thus to spend?

But I have men who wait with me,
stars pricking a song upon the sheet of sky.
I knew not men till now,
I knew not succour in a laughing word
affection in a curse;
blood-brethren now, Cain-marked or free.

Eyes slow to warn the limbs,
void where was richness and warm blood,
no path through flesh cold-weary
deaf to my bidding, rebel to my will.

All is afar, haze-hidden,
a petty thought revolves an endless trill of haste.
O bring me sleep silent and smooth,
cool coverlet of sleep
and in the end release.

Too swift a word, too kind,
respite is all free-given now,
but gift enough.
Savour of living air,
hard crust of stone against the feet,
boughs patterncurved against the stars,
quiet shuttered house, reprieve of voice:
eyes born in the dark to sweep
borders of the seen-unseen.
Limbs free to move unshrinkingly
ears sharp to laughter and O
this unremembered beauty of the dusk
when all is still to greet the moon:
slow patient cattle in the grass.
Long catalogue of smallness bursting great
upon a starved heart, day turned long life
to spend recklessly gladly
in joy in gratitude.
But there is a morrow
and this I know a scene upon a stage,
mere trick of art to cozen me
I am kin with man.

Believe it not . . . hark to the drums.

I have played at in-and-out with danger
a thousand times, grown old in craft,
plumbed hidden fear beneath the heart.
I am known to Death. His iron hand
to right and left moves quickly . . .
Hath it an end, this pilgrimage?

Bring dark bring day
scatter the stars to bridge the sky
drive cloud to hold the moon,

no liberty of flesh, the burden falls not.
My metal thins to a thread will snap
and I turned worshipper of little gods
who scatter chance to man.

This giant impotence shadows me,
Blinds me.

Llewelyn Wyn Griffith

'Just like the French'

It was curious how the attitude of the French varied towards us. One old woman insisted not without truth that but for the British the war would have been over long ago. What is more, she lived up to her belief and the inferences she made from it, contriving in a hundred and one ways to make things awkward for us. She took the handle off the pump so that unshaved and without our usual drink of hot tea we looked a sorry crowd on parade. Only a recital of the facts saved us from the wrath to come. The services of a gendarme were required before the pump-handle was restored and we were enabled to wash.

'Just like the French.' That was the comment of our men, but in the same village was another old lady. She lived in the little house, a room of which we had commandeered for the company stores, and during the weeks we spent in that neighbourhood it was an increasing delight to talk to her. There were stories of grandsons at Verdun and now and then we would persuade her to relate her experiences in the bitter days of 1870.

I had to guard the stores between the hours of 4 and 6am. The weather was cold and the wind swept through the street cutting me to the bone, greatcoat notwithstanding. Every morning without fail the old lady appeared at the door about ten minutes past five, bringing with her a bowl of hot coffee and a hunk of bread and butter. That, too, was 'Just like the French.'

Morgan Watcyn-Williams, From Khaki to Cloth

The French and the Welsh

The French and the Welsh become very friendly. It is a hard job to prevent the exchange of helmets, bayonets, caps, puttees and whatnot, to such an extent as to have our men taken for French troops on the way back from the line. In temperament the Welsh and the French seem to have much in common. The English worship the idea of the unbroken square, the unbroken line, at any rate some outward and visible sign of conformity. Not so the French and the Welsh. In the village of Loos the other day the French soldiers were strolling about in considerable numbers. There was no trace of excitement, yet no sign of uniformity of movement. On the slopes of Hill 70 when the shelling was heavy and the attack was developing we could see French soldiers moving about with so little evident purpose or control that more than once some of our men, watching, called out 'the French are retreating.'

Yet they were not. They were probably adjusting themselves to the situation in a far more elastic, and possibly more effective, way than was plain to the onlooker. In the calm self-reliance and disregard of danger, and equal disregard of external discipline in a crisis; in their impatience with what they regard as the mere formalities of soldiering the Welshmen, especially the miners of whom there are so many in the Battalion, and the French in these parts at least, seem to see eye to eye. The English Officer fails, I think, to do justice in his own mind to the Welsh miner-soldier, who has no use for the martinet officer, for clean buttons in the trenches, for arms drill and sentry-go, but who, when it comes to fighting, is absolutely imperturbable. In virtue of the very independence of spirit that makes him unhappy on the parade ground, he can be depended upon to take initiative when there is no one at hand to command.

Charles Pritchard Clayton, *The Hungry One*,
edited by Michael Clayton, from diaries collated in the 1920s (1978)

In a French Village

J.S.L.
This is all my address: 12th S.W.B.
B.E.F. France.
Thursday, 7.6.16.

My Dear Margaret,

I think I told you we were settled now in a little French village about fifteen miles from where the guns begin, and it is here we remain, in billets, very comfortable and enjoying the new surroundings immensely.

The French people are delightful; they are, as you expect, mostly women and children, and old men, as well as a sprinkling of wounded who have been discharged, or men unfit. At places we come across refugees from further east, from La Bassée and the places you see mentioned in the newspapers. What I like is their simplicity, the open intimacy of their life. They take us into their kitchens and family circles naturally. This village, as one old madame said to me yesterday, is governed by the English; it is English troops they have had here from the beginning of war, so that they know our ways and can put up with them.

They are kindly people, their houses are poor as you'd expect of peasants, yet bright and clean, and their food is always appetising. I sleep in a bed – in sheets that are white and sweet. We have all the comforts you have – newspapers, a few books; only the water is undrinkable, and light wines and ales are the staple drinks. *Estaminets* and cafés are everywhere, eggs are cheap and fresh every morning. Daily life is simple, gentle and pleasant. (I have added the pencil details since getting your letter this noon, hence all the particulars in reply.)

We are not working at all hard, as we're supposed to be resting – God knows after what. Nor are we likely to go up to the firing line till well into the end of next week. We get all the news daily, but as you say it is almost better without it, Kitchener gone and the North Sea fight only a very partial success. Russia is again the only bright spot.

Your letter is the best thing that has happened today. I can understand how you feel. But I am learning from these French people. With them the war is a close reality. One break in that line from where we can now hear the guns booming, and the Germans would be living with them, billeted where we are now. Yet day to day is entirely normal; danger and loss are so much closer neighbours than with those who are away; this is all. Every house here has a son or sons or father or brother, either killed, wounded, or fighting. The essentials remain the same with us as with you, and there is very little abnormal or even artificial.

With most of us the causes of anxiety are in England.

Au revoir, Margaret. (Just outside the window a tiny little girl is leading a calf to the stable quite alone.)

Yours, yours,
Saunders

Saunders Lewis, letter to Margaret Gilcriest,
Saunders Lewis: Letters to Margaret Gilcriest

Trench-French

A knowledge of Welsh is useful in the understanding of French – an assertion quite unnecessary to the philologist who knows how Latin has influenced both French and Welsh, though in the latter case the influence is less generally recognised. One lad from Ffestiniog – certainly no philologist – is convinced that French is only an inferior Welsh, which somehow, and at some time, strayed into the Continent and did not improve by contact with the foreign tongues. Seeking with his chum the eternal egg in a French farmhouse he addressed the farmer's wife.

'Compree, Madame, compree egg?'

'Oui Monsieur, Oui,' replied Madame, wise in the habits and requirements of the British soldier.

Turning to his friend he exclaimed, 'Myn jiawst, there's funny, mun – she said *wy** as plain as anything.' Turning to Madame he said 'Dou' and held up two fingers. The eggs were brought, Madame demanding 'Trois pence pour un' which to the Welshman sounded like 'Tri pence yr un.' He wonderingly paid the sixpence, and on his way back to the billet expounded his thesis of the ultimate origin of this corrupt Welsh . . .

. . . A big Guardsman took me to a Flemish farm. Putting his head through the window he shouted without ceremony, 'Monsieur, avez-vous hoofs to-day?'

Turning to me he said ''Ear that, kid – hoofs, that's the bleedin' word they 'ave for heggs out 'ere – hoofs.' I thanked him; it is no mean honour to have been taught French by a Corporal of the Grenadier Guards . . .

What will a civilian make of the following? 'Mae Fritz a'i bloomin' strafes no bon heddi. Daeth whizz-bang just mewn i'n dugout ni, a dowlws sopyn o fwd dros y bleedin' mangy. Mae Shoni beaucoup wind-up o achos a, ond w'i yn très bien fair play.' Probably nothing! Yet this mixture of Welsh, English, French, German and slang is perfectly comprehensible to the Welsh troops in France today. In plain English it means, 'The German shellfire is very severe today. One shell from a light field gun nearly came into our dugout, and it threw a lot of mud over our food. Shoni is frightened, but I'm not – fair play.'

This is the result of three years of war. If the war lasts yet another three years those who remain at home will have to be taught the new language when the boys come home.

Fred Ambrose, 'Trench-French',
The Welsh Outlook, vol. v, no. 52, April 1918

* *wy*, meaning *egg*, is pronounced exactly like the French *oui* in South Walian Welsh.

A Letter from 'Somewhere in France'

Dear Friend,

I probably won't have to tell you who I am as you begin to read my letter, because its untidiness will answer for itself . . . At the moment I am living in a very strange place, and it's very difficult to know what you are here. The second day after my arrival, two lads were walking slowly between the tents in the heat, and they said as they went past, 'Well, kid.' But the next day on parade the officer asked me, amongst others, 'Well, man, did you shave this morning?' Whether the two lads or the officer was right, I'll leave it to you to decide. Also I have reached a place which is full of romantic and unusual experiences. When three or four of us were complaining about the heat, a veteran with a yellow complexion came by and said: 'You've no cause to grumble, lads. What if you were in the Sudan as I was some years ago. I had a bronze helmet on my head and I wore a bronze breastplate, and sometime around two o'clock, I could see something running down my trousers, and when I looked I saw that the helmet and the breastplate were melting rapidly, so what have you got to complain about?'

This is a very beautiful country from what I have seen of it up to now – the trees high and full-leafed, and their leaves shaking, quivering and murmuring, as though they were trying to say something mysterious, or as though some nostalgic spirit from Wales was returning sadly after failing to find someone who is lying in a grave 'Somewhere in France'. I saw some rosebushes, and the lips of every rose so bright and crimson that it seemed as though a myriad kisses slept in them; and because the weather here is so fine, the sunset is a beautiful spectacle, with the sun on the far side of the battalions of trees setting as beautiful as an angel of fire. Soon after, a thin veil the colour of blood can be discerned over the horizon, with a yellowness like the colour of primroses woven into it; but the most beautiful thing I have seen since coming here is an old shell-case that had been adapted to grow flowers: a small green plant hid the upper half of the old shell, and nine or ten small flowers could be seen between the leaves. And doesn't that prove that beauty is stronger than war, and that loveliness will survive the madness? But the flowers of France in the future will be flowers of sadness, and a sad wind will blow over the land, because the flowers will be of the colour of blood and the wind will be full of the sound of mourning.

There are many kinds of people to be seen here. I have seen many Russians, and it is amusing to watch them, knowing that they have already witnessed eternity – their country, its ancient bondage and its sudden awakening. There are many Indians here also, with hair like a horse's mane, a dark, yellow-black complexion and teeth as white as marble, and the influence of their strange gods on every thing they do. I also saw some German prisoners, with the shadows in

49

Rhiwle yn Ffrainc Mef 25, 1917

Anwyl Gyfaill

... mae'n debyg nad oes eisiau i mi
ddweyd wrthych pwy ydwyf wrth
ddechrau fy llythyr ...
bydd ei hun ... ar ... ateb drostaf yn gyntaf ...
yn disgwyl eich bod yn
wella, Wel myfi yn ...
lle doniol iawn rwan ...
ambyd i chwi iw gwybo...
beth ydych yma, yr ...
ar ol i mi gyrhaedd y ...
dau hogyn yn cerdd...
rhwng y tentiau yn ...
a dyna'r ddau yn dwe...
mhalio. "Well Kid" ...
ar y Parade dymhar...

yn gofyn i mi yn mysg eraill
"Well man" did you shave this
morning i" yntau'n swpdlog. a'r
hogiau redd yn iawn cewch
chwi ddweyd, hefyd myfi wedi
digwydd disgyn mewn lle llawn
o brofiadau rhamantus a.
an ghyffredin, Dan redd, Pan
redd tri neu bedwar o honom
yn cwpro ar y fwres, daeth
hen filwr wyneb felyn heibio
a dyna fon deud, Well peidiwch
a cwyno Boys Bach beth pelae
chwi yn Soudan fel ..... nun
fath a fi, roedd ....

.... dau or gloch i chwi, gwelwn rhiwbeth
yn llifo hyd fy nhrowsys. ac arbysn
edrych roedd yr helmet ar plat yn brysur
doddi, Beth ydych chwi'n cwyno Boys Bach.
mae yma wlad rhyfeddol o dlos yn y
rhanau welais i hyd yn hyn. y coed yn
uchel a deiliog. a'i dail i gyd yn ysgwyd
crynu. a murmur fel pe baent yn ceisio
deud rhiwbeth na wyddom ni ddim am dano.
neu fel pe bai hiraeth siomedig o Gymru.
yn dod yn ol yn athrist ar ol methu cael
hyd i rhiwun ....

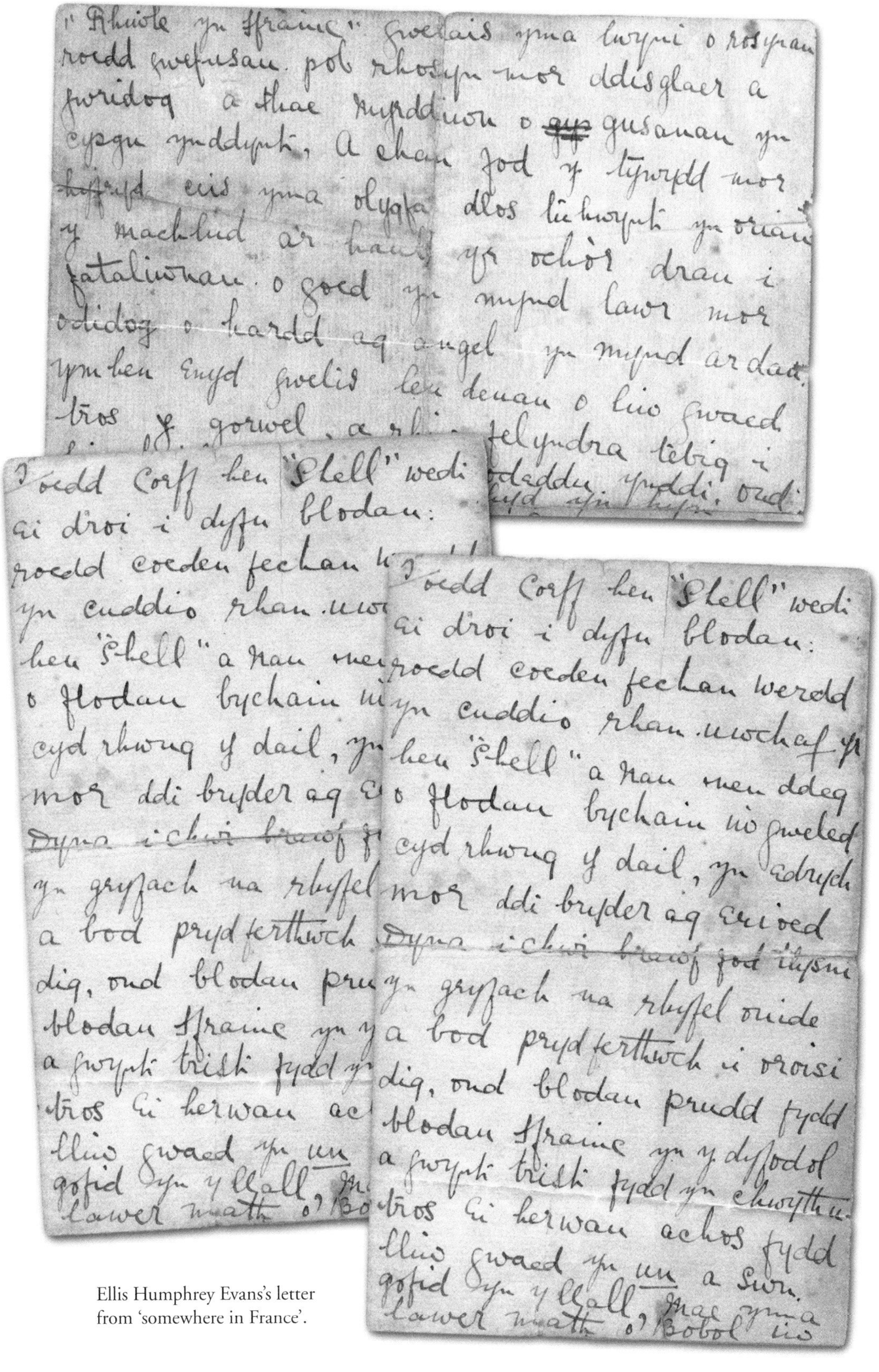

"Rhiole yn Ffrainc" Gwelais yma lwyni o rosynau
roedd gwefusau pob rhosyn mor ddisglaer a
gwridog a thae myrddiwn o [illegible] gusanau yn
cysgu ynddynt. A chan fod y tywydd mor
[illegible] ceis yma olygfa dlos [illegible] yn oriau
y machlud ar [illegible] yr ochor draw i
fataliwnau o goed yn mynd lawr mor
odidog o hardd ag angel yn mynd ar daith
ymhen ennyd gwelis ben denau o liw gwaed
tros y gorwel, a rhi[illegible] felyndra tebig i
[illegible] oddddu ynddi. Ond

roedd Corff hen "Shell" wedi
ei droi i dyfu blodau:
roedd coeden fechan werdd
yn cuddio rhan uwchaf yr
hen "Shell" a nau neu ddeg
o flodau bychain i'w gweled
cyd rhwng y dail, yn edrych
mor ddi bryder ag erioed
Dyna i chwi brawf fod bywyd
yn gryfach na rhyfel onide
a bod prydferthwch i oroesi
dig, ond blodau prudd fydd
blodau Ffrainc yn y dyfodol
a gwynt trist fydd yn chwythu
tros ei herwau achos fydd
lliw gwaed yn un a sun
gofid yn y llall, mae yma
lawer math o' Bobol i'w

Ellis Humphrey Evans's letter
from 'somewhere in France'.

their eyes reflecting the disintegration of a great empire. I haven't reached danger yet, but in the middle of the night I can hear the distant rumble of artillery guns. Perhaps I'll have more leisure and will have gained more experience to write my next letter. My regards to you and your family and to everyone else back home.

Yours, as usual,
Hedd Wyn

Ellis Humphrey Evans (Hedd Wyn), letter to H. O. Evans, Trawsfynydd,
June 25, 1917, published in *Y Rhedegydd*, July 7, 1917;
original letter kept at the Archives and Welsh Library
at the University of Wales, Bangor

Ellis Humphrey Evans (Hedd Wyn)

Life
in the
Trenches

The First Trenches

We entered Bailleul in the afternoon and the people there were very glad to see us. The place had been in possession of the enemy for a few days and the Uhlans had intended to billet there that night. At this place Stevens rejoined the Battalion. His wanderings on the retirement had been similar to my own: he had also been to Le Mans and had been in hospital a week with fever and ague, after which he had been sent up country and had been serving with another unit for a fortnight. The next morning as we left Bailleul on our way to Vlamertinghe we saw about a dozen Uhlans galloping for all they were worth back from the outskirts. We fired a few shots but they were too far away for us to do any damage. The sight of one Uhlan would frighten the French people more than if half a dozen large shells were exploding in their villages. They told us that the Uhlans were brigands of the first water and would pinch anything they could carry with them. Although the French were our allies we used to do much the same. But we had to be careful: at this early date in the War the penalty for looting was death. We were at Vlamertinghe a few days and then marched for thirteen hours, arriving at a place named Laventie the following morning; we must have come a roundabout way to have taken that time. We moved off again at daybreak and relieved some French troops the further side of Fromelles on the Belgian frontier: two days later we retired back through Fromelles and dug our trenches about four hundred yards this side of that village.

Little did we think when we were digging those trenches that we were digging our future homes; but they were the beginnings of the long stretch that soon went all the way from the North Sea to Switzerland and they were our homes for the next four years. Each platoon dug in on its own, with gaps of about forty yards between each platoon. B Company were in support, but one platoon of B were on the extreme right of the Battalion's front line. On our left were the 1st Middlesex, and on our right was a battalion of Indian native infantry. Our Company Commander used to visit the other three platoons at night; he, the Second-in-Command of the Company and the platoon officer stayed on the extreme right of our trench. We dug those trenches simply for fighting; they were breast-high with the front parapet on ground level and in each bay we stood shoulder to shoulder. We were so squeezed for room that whenever an officer passed along the trench one man would get behind the traverse if the officer wanted to stay awhile in that bay. No man was allowed to fire from behind the traverse: because the least deflection of his rifle would put a bullet through someone in the bay in front of him. Traverses were made to counteract enfilade rifle-fire. Sandbags were unknown at this time.

Frank Richards, *Old Soldiers Never Die*

From the Ypres Salient

People out here seem to think that the war is going to be quite short, why, I don't know; personally, I see nothing here to prevent it going on for ever. We never attack the Germans, and simply do our utmost to maintain ourselves; when we seem to advance it is really that the Germans have evacuated the place. Someone once said that war was utter boredom for months interspersed by moments of acute terror – the boredom is a fact . . . Except for a belt of about twelve miles where the battle is being waged, the whole country shows hardly a sign of war. In many places the inhabitants return the day after the battle . . . We have had a lot of fighting all in trenches and look like having more . . . The other day we were evacuating some trenches and the question was if we could cross a piece of much-shelled ground safely – i.e. Was it under direct observation of their gunners? 'Send on one troop and see' was the order. I was first, and I saw the men's faces look rather long. I had no cigarettes, so I took a ration biscuit in one hand and a lump of cheese in the other and retired eating these in alternate mouthfuls to 'restore confidence'. We escaped without a shell, but I almost choked myself! It looks to me as if we shall have a busy time now . . .

Colwyn Philipps, letter to his mother, March 12, 1915,
Verses: Prose Fragments: Letters from the Front (1916)

Life in the Trenches

9th R.W.F.,
B.E.F. France,
28th August, 1915

My Dear Brother,

. . . The trenches are now for the most part not cut into the ground but built of sandbags above the ground so that it is really more comfortable. In front of the trenches are listening posts where men are stationed, especially by night, to watch for any hostile movement.

There are of course lots of dead between the trenches and half-buried bodies – an arm or a leg sticks out here and there. There are, to add to the general discomfort, any number of large rats.

Patrols go out from each company by night and sometimes by day, generally consisting of 1 officer and a N.C.O. These patrols go right close up to the German lines. One of our officers went out the other night and got into an old German trench which was full of dead who had been there for several months. He crawled along over their faces! Some of the remarks made by the Germans are very funny and more funny as reported by our men whose letters we censor. Here is an extract from a letter: 'The Germans shouted out "Hoch der Kaiser" and we shouted back "Oh! B . . . r the Kaiser" and the Germans answered "You are no gentlemen".' Many such choice epithets as 'You Welsh Bastards' are hurled at our lines. It really is rather comic.

Bombs are now, of course, much improved, but they have to be carefully handled. One of our officers was accidentally killed with one. There are also used by both sides, as I suppose you know, rifle grenades and trench mortars. The rifle grenade is very good . . .

Soft hats are the rule. It was in orders that the men were to take the wire out of their hats. A Sam-Browne is very necessary here. Also a bath is very essential to bring out with one.

A lot of officers out here wear Tommy's tunics and trousers. The rule out here seems to be dress as you jolly well like.

Best luck,
Glyn

Glyn C. Roberts, letter to his brother, P. Aubrey Roberts,
Witness These Letters: Letters from the Western Front 1915-18,
edited by G. D. Roberts (1983)

Day by Day in the Trenches

Front Line.
July 13, 1916.

My Dear Margaret,

There are all kinds and conditions of dugouts, and up to this time I have been very fortunate. But this one is one of the bad ones. It is very deep down (about 30 feet) but there is a foul smell about it always, and no light comes from the day to cleanse it and so little fresh air that my candles all burn very low here. It has three classes of inmates beside myself. The rats course over the floor, the mice forage about the table and rafters, and vermin drop in swarms wherever you lie or sit. So I shall not be sorry to leave it as I shall do on Saturday.

Would you like to have the story of how a quiet day in the front line passes. To begin with, we turn night into day and day to night. The day begins at 8.45 in the evening when it is still light. I inspect all the rifles of my platoon then, and see that they are all fit for use.

Three quarters of an hour later it is quickly darkening, and the word comes to 'Stand-to'. Every man then mounts the fire-steps of the front line and is on guard with fixed bayonet and rifle loaded to assure that no raiding party from the opposite trench creeps towards us.

As soon as it is full night, the whole line turns to work. The trench needs deepening, and picks and shovels are busy; the wire in front of the line is weak and a patrol goes out over the parapet to repair and strengthen it; sandbags are filled and piled up to make better bays and rests for men to fire over the parapet.

So right up to the first paling of night into the grey of dawn the work continues, and the N.C.Os are generally relied on to see all goes well. The officer has other work. He is responsible for his length of trench, that it is kept in condition and that it is not attacked and that the men working shall not be surprised by the enemy.

So patrols and listening groups and fighting parties are organised and led out beyond our wire entanglement, to prowl the dark long in No Man's Land, watching the Hun lines, listening for any sound from them, crawling as close to their wire and trenches as is safe and possible, sometimes making small bombing raids on their saps.

This until about 2.30 in the small morning, when all the parties are called in before the light should give them to the enemy. A little after 3 it begins to whiten, the Very light illuminations that shoot out all through the dark hours making the long parallels of trenches a ghostly scene, die down gradually; and this is the hour when, if the Germans have been cunning enough to evade our defences during the blackness, they will with the guidance of the dim dawn rush upon us.

So again everyone 'stands-to' on the fire-steps until at last the sun stands out east to make the dangers that hover by night of no avail. We stand down. Rifles that have been fired through the night are cleaned, I have again to inspect them. Breakfast follows at 5.30am, and then the men turn in to sleep until noon. An officer must be on duty with the day sentries always however, and when he promenades up and down the line during the hours before midday in each dugout prone men sleep silently and heavily.

After sleep dinners are served hot, and the afternoon is given to clearing up the trenches and working at the communication and support lines. Tea follows, then until 8.45 a spell of rest, to the beginning of another twenty-four hours.

That is a day of quiet. I cannot describe a day of 'strafing', for then anything may happen. During a quiet day of course we get artillery fire all through, but unless it gets very fierce it does not much disturb us. The only pity is that thus from day to day we occasionally suffer losses.

Well, this is a letter written when not inclined for sleep, so goodbye for a while.

Your loving
Saunders

Saunders Lewis, letter to Margaret Gilcriest,
Saunders Lewis: Letters to Margaret Gilcriest

In the Front Line for the First Time

We moved up to Béthune and Beuvry on the La Bassée road, and on Sunday, November 21, 1915, we went up to the front line for the first time. There the Warwicks and the Staffords, of the famous Seventh Division, made us at home in their shelters and put us through our paces. They instructed us in the mysteries of our craft, of which 'bagging a bougis' seemed the most important. Everywhere in that area the engineers, English and German, were engaged in desperate sapping, and as they used thousands of candles to illuminate their main shafts, the infantry never lost a chance of 'bagging a bougis'. A candle made all the difference in a dugout. It helped us to see the rats instead of merely hearing or feeling them.

The trenches were long, narrow ditches in the ground, twelve or fourteen feet deep, with communicating alleys branching off here and there. They were for the most part one quarter filled with mud, which stank with a stale stench. Great fat rats darted in and out of our shelters or ran along the parapet. Scores of them were shot by the simple device of placing some cheese at the end of a bayonet, and pressing the trigger of one's rifle as they came to feed. Loathsome, foul things, they seemed to me the very incarnation of war, seeking whom they might devour. Beyond lay the barbed wire – strand upon strand protecting us from sudden attack.

No more wretched job greeted the new recruit than joining a wiring party. We crawled from the comparative safety of the trench and began to run out yards of wire to fill in the gaps made by shells. Every few minutes a machine gun would start to stutter, bursting out into a torrent of bitter comment which reeked of the pit. If the artillery was Saul slaying its thousands, machine guns were David wiping out tens of thousands. Flat on our faces we fell waiting for the Very lights to die down, and having finished our task we returned to our dugouts and the fitful sleep of exhaustion in the cold.

The first casualty I saw seared my memory. His name is written in my book of death and there it shall remain. He was the son of a clergyman in a town where I had once lived, but although I knew his father well I never met the lad until we had both joined the army. He lay very still on his stretcher scarcely scarred by the blow which had struck him. Many such scenes were to haunt me in the months that followed, but the stark horror and suddenness of the first abides. This was war and it stalked the earth, bludgeoning life without sense or reason. Of all the millions it slew none was more childlike and innocent than that quiet boy from a mining vicarage, brought up in the paths of peace and apparently incapable of hurting a fly. There were few thrills.

Morgan Watcyn-Williams, *From Khaki to Cloth*

Division of the Spoils

B.E.F. France,
16th September, 1915

My Dear Brother,

I believe the date above is correct. I am sure I can't remember. Anyhow it is Thursday.

I write these lines to you from my dugout in the firing line. We came in last night. We are to have another spell of fifteen days in the trenches and five in reserve again. Then I believe we shall go into Divisional Reserve for about 20 days. We shall have been in then for 40 days – 30 days actually in the trenches and 10 days in Brigade Reserve. In Brigade Reserve, of course, as I told you before, we are under shellfire.

Half a dozen shells burst within two hundred yards of us the other day. Since we came in last night we have had two casualties in my company. Both were caused by trench mortar bombs.

You can see bombs coming through the air easily. We have sentries on watch for them. You first of all see a heavy puff of smoke and then you see the bomb (which looks very like a champagne bottle) coming, turning over and over as it flies.

One of the sentries shouts out 'Coming over, Right' or as the case may be, and the men clear into dugouts.

Unfortunately this morning the men got blocked at a corner and the bomb exploded under a man. It broke the bone completely at the ankle so that his foot was hanging by the skin and broke the leg in three or four places as well, besides inflicting a severe gash in the stomach. The poor fellow died in twenty minutes. The other casualty (by the same bomb) was fairly slight – a head and breast wound.

After that we were more on the alert. They threw about fifty altogether but did no further damage.

Our second battalion is only separated from us by the frontage of our two battalions.

The great thing about this part of the line (we have relieved another battalion of the Brigade) is that it is comparatively free from dead bodies and there are not so many horrid stenches which makes it comparatively cheery work visiting saps and prowling about in front of the line.

We have not had our mail of yesterday yet, so that I don't know whether there are any letters for me.

I have got a very rotten dugout here. It is hardly splinter-proof. But as for our Mess, it is a palace. Why, six people can sit in it at once! The only disadvantage about it is that there are any amount of frogs in it. They peep out of every nook and cranny between the sandbags. There are additional disadvantages. For one thing it seems to be a pet target of German snipers and also it is rather too near the Officers' latrine, which is also a very special target of the Huns. At any rate they put an 18 pounder shell plum in the centre of it the other day.

Strolling round the trenches this morning I found a few stray green peas. I enclose you a specimen which would, I am sure, almost win a prize in the *Daily Mail* Competition! Don't say I don't send you souvenirs!

I believe the Huns opposite us are Saxons, at least they say they are. They shout it out at night time. Certainly they are extraordinary quiet. Some of them are perfectly extraordinary. Two or three of them came right up to the wire in front of the Welsh Regt the other day. The sentry saw them and killed one of them. He wore the uniform of the Prussian Regt.

Some of them brought him in and they fell on him like wolves (of course he was dead) and there was almost a fight about the division of the spoils – his watch, badges, buttons etc. I believe the man who shot him actually got least. Don't you think I have improved as a letter-writer? Tell me honestly, do you find my letters at all coherent and interesting?

If I leave out anything which you would care especially to know, please ask as many questions as you like. You ought by this time to have a fairly complete record of my wanderings and doings in France.

I hope you keep them so that they may be a record to future generations!

Your affectionate brother,
Glyn

Glyn C. Roberts, letter to his brother, P. Aubrey Roberts,
Witness These Letters: Letters from the Western Front 1915-18

A German Boy

Festubert was a death-trap. In its swamps friend and foe alike lay waterlogged with no more than a hundred yards between them. Several men came near to drowning in the deeper water through which a road of trench boards led to the front line. Through a slit in the revetment someone noticed a German boy, cold and half-frozen, swinging a brazier round and round to force it into flame. We could have picked him off more easily than hitting a wicket, yet when one of the men turned to raise a rifle the others bade him desist. 'Poor ——'s as cold as we are,' was the verdict, and in a minute or two he dropped back into his trench with his fire-bucket burning merrily.

I thought much on the incident. What would happen if that spirit spread? Both staffs had forbidden fraternisation, but there were moments when humanity could not be denied. You may call it bad discipline but when human life is so disciplined and dragooned that it cannot rise to such an attitude, hell will have seized the reins for aye.

Morgan Watcyn-Williams, *From Khaki to Cloth*

Conversations with the Enemy

During this time we often carried on conversations with the enemy, and one night one of them shouted across in excellent English: 'Hello, Second Royal Welch Fusiliers, how are you?' We shouted back and enquired who they were. 'The same regiment that you spent your Christmas day with in Houplines,' came the reply. The enemy always seemed to know who was opposite them in the line. We were never opposite a German regiment during this time but what didn't have a few men who could speak English. In one German regiment they had a wonderful violin player who often played selections from operas, and in the summer evenings when a slight breeze was blowing towards us we could distinguish every note. We always gave him a clap and shouted for an encore.

Frank Richards, *Old Soldiers Never Die*

Trenches in Flanders
June 17, 1915

I have just come back from a little walk to view the German lines. Hitherto, I confess, I have been a little chary of the idea of exposing myself to the direct view of the enemy, even at a long distance. But this morning three of us started to seek what we could see, and took the road outside the ruined public house in which the Officers' Mess has found a home. This road is a favourite one in the enemy's eyes. Besides 'Suicide Corner', just a couple of hundred yards away from the Mess, there are other points at which it is pitted with shell-holes particularly one section to which the Germans devote their evening 'hate', lasting from about 3pm, sometimes, until dark. Just there the top part of a tree is lying across the road, while close beside it another is half overthrown, with a huge cavity laying bare its roots. Now we turn to the right, and after a hundred yards we come to the high banks of the Yser Canal. These present a remarkable spectacle. First comes a huge bank, rising out of the surrounding country to the height of about 40 feet. Then there is a descent of over 50 feet to the canal, which has on each side of it a towpath. A similar bank to that on the near side rises beyond the canal. It is the banks which excite comment. For each is honeycombed with cave dwellings, until it resembles a gigantic rabbit warren. Every kind of burrow is there large and small, square and round, crude and finished. As we approach, it looks as though one wall had fallen from a block of tiny tenements, disclosing the interiors. On the sheltered side of the far bank it is the same. And here, above, are fighting trenches, which I may not describe, and shall not attempt to. In the middle runs the canal, and today the men are bathing like schoolboys, splashing and shouting in the midday sun. On the far bank they are standing or sitting outside their dwellings, like rabbits at the mouth of their holes, some cleaning equipment, some writing letters, some asleep. A few wooden crosses mark the sites of soldiers' graves. We cross the canal and mount the other bank. At the top the whole stretch of country comes into view.

'Are the German trenches in view?' I ask.

'Yes,' says the Major, who is conducting us; 'there they are, about 1,500 to 2,000 yards away.' And there indeed they are, grey-brown ridges on the green. I take out my glasses and look. No human being, only those ridges of earth. 'They don't fire at one or two people?' I inquire, aware that I am in full view of the Bosches. 'No; it's not worth it.'

I feel safer!

It is extraordinarily interesting. The whole field of battle lies stretched out before one. First the long lush grass and bending corn of the fields of Flanders, lying peaceful and beautiful as if the horrors of war never existed. Beyond, the charred and shattered walls of ruined farmsteads. Beyond, again, the network of trenches, first our own; then, hardly distinguishable from them, the Germans'. Lastly, on the horizon, rows of poplars, little deserted farmhouses, and more rows of poplars. All is absolutely still in the midday heat, save where single khaki figures here and there move down a road across the fields. But, as we look, suddenly a black splash of smoke appears low down in the blue sky, and almost simultaneously another, black and brown, spreads to its left. Two 'Black Marias', one in air, one on graze. The double report has hardly reached us before there is a crash from behind us, and a shell from one of our heavy Batteries goes screaming overhead in an ever-dying wail till, far away beyond our ken, there is a dull rumbling report. We sit on the top of the bank and enjoy the view and the sensation of nearness to the centre of things. A little later, and we also shall wend our way, like those solitary figures, over the fields and up to the advanced trenches, with perhaps the 'couple of bullets', that the Major refers lightly to, singing past us. But now we make our way home to lunch, over a pontoon, past some French soldiers' graves, and past, too, a smell which suggests that burial cannot always be carried out so efficiently as greater leisure would permit.

Eliot Crawshay-Williams, *Leaves from an Officer's Notebook*

Retaliation

At night a trench mortar officer set his guns in a derelict trench about twenty yards behind the line and carried up his ammunition, heavy globes of iron with a little cylindrical projection like a broken handle. In the morning I moved the men from the bays between the trench mortars and their target, to lighten the risk of loss from the retaliatory fire. A pop, and then a black ball went soaring up, spinning round as it went through the air slowly, more pops and more queer birds against the sky. A stutter of terrific detonations seemed to shake the air and the ground, sandbags and bits of timber sailed up slowly and fell in a calm deliberate way. In the silence that followed the explosions, an angry voice called out in English, across No Man's Land, 'YOU BLOODY WELSH MURDERERS.'

The trench mortar team hurried away, pleased with their shooting – as they always were – and left us to wait for the shelling of our line. It did not begin immediately, as we had expected. An hour passed, then another, until the suspense became harder to bear than a bombardment. In the late afternoon, when we had decided that the enemy was going to swallow this insult and we had resumed our mud-building and irrigation, a sudden fury of shellfire turned our poor trench into a field of spouting volcanoes, spattering mud up into the air. The angry hiss, of 7.7s, the ponderous whirr of 5.9s, the dull empty whack of bombs and the whipping crack of shrapnel all merged into a sea of noise. Ten minutes of this drove us into a stupor of fear, and fear brought its terrible thirst; there was nothing to do but to sit still, half crouched against the wall of the trench, waiting, waiting. Every moment we expected to hear a shout of 'Stretcher-bearers at the double,' but it never came. The storm ended as suddenly as it began; now was the time to count the cost. By some uncommon stroke of luck, not one man was wounded or killed, and in ten minutes we drank the best cup of tea ever made on this earth.

Llewelyn Wyn Griffith, *Up to Mametz*

Morning in the Trenches

John Ball, relieved for sentry, stood to his breakfast. He felt cheese to be a mistake so early in the morning. The shared bully was to be left in its tin for the main meal; this they decided by common consent. The bread was ill-baked and sodden in transit. There remained the biscuits; there remained the fourth part of a tin of jam; his spoonful of rum had brought him some comfort. He would venture along a bit, he would see Reggie with the Lewis-gunners. He stumbles his path left round traverse and turn.

At the head of the communication trench, by the white board with the map-reference, the corporal of a Vickers team bent over his brazier of charcoal. He offers an enamelled cup, steaming. Private Ball drank intemperately, as a home animal laps its food, not thanking the kind agent of this proffered thing, but in an eager manner of receiving.

After a while he said: Thank you sergeant – sorry, corporal – very much – sorry – thanks, corporal.

He did not reach the Lewis-gunners nor his friend, for while he yet shared the corporal's tea he heard them calling down the trench.

All of No. 1 section – R.E. fatigue.

He thanked these round their brazier and turned back heavy-hearted to leave that fire so soon, for it is difficult to tell of the great joy he had of that ruddy-bright, that flameless fire of coals within its pierced basket, white-glowed, and very powerfully hot, where the soldiers sat and warmed themselves and waited to see what the new day might bring for them and him, for he too was one of them, shivering and wretched at the cock-crow.

Give the poor little sod some char – that's what the corporal had said.

No. 1 section were already moving off, he fell in behind, and followed on. Slowly they made progress along the traverses, more easy to negotiate by light of day. Not night-bred fear, nor dark mystification nor lurking unseen snares any longer harassed them, but instead, a penetrating tedium, a boredom that leadened and oppressed, making the spirit quail and tire, took hold of them, as they went to their first fatigue. The untidied squalor of the loveless scene spread far horizontally, imaging unnamed discomfort, sordid and deprived as ill-kept hen-runs that back on sidings on wet weekdays where wasteland meets environs and punctured bins ooze canned meats discarded, tyres to rot, derelict slow-weathered iron-ware disintegrates between factory-end and nettle-bed. Sewage feeds the high grasses and bald clay-crop bears tins and braces, swollen rat-body turned-turtle to the clear morning.

Men-bundles here and there in ones and twos, in twos and threes; some eating, others very still, knee to chin trussed, confined in small dug concavities, wombed of earth, their rubber-sheets for caul. Others coaxed tiny smouldering fires, balancing precarious mess-tins, anxious-watched to boil. Rain clouds gathered and returned with the day's progression, with the west wind freshening. The south-west wind caught their narrow gullies in enfilade, gusting about every turn of earthwork, lifting dripping groundsheets, hung to curtain little cubby-holes. All their world shelving, coagulate. Under-earth shorn-up, seeled and propt. Substantial matter guttered and dissolved, sprawled to glaucous insecurity. All sureness metamorphosed, all slippery a place for the children of men, for the fair feet of us to go up and down in.

David Jones, *In Parenthesis*, part 4

Service in the Brewery

After coming out of the line for a short period the Reverend Evan Mathias and myself went on our bikes to Noux les Mines to visit the Reverend Cynddelw Williams, who had only just returned from the hell of the Somme. He told us about the heavy losses that the 10th Royal Welch Fusiliers had suffered there. Of the numerous many who had gone over to France, he said that only twenty were alive. A short while before this we had invited the Reverend Dyfnallt Owen (later to become the Archdruid of Wales), who was serving with the Y.M.C.A. at Béthune, to hold a service with us in Petit Saens. Because the Catholic church there had been utterly destroyed, the service had to be held in the local brewery. The service was conducted entirely in Welsh, because the majority of our officers were Welsh-speaking, as were most of the ordinary soldiers. It was a service of blessing. The Reverend Dyfnallt Owen asked to see for himself what kind of conditions our lads had to contend with every day in the trenches. This made a deep impression on him, and within a few days he sent the following lines ['No Man's Land'] to the Reverend Evan Mathias to commemorate the occasion.

E. Beynon Davies, *Ar Orwel Pell: Atgofion am y Rhyfel-Byd Cyntaf 1914-1918*
(On a Far Horizon: Reminiscences of the First World War 1914-1918), (1965)
(Translated from the Welsh)

No Man's Land
(Dedicated to Chaplain Evan Mathias)

Only a wall made of mud
And bags full of sand overhead,
And the corpse of a battered wood
Protect me from steel and lead.
Who owns this barren mire,
This cratered, pock-holed terrain –
The corpse by the steel-edged wire –
In this, death's final domain?

The purple-red poppy grows
At the edge of the trench, shell-torn,
And wildly the sunlight glows
On its cheek as dark becomes dawn.
I would not afflict its cheek
Nor its tranquil hour destroy
Lest the hidden sniper who seeks
Fulfilment should find true joy.

Did someone stir over there?
What was it? Phantom or foe?
Now devils shout everywhere,
Awake in this Kingdom of Woe.
To whom does this slough belong?
No one, except the strewn
Corpses who sleep and dream long
Of war under sun and moon.

J. Dyfnallt Owen
(Translated from the Welsh)

'Is there anything happening?'

In that world we all returned suddenly to the primal solitude of the forest and the wilderness. We threw away all those centuries of civilisation. Our fellow-men become strange and incomprehensible to us. I never had a stranger experience than when walking along the trenches at night, nudging a sentry here, another one there, every single one of them turning to face me with a weary, half-crazed expression, and stamping the ground with his feet to awaken the blood in them. 'Is there anything happening?' I would ask. 'No, nothing.' And he would turn away from me. I felt myself sinking into hopelessness. The spectre that had answered me was so far away from me, and nothing in the language that we used could bridge the void between us. There, every man faced his own mad confusion. Compassion waned, because of our inability to comprehend a comrade's look, and when a man was killed, a whole world was lost with him, a world which was completely alien to everyone else.

Saunders Lewis, 'Profiad Cymro yn y Fyddin: Ar Ddaear Ffrainc'
('The Experience of a Welshman in the Army: On French Soil'),
Y Cymro, August 6, 1919. (Translated from the Welsh)

On Sentry Duty

You can hear the silence of it:
You can hear the rat of no-man's-land
rut-out intricacies,
weasel-out his patient workings,
scrut, scrut, sscrut,
harrow out-earthly, trowel his cunning paw;
redeem the time of our uncharity, to sap his own amphibious paradise.
You can hear his carrying-parties rustle our corruptions through the night-weeds – contest the choicest morsels in his tiny conduits, bead-eyed feast on us;
by a rule of his nature, at night-feast on the broken of us.
Those broad-pinioned;
blue-burnished, or brinded-back;
whose proud eyes watched
            the broken emblems
droop and drag dust,
suffer with us this metamorphosis.

These too have shed their fine feathers; these too have slimed their dark-bright coats; these too have condescended to dig in.

The white-tailed eagle at the battle ebb,
        where the sea wars against the river
the speckled kite of Maldon
and the crow
have naturally selected to be un-winged;
to go on the belly, to
sap sap sap
with festered spines, arched under the moon; furrit with
whiskered snouts the secret parts of us.
When it's all quiet you can hear them:
scrut scrut scrut
when it's as quiet as this is.
    It's so very still.
        Your body fits the crevice of the bay in the most comfortable fashion imaginable.
    It's cushy enough.

The relief elbows him on the fire-step: All quiet china? – bugger all to report? – kipping mate? – christ, mate – you'll 'ave 'em all over.

David Jones, *In Parenthesis*, part 3

'Dead Rats, Ploegsteert (1916)' by David Jones

69

To the Trench Again

We are soon well on our way back to the region of fire, singing with great heartiness 'Keep the Home Fires Burning', and shouting, 'Are we downhearted – no.' There is one thing about Tommy Atkins – he is always happy and contented wherever he goes, and whatever dangers are staring him in the face . . .

Obliged to carry full kit, our packs are now getting a bit heavy, so a considerate Commanding Officer cries 'Halt!' to give us a breather. The rest is brief. On we go, now separated into companies, so as not to appear a mass to the Hun observer, who is always on the look-out. We are soon well within sound of the guns. A loud report is heard on our left. It is one of our own heavy batteries sending 'Lloyd George's' over. Further on we hear the sound of the French 75s on our left. The French idolise the 75 guns, and are justifiably proud of them, as they have done great executive work with them – and the Huns know it, too. On our journey we meet an ambulance coming down with wounded, and the remark is casually heard, 'They are all right for Blighty.' It is now getting dusk, and we see vivid flashes in our rear. They are our howitzers sending some 'hot 'uns' to the German trenches.

We have now arrived within range of the Huns' death-dealing shells, and a 'coal-box' has just dropped about 100 yards away as a reminder of their close proximity. We are also near our 18-pounders, and they are sending some over like old boots. It's pretty hot; the Huns are after our batteries, and the ground is ploughed up in many places by the enemy's shells. It is quite evident from the withering fire and the evidences about that the enemy is not short of ammunition. Darkness having set in, we are now at ———, the nearest point to the firing line in the locality to which we are destined. The place is full of dugouts, and it is in these and the cellars of the destroyed houses that the troops billet. We have made a kind of a stores here. The Royal Army Medical Corps have installed a first-aid post, and they are busy giving succour to the wounded. The place is in a terrible state; there is not a house left that has not been struck by shell. Pathos is not wanting even among troops who are seasoned to hardships. We see a chaplain coming from a cemetery after paying the last respects to a fallen hero. It may have been one of my own pals – and I have lost many since landing in France – and whose body was only recently recovered.

. . . We have left ———, and are now in the communication trench, leading to the firing line. These trenches are not a straight cutting in the earth, but they thrust in all directions – one has to go through them for himself to realise what they are like. The trenches are so narrow that we have to proceed through them slowly; it is impossible to walk fast. The rain – our ever-constant friend (?) – has come on, and the sides of the trenches become wet with white slime, whilst the floors are ankle deep in mud and water. There is positively no place so miserable as the trench in wet weather. Having arrived in the firing line it is not safe to put one's head too high, as there are snipers about, and we hear a 'ping, ping' above our heads. We are now in the reserve trench, and we pass a party of Royal Engineers building up the walls of a trench which has been damaged by enemy shells. We stop here for a while, as it is getting pretty hot. A Hun star shell has gone up and illuminated the whole place, and, accompanying it, the Huns let fly five rounds 'rapid' in the hope of catching the unprepared. A little later one of the enemy's trench mortars sends a 'whizz-bang' over, but, thank goodness, it falls on top.

One is quite safe unless these 'whizz-bangs' drop actually in the trenches. It is evident the Huns have got the wind that we are relieving the ———, as they keep on sending over whizz-bangs and a steady rapid fire. We have passed the support trench, and we are now in the firing trench. It was a long journey up, and we feel tired, but, realising that we are the relief, we have to go about our duty right away.

The sentries are posted, and the remainder of us go into our dugouts to rest, but ready at a second's warning to turn out in the event of anything moving. Some of us cannot doze off – we are too tired – and we overhear an 'old hand' giving advice to one of the reinforcements who has not been in the firing line before.

It was such good advice that I repeat it for the benefit of all soldiers in South Wales who have not yet been in the firing line, but hope to be there before this great war is over.

The advice of the trained man is:

'Don't be too inquisitive.'

'Don't jump up and look where a shell bursts.'

'Keep your head well down.'

Briefly, this is how one battalion relieves another, and the same process will go on until this great trench war is over. Every time a battalion comes out of the trenches it is a good many men short. No wonder the call is for 'more men and still more men'. This is a terrible war, the like of which history is unable to point to a parallel. With all the modern appliances that are used to kill men, it seems to me like the uncivilised race looking on at the civilised races killing one another.

Sapper Llew Bassett (South Wales Royal Engineers),
'To the Trench Again',
Western Mail, January 6, 1916

All-conquering Fatigue

While the mind was spinning slowly round a pivot of 'How long?' the muscles were carrying an aching frame back and fro along a wet and sour-smelling trench, finding each journey more difficult than the one before. How long must we wait for the relief? How long could one hope to live, after two months of daily escape? How long would it be before we could get leave? How long could this war last? This was the series of concentric circles of sentences passing through a deadened mind, each one repeated again and again, a new way of 'counting sheep', dulling the brain into a half-sleep. Four days in the line can be written down as a rapid fall along the slope of vitality into a stupor of weariness; on the path, some sharp crests of fear, but the end was overwhelming fatigue. Now that the war is half-forgotten, many men have described trench life, some with a wealth of remembered detail both of doing and of saying, rebuilding for the reader a day, a place and a people. Some clever writers have found in an early morning visit to the line material enough to furnish a vivid background for a long play of wit and character. But to most of us who served in the infantry, the thought of a trench brings back that long span of damnable tiredness, broken here and there by a sudden dry-tongued spasm of fear. Cold nights, the discomfort of wet clothes, dragging minutes of anxiety on patrol, the sufferings of men . . . these are all fading with the passing years, but nothing can efface the memory of that all-conquering fatigue.

Llewelyn Wyn Griffith, *Up to Mametz*

In Reserve

3/10/16.

My Dear Margaret,

I have very little to say and this morning I'm almost too tired to say it. Being in reserve has this disadvantage that if the front trenches fall into bad condition through rain or shell, the battalion in reserve has to provide the party to repair the damage. It is always night work and a march there and back of some miles, and I was very tired when I came back in the early hours of this morning after being out since the previous evening.

The rain has broken in on a fine spell of Indian Summer, and now we are having a sort of October mist hanging and drizzling about us like a warm moist blanket steaming. It has a strange effect on the Very lights at night. You see them shoot up from the opposite line and climb out of sight in the fog, then after a moment they fall slowly and dimly on our side and fizzle out dejectedly. There is only a little nervous spasm of machine-gun fire now and again, a trench mortar whistles away and explodes, a rat scurries over the fire-step where the sentry watches and shivers. So we wait for the daybreak.

Yours,
Saunders

Saunders Lewis, letter to Margaret Gilcriest,
Saunders Lewis: Letters to Margaret Gilcriest

In the Trenches at Cambrin

Our guide took us up to the front line. We passed a group of men huddled over a brazier – small men, daubed with mud, talking quietly together in Welsh. They were wearing waterproof capes, for it had now started to rain, and cap-comforters, because the weather was cold for May. Although they could see we were officers, they did not jump to their feet and salute. I thought that this must be a convention of the trenches; and indeed it is laid down somewhere in the military text-books that the courtesy of the salute must be dispensed with in battle. But, no, it was just slackness. We overtook a fatigue-party struggling up the trench loaded with timber lengths and bundles of sandbags, cursing plaintively as they slipped into sump-holes or entangled their burdens in the telephone wire. Fatigue-parties were always encumbered by their rifles and equipment, which it was a crime ever to have out of reach. After squeezing past this party, we had to stand aside to let a stretcher-case pass. 'Who's the poor bastard, Dai?' the guide asked the leading stretcher-bearer. 'Sergeant Gallagher,' Dai answered. 'He thought he saw a Fritz in No Man's Land near our wire, so the silly booger takes one of them new issue percussion bombs and shots it at 'im. Silly booger aims too low, it hits the top of the parapet and bursts back. Deoul! man, it breaks his silly f—ing jaw and blows a great lump from his silly f—ing face, whatever. Poor silly booger! Not worth sweating to get him back! He's put paid to, whatever.' The wounded man had a sandbag over his face. He died before they got him to the dressing station.

I felt tired out by the time I reached company headquarters, sweating under a pack-valise like the men, and with all the usual furnishings hung at my belt – revolver, field-glasses, compass, whisky-flask, wire-cutters, periscope, and a lot more. A 'Christmas-tree' that was called. Those were the days in which officers had their swords sharpened by the armourer before sailing to France. I had been advised to leave mine back in the quartermaster-sergeants' billet, and never saw it again, or bothered about it. My hands were sticky with the clay from the side of the trench, and my legs soaked up to the calves. At C Company headquarters, a two-roomed timber-built shelter in the side of a trench connecting the front and support lines, I found tablecloth and lamp again, whisky bottle and glasses, shelves with books and magazines, and bunks in the next room. I reported to the company commander.

I had expected a grizzled veteran with a breastful of medals; but Dunn was actually two months younger than myself – one of the fellowship of 'only survivors'. Captain Miller of the Black Watch in the same division was another. Miller had escaped from the Rue du Bois massacre by swimming down a flooded trench. Only survivors had great reputations. Miller used to be pointed at in the streets when the battalion was back in reserve billets. 'See that fellow? That's Jock Miller. Out from the start and hasn't got it yet.' Dunn did not let the war affect his morale at all. He greeted me very easily with: 'Well, what's the news from England? Oh, sorry, first I must introduce you. This is Walker – clever chap from Cambridge, fancies himself as an athlete. This is Jenkins, one of those elder patriots who chucked up their jobs to come here. This is Price – joined us yesterday, but we liked him at once: he brought some damn good whisky with him. Well, how long is the war going to last, and who's winning? We don't know a thing out here. And what's all this talk about war-babies? Price pretends ignorance on the subject.' I told them about the war, and asked them about the trenches.

'About trenches,' said Dunn. 'Well, we don't know as much about trenches as the French do, and not near as much as Fritz does. We can't expect Fritz to help, but the French might do something. They are too greedy to let us have the benefit of their inventions. What wouldn't we give for their parachute-lights and aerial torpedoes! But there's never any connection between the two armies, unless a battle is on, and then we generally let each other down.

'When I came out here first, all we did in trenches was to paddle about like ducks and use our rifles. We didn't think of them as places to live in, they were just temporary inconveniences. Now we work here all the time, not only for safety but for health. Night and day. First, at fire-steps, then at building traverses, improving the communication trenches, and so on; last comes our personal comfort – shelters and dugouts. The territorial battalion that used to relieve us were hopeless. They used to sit down in the trench and say: 'Oh, my God, this is the limit.' Then they'd pull out pencil and paper and write home about it. Did no work on the traverses or on fire positions. Consequence – they lost half their men from frostbite and rheumatism, and one day the Germans broke in and scuppered a lot more of them. They'd allowed the work we'd done in the trench to go to ruin, and left the whole place like a sewage farm for us to take over again. We got sick as muck, and reported them several times to brigade headquarters; but they never improved. Slack officers, of course. Well, they got smashed, as I say, and were sent away to be lines-of-communication troops. Now we work with the First South Wales Borderers. They're all right. Awful swine, those territorials. Usen't to trouble about latrines at all; left food about to encourage rats; never filled a sandbag. I only once saw a job of work that they did: a steel loop-hole for sniping. But they put it facing square to the front, and quite unmasked, so two men got killed at it – absolute death-trap. Our chaps are all right, but not as right as they ought to be. The survivors of the show ten days ago are feeling pretty low, and the big new draft doesn't know a thing yet.'

'Listen,' said Walker, 'there's too much firing going on. The men have got the wind up over something. If Fritz thinks we're jumpy, he'll give us an extra bad time. I'll go up and stop them.'

Dunn went on: 'These Welshmen are peculiar. They won't stand being shouted at. They'll do anything if you explain the reason for it – do and die, but they have to know their reason why. The best way to make them behave is not to give them too much time to think. Work them off their feet. They are good workmen, too. But officers must work with them, not only direct the work. Our timetable is: breakfast at eight o'clock in the morning, clean trenches and inspect rifles, work all morning; lunch at twelve, work again from one till about six, when the men feed again. "Stand-to" at dusk for about an hour, work all night, "stand-to" for an hour before dawn. That's the general programme. Then there's sentry duty. The men do two-hour sentry spells, then work two hours, then sleep two hours. At night, sentries are doubled, so working parties are smaller. We officers are on duty all day, and divide up the night into three hourly watches.' He looked at his wristwatch. 'By the way,' he said, 'that carrying-party must have brought up the RE stuff by now. Time we all got to work. Look here, Graves, you lie down and have a doss on that bunk. I want you to take the watch before "stand-to". I'll wake you up and show you around. Where the hell's my revolver? I don't like to go out without it. Hello, Walker, what was wrong?'

Walker laughed. 'A chap from the new draft. He had never fired during his musketry course at Cardiff, and tonight he fired ball for the first time. It went to his head. He'd had a brother killed up at Ypres, and sworn to avenge him. So he blazed off all his own ammunition at nothing, and two bandoliers out of the ammunition-box besides. They call him the 'Human Maxim' now. His foresight's misty with heat. Corporal Parry should have stopped him; but he just leant up against the traverse and shrieked with laughter. I gave them both a good cursing. Some other new chaps started blazing away too. Fritz retaliated with machine guns and whizz-bangs. No casualties. I don't know why. It's all quiet now. Everybody ready?'

When they went off, I rolled up in my blanket and fell asleep . . .

Robert Graves, *Goodbye to All That* (1929)

In the Trenches

Tonight over these fields the moon will rise,
Rise, as I've seen her often, large and slow,
With faint stars far behind her, and heaven will grow
Under her flowering strange to its own skies.

Here we shall stand the night long, ears and eyes
Wary to danger, swift to anticipate woe,
And over there, watchful as we, the foe,
Till wonder and horror fill me with surmise.

The moon that lays her calm upon our dead
Is kind because she knows not, the mild earth
On whose green breast our many lives are bled
Receives them nor in pity nor in mirth;
'Neath all the beauty that this night does shed
We alone feel the mystery of our birth.

Saunders Lewis

'Next, Private Morgan,' shouted the Sergeant-Major. 'Quick march! Left wheel! Halt! Right turn.'

'Sir (to the Colonel), Private Morgan, sir, who is reported by Corporal Thomas for not complying with an order. The offence took place yesterday afternoon at 4.30pm near the man's billet, sir.'

'H'm, yes,' said the Colonel, 'very serious charge indeed – especially on Active Service. Give me his conduct sheet, Sergeant-Major.'

As the Sergeant-Major searched his wallet, the Colonel turned to the Corporal who made the charge. 'Well, Corporal, what was the trouble?'

'It was like this, sir. The Surgunt-Major said some officer from Headquarters – sanitary or something – 'ad complain about our billat bein' untidy -- tins an' things about the place, sir – an' he was blamin' me because the place was so dirty, so I ordered Shoni Morgan – Private Morgan, I mean, sir – to burn the tins an' then bury them. He refuse to obey the ordar, sir. He said what was the good of burning the tins if they was to be buried after. He said he would burn them tins or bury them, and last of all he did say that he wouldn't bury or burn them, sir. So he did refuse to obey ordars, sir.'

By this time the Sergeant-Major had found the elusive conduct sheet. By no stretch of leniency could Private Morgan's record be regarded as creditable – C.B., Stop-pay, Field Punishment, Nos 1 and 2, figured largely, while the numbers of a few 'Drunk' entries in red ink stared up from the paper.

The Colonel glanced at the sheet, frowned slightly, and looked up. 'Well, Morgan, what have you to say for yourself?'

'They are always on to me, sir, an' it isn't fair to put all the work on to the same chap all the time. There was a lot of chaps sittin' in the billat doin' nothin' and the Copral ought to ask them to 'elp too, an' that is what I told 'im. He always do pitch on to me for the dirty work sir . . .'

'Yes, Morgan,' said the Colonel, 'but being in the army . . .'

'I know, sir, I'm in the army, but I didn't join . . .'

'Silence,' thundered the Sergeant-Major; 'Don't interrupt the Colonel when he is speaking.'

But Private Morgan would not be silenced: he commented with extraordinary fluency upon the unfair division of labour in the Battalion in general, in particular upon the unnecessary amount of labour that was the portion of his platoon. He asserted that the Sergeants had their favourites, and the Corporals their pets. Taking a wider survey, he was beginning to develop the thesis that nepotism was widespread in the Army, when the Colonel cut him short with, 'Very well, I sentence you to Field Punishment, No. 1 for fourteen days. In future you will obey orders first, and make your complaints afterwards.'

The Colonel nodded, and the Sergeant-Major addressing the culprit as if he were a regiment of soldiers, shouted, 'Right turn! Quick March! Right Wheel!' and Private Morgan disappeared.

This was my first acquaintance with Morgan, who was known to his comrades as 'Shoni'. On the short side, with black hair, and rather squarely-built, he was a typical Welsh collier.

I had but recently joined the Battalion from the Depot, and I was beginning to find it no easy matter to aid in administering justice to a Battalion with such a curious psychology. Formed at the beginning of the war, the Battalion had had the usual training, and had now been some time in France. The men were quick and smart, but they had no discipline – I mean they had no 'sense' of discipline. They obeyed orders, but they were outspoken in their criticism of authority in any shape or form. I put it down to the years of tuition they had received in Trades Union and Socialistic principles in the South Wales coalfield. And 'Shoni' Morgan was more than representative of the type!

Of Morgan I was destined to see more than was enough. He was a 'grouser' – the super-grouser of the Battalion. It is the privilege of the British soldier to grouse, but grousing was more than a privilege to him: it was an obsession. One day it was the rations – he did not get his fair share. For this he blamed everybody from the Corporal to the C.Q.M.S. Another day it was fatigues: they always pitched on him. What were the Pioneers for? They were paid for doing navvy's work. He had joined to fight: he was an Infantry man, not a navvy.

He was selected for reconnaissance work one night, and orders were given to leave the rifles behind. He remonstrated, as he always did: he did not see why he should not take his rifle. How was he going to defend himself? It was useless to assert that the object of the patrol was to discover without being discovered: he would not be silenced, and even in 'No Man's Land' audibly protested that it was folly to leave his rifle behind.

The Bosches must have heard him, for a machine gun was turned in our direction, and we had to lie flat for half an hour before we could continue our work. 'Shoni', in his perversity, seemed most active when the Very lights went up, and he was cursed silently, but fervently, by every man in the patrol. We got back eventually, apparently without losing a man, the only casualty being my sergeant, who had received a bleeding nose through falling flat with too much celerity when the machine gun forced us to take cover. When I mustered the little party in the trench, 'Shoni' could nowhere be seen, and no one knew anything about him. Blessing him, I was about to return when the crack of a solitary rifle was heard from the direction of a Johnson hole we had crept past a little time before. I remembered remarking in an undertone how it overlooked a German trench and would make a fine sniper's post. Our Very lights showed 'Shoni' lying prone, and putting in some 'rapid fire' – probably hopelessly ineffective – at the Bosches. When he had emptied his pouches, he crept back to our trench. I admonished him for his conduct, but he was, as usual, staunch in his defence. He did not think it fair to go out without his rifle to protect himself. What was his rifle good for? He had gone back 'to get a bit of his own back.'

Another grievance was not long in presenting itself, for one afternoon, marching back from our billets to the trenches, we saw a string of London omnibuses taking down a company of Scotch Bantams from the trenches, where they had been training, and we learnt that they were soon bringing back a fresh Company. Whether his equipment galled him more than usual, or whether his feet were more than usually sore I do not know: I know I was surprised by the force of his language. Why should he walk while those —— Scotchmen were carried? He was as good as any —— Scotchman any day. Macalister, looking sourly in his direction, brought a torrent of abuse upon himself, and hurriedly disclaimed his obvious Scotch ancestry before 'Shoni' turned his attention from his luckless fellow private to his general grievances. The whole army was in a rotten condition. Favouritism was rampant: it was not fair that one should march while another was carried: all should march, or all should be carried. It was the Sergeant who cut him short with a gruff 'Silence in the ranks.'

I well remember that march. We were returning from billets along the old Rue de Bois. There was a battery of 6in. guns roaring away on our left, while behind us, the sun was setting in a blaze of red, against which were silhouetted the quaint red-tiled cottages with their attendant poplar sentinels. The crimson glare shone on the filled ditches and the pools which pitted the roadway. From the fields, weary with their day's toil, came the workers – old and bent peasants, soldiers broken in the war, soldiers on leave, and young girls and lads. We passed their peculiar three-wheeled carts, the driver persisting in his habit of driving in the middle of the road in spite of loud shouts of '*À droit!*' The motor transports squelched past us, sending up streams of mud to the accompaniment of curses from the infantry. As it grew darker, the gun limbers hurried past – a long train, stretching out into the gathering night. As we neared the trenches we saw the familiar star shells and Very lights rising and falling, showing up the 'line' as a black ridge. Shrapnel began to find us out, and we separated into small parties. This, apparently, was the opportunity for which Private 'Shoni' Morgan had been looking, for he dropped out. In the dusk and the bustle he was not observed, and he was not missed until we began the inter-battalion relief. Half an hour later he turned up with a platoon of Bantams up for training. He did not see it fair to march while others were being carried, so he had stopped on the road until a bus had picked him up. How to punish him puzzled me. Field Punishment, or loss of pay, seemed not to influence his actions in the least, and yet his offence was flagrant. During that period in the trenches I kept him on fatigue duty all the time, supplying him with sufficient material to grouse about for an average lifetime.

After this he determined to transfer. The formation of a new tunnelling company gave him his opportunity. He, and several of his comrades, applied to the Colonel for the necessary permission, and in his particular case it was readily granted. So 'Shoni' Morgan joined the 'Moles', and the Battalion, officially, knew him no more.

We were, however, not without news of him. The Sergeant-Major, some time afterwards, told me that he had seen him in a working party coming back from the trenches. He looked well, and was singing. Knowing his officer, a mining engineer, I went across to his billet for a chat. He was most favourably impressed by Morgan. 'He is one of the best miners we have,' he said, 'the most willing, and the most daring.' I was discreetly silent. He stated, further, that he was recommending him for promotion. In the narrow galleries of the mine, it seemed, he had again found his element.

Hearing that he had been seen, with a stripe on his arm, in charge of a small working party, I sent him one of those all-embracing F.S. postcards, addressed to Second Corporal J. Morgan, R.E., scribbling 'Congratulations' where the Regulations state 'Signature only'. I wonder if he ever guessed who sent it.

Weeks passed, and I lost sight of him: his Company had, somehow, been attached to another Brigade. Cares multiplied, and I forgot his existence, until one day I saw him again – this time at a Battalion Aid Post – coming in on a stretcher. I can see him now, all clay-covered, with his head all battered and bleeding. There he lay, dead, the stretcher dripping with the sticky, brown blood of him.

I turned to one of the stretcher-bearers whom I recognised as having transferred from the Battalion at the same time as Morgan.

'Shoni?' I queried.

He nodded his head, and said, 'Blown up in a mine, sir.' The bearer assisted in carrying the body and returned to me.

'How did it happen?' I asked.

He answered my question with all a Welshman's circumlocutions and irrelevancies, and this was his story:

'Yes, sir, "Shoni" was one of the best minars in the Company – he was a better minar than soldiar, sir, and the Captun said he was one of the best men he 'ad, beggin' your pardon, sir. "Shoni" was a good colliar, an' I remember 'ow 'is stall in the Dyffryn pit was one of the tidiest in the place. Well, sir, it was like this. We was drivin' a headin' – I mean a gallery, sir – towards a German sap, and we 'ad got well under it, and there was three Engineers workin' in the cross headin' preparin' for the mines and the connections. But the Germans 'ad countermined, an' all at once part of our gallery fell into theirs, shuttin' up the Engineers in the far end. Our top fell in, and there we was in the gallery not knowin' what to do, and every minute we was expectin' the Germans to blow up their mine. To stop

80

in the gallery was dangerous, an' to leave it was to leave them three to be buried alive. The ground was so loose, an' the boys was afraid, and we was beginnin' to make for the shaft when "Shoni" came up. "Where are you goin'," he said, "you aren't goin' to leave them boys there. Come on, Twm," he says to me, "We can get a hole through that fall in ten minutes. I've been lookin' at it." So we went back, an' dug away at that fall like anythin' – all the time expectin' that German mine to go off. I was all nerves, but "Shoni" was as cool as anything – workin' away as if he was in his own pit at 'ome, diggin' an' proppin' with flats an' other things at full speed. At last 'e shouted 'e was through, but we could see that the fall would be settlin' again as the top was working like anything. "Twm," he says to me, "me an' you will get them out – we are used to it. You others get back now." They didn't want to go then, sir, but "Shoni" made them go, sayin' they was only in the way. So we worked our way in, an' we found them: two was very weak an' exhausted, an' the other like dead. We got them out to the top of the slant, and then "Shoni" said, "Twm, it's no use you comin' back again: I'm goin' back for the dead one. We'll try artificial respiration on him." It was no use me arguin' – he would go in himself. So I went back to the neck of the slant, an' 'eard 'im creeping back an' draggin' the body along. He was just pullin' 'im through the hole in the fall, when the mine went off. The wind of the explosion came up the gallery, an' hit me against the trench, an' left me gaspin'. They all rushed up, an' by then I was all right, but a bit shaky. The Germans 'ad fired what is called a "camouflet", which is a small charge which will blow up a gallery, but not make a big crater like a mine would do. They 'ad blown it up just as "Shoni" was clearing the fall, an' 'e didn't have a chance. It had exploded nearly under 'im, an' had blown 'im yards towards the mouth of the gallery before the roof came down an' buried him. We dug like devils an' got 'im out: he was still conscious when we brought 'im out, but 'e was nearly gone. He couldn't speak, an' then 'e went unconscious. He wasn't long, sir, before he died. He was back in the mine again, an' 'e was in awful pain, an' he was moanin'. "Tell the manager," I heard 'im sayin', "I nearly got 'im out. I done my best" – and he was dead.'

And the bearer's voice broke, and the big tear drops coursed down his cheeks.

*   *   *

I went to his burial at the British Cemetery at Windy Corner, where those rows of simple wooden crosses mark the last resting-place of many, whose heroic deeds no pen will record. As the Chaplain read those undying words of the Burial Service over the poor, shattered body in the blood-stained blanket, lying in the shallow grave, the snow fell steadily and wrapped it gently in a pure white coverlet: his winding-sheet was of the purest white . . . And there I left him. Far from the Land of his Fathers he sleeps well among the brave.

At the crossroads the German shrapnel was beginning to burst at the usual time; where the road bent sharply to the right passed a working party bound for the trenches; behind us a battery of 18-pounders suddenly opened fire, as if in honourable tribute to the poor clay that was Second-Corporal John Morgan, R.E., grouser, and man.

Fred Ambrose, *With the Welsh* (1917)

Rats

At last something happened to rouse us a little. We heard that a platoon of Bantams was coming to us to serve an apprenticeship in the line. Were we already old enough in the ways of war to teach others? It was not difficult to persuade ourselves that we were veterans, for years seemed to have passed by since we 'came out of our time' with the Guards. A whole platoon of fresh men to help us in carrying and in digging was a great reinforcement. The Bantams were small, but very sturdy and self-possessed; on parade they seemed to be all equipment, and on the march, walking bundles of gear. The Londoners gave them a great welcome, and I heard many a traveller's tale being told to the newcomers. This I overheard in a dugout in Festubert.

'I tell you what, kid, the shells ain't so bad, nor the bullets ain't, nor the blarsted fatigues. It's the bleedin' rats as does it. When you're standin' on guard at night they runs abaht on the parapet and lashes out at yer with their bleedin' 'ind legs and if you ain't careful they knocks yer off the bleedin' fire-step back inter the trench.'

'And it ain't only that,' said another. 'Look what they did to Sergeant Tracy. Now 'e was farst asleep in a dugout, 'e was, and when 'e woke up, blowed if a rat 'adn't bitten off 'alf 'is blinkin' ear.'

''Ave yer seen the Cap'n's mackintosh?' asked a third. 'Just you look at the collar when 'e comes round tonight. You'll find one 'alf of it all gone, all chewed away by a rat when 'e was sleepin'. Big fat things they are, big as dogs, and fat as 'ell.'

Llewelyn Wyn Griffith, *Up to Mametz*

With a Working Party

My first visit to the region of the trenches still haunts me like a nightmare. I can still see that shell-scarred plain, with its hideous skulls, whitened bones, rusty rifles and bayonets shown up in bold relief by the pale moonlight, and I conjure up visions of the hundreds of brave men who fell there on the occasion of the British advance at this spot. Every gruesome relic – and there were many strewn about there – seems to tell its own sad tale, bearing testimony to the heroic deeds performed by our countrymen on that memorable day. This, however, was not a healthy vicinity for meditation.

I was one of a working party toiling behind our front line trenches, and the Huns were far too close to us for our liking. Work under the most favourable conditions is unpleasant, but when bullets and shells are flying about, it is a very trying occupation indeed.

From the moment our guide led us from the ruined house where we picked up our spades and picks, we were greeted with an ominous ping, ping, ping just above our heads. A working party is the favourite mark of the German sniper, and, in our nervousness, we imagined that a few playful Huns were indulging in an evening's 'strafe' at our expense. Those deadly little bullets as they sped by seemed to whine mournfully, like an injured animal.

As we crept nearer our working-place we came within the zone of a new peril – the machine gun and its ally, the star shell. As the latter's light illuminated the parapets and the ground behind, the vicious rat-tat-tat of the Maxims rang out, sweeping a wide area with a hail of lead. Woe betide anyone within the range of that devastating sweep!

We had very little heart to wield the pick and shovel when those star shells were falling every few minutes. As they burst we flung ourselves on our faces, but this 'bobbing-up-and-down' business became so tiring at length that we adopted the saner course of simply remaining quite still and trusting to luck. The British machine-gunner in our immediate vicinity had a grim sense of humour, using his deadly weapon as a musical instrument.

Now and again the gun would spit forth to the tune of rat-tat-tat–tat, tat, tat–tat-tat, each report sort of indicating the time and tune of a popular melody such as 'Yankee-Doodle'.

The Huns evidently did not appreciate this sort of humour – no more did we – for they always retorted with a furious volley, and we lay on our stomachs to escape the consequences of 'Tommy's' practical joke.

My nerves were severely tested that night. The first time I flung myself on the ground a grinning skull, with bullet-holes through the forehead, lay within six inches of my face. And I had to lay there perfectly still for three minutes to escape the too ardent attentions of a sniper.

When I returned to the barn that night it needed a good stiff tot of rum to produce a dreamless sleep. Familiarity, however, breeds contempt, and one can soon work under those conditions as unconcernedly as on England's peaceful shore.

Shellfire at a respectable distance is soon got accustomed to, but it needs nerves of steel to undergo a bombardment coolly. The Germans are right when they say that the nation with the strongest nerves will triumph, and although statistics prove that shells cause comparatively few casualties, they undoubtedly have a very demoralising effect even on the best troops.

I can speak from experience, and with all honesty I say I do not wish again to undergo the ordeal which I am going to relate.

We were a working party at a particularly warm part of the line, engaged on a job in an abandoned traverse. We were not aware it was an 'unhealthy' spot – it was all so peaceful and quiet that morning. Some of the boys at our lunch interval strayed into the open in search of souvenirs, and it was then that the storm burst. They must have been 'spotted' by a German artillery observer, for suddenly a salvo of half-a-dozen shells screamed through the air and burst twenty yards away. The boys outside scampered back and jumped into the traverse just in time to escape another half-dozen, this time only ten yards away. Lying down flat, we waited anxiously for the next dose, and it came in a few seconds so near our parapet that we were smothered in débris, and our rifles were hurled from one side to another. For the succeeding ten or fifteen minutes projectiles fell all round us, but, fortunately, none fell in the trench, otherwise I would not be writing this epistle, and my comrades would not be eating their evening meal at this moment. We all knew during those awful moments that it was touch and go, and we heaved a mighty sigh of relief when it was all over. We were told afterwards that the bombardment lasted half an hour – but I was oblivious of the flight of time. It seemed like ages to me.

Unnamed Member of the Welsh Cyclist Scouts, letter to a friend in Cardiff,
Western Mail, February 11, 1916

The Unseen Enemy

There was always something to be done, involving a movement and a standing about. Digging, filling sandbags, building, carrying stores and ammunition, repairing the walls damaged by shellfire, scheming against the insidious attack of water, strengthening the barbed wire, resetting duckboards; an officer did none of these things with his own hands, or but rarely. He was there when such things were done, and being there demanded a presence of body and of mind. These tasks, in our early days, seemed to be of such importance that their supervision became an occupation capable of absorbing one's entire stock of energy. They filled the mind so fully that a bombardment became a troublesome interruption of the serious business of life in the trenches.

Later, however, the redistribution of mud took the second place, for the men knew what to do; the zeal of the beginner faded into the semi-drudgery of the journeyman. Days and nights passed by in an oscillation between a suddenly roused fear of instant death and a slowly increasing dread of the continuance of this life of atrophy. An enemy we never saw – no, not an enemy, for maiming or extinction came from a bursting of iron in a ditch, the result of a mathematical computation made some miles away, tragically wrong to us, while the arithmetician knew not whether his answer were right.

Across No Man's Land there were men sharing trouble with us, fighting the same losing battle against water, powerless before the sudden storm of bursting metal, and longing to be home again with their children. Were they an enemy? A scrap of song floating across at dusk, or a grey helmet seen for a moment through a periscope – were we to freeze into hatred at these manifestations of a life so like our own? An unrelieved weariness drugged us into a dullness of mind so overpowering that the brain declined a metaphysical battle on these issues. Everything was unreason, and it profited not to refine the ridiculous into the mad. On the other side of Aubers Ridge a German gunner twirled a few wheels into a new position, moved a bar of iron, and sent death soaring into the air; he went to his dinner. While he was moving his wheels and dials, three Londoners were filling sandbags in a ditch on the plain, arguing about Tottenham Hotspur. A flash, a noise, and a cloud of smoke.

'Blast 'em, they've killed old Parkinson – blown 'is 'ead off, they 'ave, the bastards.'

Blast whom? The unseen German, going to his dinner? The man who sang, over the way? No. Blast everybody and everything; blast all who contributed to the sending of this quiet middle-aged Londoner to die in a ditch, in no combat between men, but in a struggle between two sets of mathematical equations. Did we think out this bitter problem, or discuss the ways of bringing an end to this distemper? No . . . we were too tired. Blast them, and back to the weary lifting of mud, this time passing a stretcher covered with a blanket hiding all but a thin trickle of blood. Four children, and his wife's name was 'Liz' . . . must write to her tonight . . . Oh, blast them!

Llewelyn Wyn Griffith, *Up to Mametz*

The Salient

The Ypres Salient no longer exists. The battles of the summer campaign of 1917 have extended the British line forward to the Passchendaele ridges and have widened out of recognition the narrow loop of defences that swung round to the north and south of Ypres. But the memory of the Ypres Salient will never fade from the minds of those who knew it in being.

The early battles against the westward advancing Germans barred their progress to the sea. The thin khaki line of British regulars and territorials held the beautiful old Belgian town against the most desperate attacks of the flower of the German Army, and in the varying fortunes of that period was the Salient formed – a settled integral part of the British line. The holding of the Salient was rather a matter of British honour and pride than of military importance. While it was held, there was still a Belgium; still was Belgium in part free. The cost of its holding will never be told – this sector with a sinister reputation which claimed a constant heavy toll of British men. When on the Laventie stretch farther south or in the Festubert 'islands' the first of Kitchener's men groused about the heavy German gunfire, the old 'sweats' would smile grimly, saying 'Wait till yer gets to Wipers chum, ye'll have something to grouse about then. They shoot yer in the back as yer walks towards the line there.'

And the new divisions came to regard the Salient as a Hell amongst Hells.

If you have ever visited the Fen country you will be able to picture the interior of the Salient. Low-lying, marshy, a sea of mud in winter, a few rare and scattered undulations which are a little less wet and muddy, frequent copses of stunted oaks, and fields of hop-poles – gaunt and bare in winter, but in summer clothed with wondrous green foliage; these are the characteristic features of that spit of land which was the foremost bastion of the British defences.

Round Ypres the line swept like the edge of an open fan. Where its radiating ribs met stands Poperinghe, a little town with cobbled streets and houses of quaint Flemish design with truncated gables and red-tiled roofs. Eastwards through Poperinghe passes the main road from Calais to Ypres. Halfway between Poperinghe and Ypres it runs through the village of Vlamertinghe. Elverdinghe and Woeston on the north, and Kemmel and St Eloi in the south, flank the Salient.

Surrounding the low land held by the British, rose arrogantly the Pilkem ridge on the north, and the Messines ridge to the south – ridges upon which for nearly three years the German positions were established. They looked down upon us as into a cup-shaped hollow: they mocked us: they gave us the feeling that our every movement was being watched and all that was done was done by the tacit permission of the Germans. That hollow one entered as one would enter the Valley of the Shadow, conscious of malevolent eyes, dreading every moment evil from an invisible, ever-vigilant foe. Within the Salient to the south rose one low ridge, relieving the flat monotony, and when the air was clear on this could be discerned the old monastery of Mont des Cato, and along the edge of this ridge the canvas sails of the Flemish windmills revolved slowly in the breeze, and peacefully ground the corn into meal. In the fields toiled the peasants, on the ridge the windmills turned lazily – and from the copse near by came the full-throated roar of a big gun battery. A strange mingling of Peace and War!

Often I have lain awake under the brown blankets in my billet in the Salient, seeing the yellow glare of the Very lights, and listening to the monotonous rattle of the ration limbers returning empty from the line over the cobbled (*pavé*) roads. *The car rattling over the stony street* – Byron's line revealed then its full meaning to me. At night the guns concentrated in the hollow roared their thunder, and lit up the darkness with their lightning flashes. It seemed as though a thousand thunderstorms were concentrating their fury upon the Salient. And the ruined city – guiltless, martyred, immortal Ypres – has been exposed for three years to the fury of the storm of steel. At times an uncanny silence brooded over its pitiful streets of houses, now masses of formless débris. Now and then a gun spoke hollowly amidst its ruins making the silence more intense. Then would come the storm periods with their hissings of angry projectiles, the roar of concealed batteries, and the heart-clutching detonations of the shells that daily, and not without success, sought their mark. Then like an April shower the storm would pass, ending in a few desultory rounds from the guns, answered by stray shells whining like souls lost in the brooding silence.

Coming from the 'Ramparts' near the Menin Gate we traversed the ruined streets as far as the Square. As we walked the sun shone serenely, pitilessly upon that naked heap of ruins. Through the Square flanked by the shattered Cloth Hall rode a cyclist-soldier, whistling cheerfully for he had nearly attained his journey's end. Another whistle – louder and ominous – stifled it and then a crash as a huge shell burst a little to one side of him, sending up a soot-black acrid cloud of smoke. The cyclist fell headlong from his cycle and lay upon his back on the cobbled stones in the sun, his knees drawn up nearly touching his chin, and his legs kicking feebly. A piece of the shell had cut across his body and had almost disembowelled him. He kicked a little more, frothed at the lips – bloody froth – and, crouched up in that horrible attitude, lay stiff and still. And the sun shone on, warming the *pavé* stones with its rays. Everything was just the same except that lad, who, but a few moments before, was whistling cheerfully, and now lay dead. The sun shone on serenely seeming to smile through death. That lad was just one of the daily toll of men who died that we might still say, 'We hold Ypres.'

Along the banks of the little Yperlee which flows northwards from Ypres for some distance parallel to the Yser were the dugouts – now little needed – of the

British troops who had sapped into the banks and constructed innumerable sandbagged shelters for themselves. Endless tracks of duckboards stretched along its banks and that of the Yser, and here in a prehistoric fashion lived for nearly three years the troops who held the northern portion of the Salient. This dugout town was self-contained; it had its bath, its hospital, its kitchens, its stores, its canteens, its railways, and its cemetery, in which an ever-increasing number of wooden crosses grew out of the soil, and in which there were always a number of ready-delved graves for the occupants that never failed them. And within a stone's throw there was gay laughter and song, jokes and harmless horseplay, amongst those for whom those graves yawned insatiate.

Elverdinghe – the fortress village surrounded by batteries which spoke often and seldom were wanting of their reply! The church is a broken ruin, the churchyard a chaotic mass of broken stone, plaster, glass and the bones of men long since dead. From the cellars, roofed with sandbags, peeped the bronzed faces of the garrison. They greet passers-by with a cheerful hail, 'Cheero, chum! Any news? When is this bloody war going to end?'

At night the Very lights rose and fell around one in a wide curve. From the apex of the Salient near Hooge it seemed as though they surrounded one and this intensified the feeling of helplessness and impotence which possessed one during the day. These arcs of light rose and fell all through the night, while, at intervals, various coloured lights signalled to the artillery behind. It was a beautiful spectacle, but life in the Salient does not conduce to artistic appreciation.

When the moon was full, and in the dull grey dawn, enemy planes came over and dropped their burden of deadly bombs on the canvas camp and hutments built by the troops for their shelter in the cold wet weather. When the wind was 'dangerous' – no rare occurrence in the Salient – the deep note of the Strombos Horn often roused us from our sleep. This heralded an enemy gas attack and the Salient was instantly a Pandemonium. Shell-case gongs were beaten, ringing lengths of steel rail hammered with metal strikers by lusty sentries, bugles were blown, and horns blared, and a little later the artillery would partially drown the inferno of noise in an attempt to smother the enemy sector from which the gas came. From the dugouts, tents, and huts flowed a bustling, cursing stream of men obeying the call to 'Stand-to' with their box-respirators worn on the chest in the 'Alert' position.

The soldier 'on pass' into Poperinghe was rarely allowed to feel, even for an evening, that he could shake off the hateful dread of the Salient. After a long period in the line he would walk the cobbled streets and would visit the concert party and the pictures at the Divisional Cinema near the station. Rarely was the evening's enjoyment unbroken, for from the north-east would come the unmistakable hollow crack of a German long-range high velocity gun, and the scream of the 8-in. shell that burst with an appalling crash in the cobbled square. Four minutes later, and then came another – this time perhaps perilously near the crowded cinema hall and the soldier-manager would deem it prudent to dismiss the audience – an audience that trudged despondently cursing back to the camps, while panic-stricken civilians and women bearing children in their arms hurried past them out of the town into the open country and safety.

Of such was the Salient. During the day it pulsated with toil; at the A.S.C. dumps, and at the R.E. yards refugees prepared war material for the line which prohibited the invader from the last corner of their beloved Belgium; at the numerous ammunition dumps huge and innumerable shells were loaded into lorries bound for the gun positions. New railways were being laid down, and new roads constructed for the grand advance to come. Innumerable hutments and camps sprang up amid the copses and woods of the Salient. Fritz, his path marked by a row of white puffballs in the sky, would come to view it all, and busy workers craned their necks to see his plane flashing in the sun, and hoped that one of our airmen would attack him. An aerial fight never proved monotonous, though it was a fairly common occurrence in the Salient.

Along the roads the refugees built themselves rows of little cabins from any and every material – from hammered-out petrol cans, packing cases, biscuit tins, from mud and wattle. There they lived making honest pennies by selling eggs and chips, doughnuts, embroidered postcards, aluminium rings and such like articles to the soldiers.

And always shells, and gunfire, and the rattle of a myriad machine guns, and the constant menace of the poison gas. And often at night the thunder of a German armoured train with its leviathan guns shelling a village or our big-gun positions. And always in the distance the black puffballs of smoke from German shrapnel bursting over Ypres.

With all its dread horror the Salient will ever be hallowed ground to Britain. Her many brave sons who lie buried there have made it 'for ever England's'.

Fred Ambrose, 'The Salient', *The Welsh Outlook*, vol. v, no. 49, January 1918

Waiting for the Battle

My dear Eleanor,

As everybody is sleepier than I and I am alone, I am going to drink hot brandy and water with you for a quarter of an hour. The gramophone (and Raymond Jeremy) is silent, and the guns are mostly half-a-mile off or more, and nothing is coming over. But these are busy times. Again the battle is promised us and we long to be into it, I suppose because then it will be nearer over. We are up late and down early. We do all kinds of things. Today I solemnly took 10 men and an N.C.O. and a trench cart to steal a small truck for carrying shells on rails. I had to guide them and stand by officially as if it were an official act while they loaded the cart and marched off. The other things I did were more technical, and in doing them I dashed about over a copse and made extra paths that the Hun will photograph. Just for 5 minutes Thorburn and I looked for primroses – in vain among the moss and ash trees. We have to cut off 10 feet from the tops of the prettiest birch trees, because they are dangerously in our way. Not one shell – touch wood – has fallen into the copse yet, though a quarter of a mile off they crack every day.

Yet we have pleasant and even merry hours and moments . . . I keep feeling that I should enjoy it more if I knew I would survive it. I can't help allowing it to trouble me, but it doesn't prey on me and I have no real foreboding, only occasional trepidation and anxiety. The men are better but then they are comrades and I am usually alone or with them. I wish that what is coming would be more than an incident – the battle of [Arras] – Still I can't wait a great while, though of course what is coming is to be worse than anything I know so far.

Edward Thomas, letter to Eleanor Farjeon, March 27, 1917;
quoted in *Edward Thomas: the Last Four Years*

In Fort Erith

We stepped down into a communication trench, and although we were so much nearer the enemy, there was a sign of safety in these muddy walls. The duckboards underfoot were unevenly set and covered with a slimy layer of mud, the trench turned right and left in a maze of windings, here deep and there shallow. What was this peculiar smell, so persistent in its penetration that the mouth tasted of it? Why was I so thirsty? Suddenly we found ourselves pushing past other soldiers leaning against the wall of the trench; we were in Fort Erith. The moon came out again, and I saw a wet straggling trench with bulging sides, uneven fire-steps and ramshackle dugouts. This was the bastion, the wonderful fort of my imagining! A child had begun to build this mud castle and had tired of his play – were men to fight for this thing? Did it rank as a strong point? Was this a part of England's defence?*

We stooped through a narrow doorway leading into a dugout, and before I had removed sufficient of my equipment to allow me to sit down, the formalities of handing over the command of the fort were finished. Two tired men were bidding each other goodnight – how tired they seemed, tired in mind and jaded. A sackcloth curtain covered a small window, another made a *portière* across the door, and a new candle stood in its grease on the middle of the table. I studied a plan of the redoubt, while its commander gave orders to a sergeant. We were in the trenches, a little behind the front line, but where was the great change, the rebirth that was to follow this initiation? Why was I not afraid? I was thirsty, but in no other way different from the man who had imagined an upheaval in his whole way of thinking, a warping of his direction now and for ever. The great transformation that I had so dreaded in advance had dissipated itself into a sequence of minute experiences, each in its turn claiming a concentration that forbade any remembering of its predecessor. A heavy pack, a pitted road, uneven duckboards in a trench, the steering of an awkward body past the projecting walls and its balancing on a slimy foothold – this was the sequence of problems, large in their moment, that had overshadowed the greater ordeal, dwarfing it into the insignificance of a dream.

Wyn Griffith, *Up to Mametz*

* cf, Rudyard Kipling, '1915: Loos and the First Autumn', *The Irish Guards in the Great War*, Vol. II (1923):

On the 14th [December] they moved to a more southerly sector to take over from the Welsh Guards, and to pick up a company of the 13th R.W. Fusiliers; one platoon being attached to each company for instruction, and the Fusiliers B.H.Q. messing with their own. There is no record what the Welshmen thought of their instructors or they of them, except the fragment of a tale of trench-fatigues during which, to the deep disgust of the Irish, who are not loudly vocal by temperament, 'the little fellas sang like canary-birds.'

Their new lines, reached across mud, from Pont du Hem, were the old, well-known, and not so badly looked-after stretch from North Moated Grange Street to Erith Street at the lower end of the endless Tilleloy Road which faced south-easterly towards the Aubers Ridge, then held by the enemy. The relief was finished without demonstrations beyond a few shrapnel launched at one of the posts, Fort Erith.

The Vandalism of it All

24.1.17.

My Dear Margaret,

If it were not for the trenches these would be glorious days, with snow and ice everywhere, and bright sunshine and blue sky. But they are spoilt by this job. Our ears are too frostbitten, snow and ice are too splashed and cut up by shell, and the sky is full of aeroplanes always throbbing and ominous.

Dugouts are very good in their way, but to think that we must be spending our leisure and finding rest and light in burrows thirty feet underground with only the flickers of candles for seeing by – when sun and snow if left alone would work us such magic . . . it's the waste of richness and goodness, the vandalism of it all, even were there no blood spilt, and no actual ugliness, no positive evil or loss. And one gains nothing by it.

I remember how once I was glad to go. Particularly glad to leave you, to leave home, dreaming in my absurd young way of winning strength, character, power, conviction – and especially depth. Well, it was like most of my dreams, but hollower than most. I have gained no more than If I'd spent three years in the rose garden at Wallasey, discussing Rousseau among the mail-carts.

– However, I think I'm writing rot, so I'll shut up.

Yours, as you see, well enough to be ridiculous,
Saunders

Saunders Lewis, letter to Margaret Gilcriest,
Saunders Lewis: Letters to Margaret Gilcriest

From the War Diary of Edward Thomas

[February 15, 1917]. With Captain observing for a B.T. shoot on Ficheux Mill and edge of Blairville Wood. Fine sun but cold in trench. With working party in afternoon. Letters arrived at 6. We sorted them and then spent an hour silently reading. 750 letters for men; 17 for me – from Helen, the children, Father, Mother, Eleanor, Freeman, Mrs Freeman, Guthrie, Vernon and Haines. Evening, reading and writing letters. A quiet evening indoors and out. Taylor says as he mends the fire, 'Well, we have to put up with many discomforts. We are all alike, Sir, all human.' A still starry night with only machine guns and rifles. Slept badly again, and then suddenly with no notice got up from breakfast on the . . .

[February 16]. 16th to do fire control on aeroplane shoot (only 10 rounds, observation being bad). Dull day. Left Thorburn on guns at 11.30. Bad temper. Afternoon up to O.P., but too hazy to observe. A mad Captain with several men driving partridges over the open and whistling and crying 'Mark over.' Kestrels in pairs. Four or five planes hovering and wheeling as kestrels used to over Mutton and Ludcombe. Women hanging clothes to dry on barbed entanglement across the road. Rain at last at 4.15. This morning the old Frenchman living in this ruin burst into our room while we were dressing to complain of our dirt and depredation, and when Rubin was rude in English, said he was a Frenchman and had been an officer. Nobody felt the slightest sympathy with his ravings, more than with the old white horse who works a mill walking up and up treadmill.

[February 17]. A dull muddy day. No observation, no shooting. On guns all day and in dugout, writing up our fighting book. Another letter from home. Could only just see A.P. Kit arrived late last night. I slept badly, coughing. Very mild and the roads chalk and water, Grandes Graves 2.50 a bottle. Thorburn asks where he shall put the letters he has censored – decides on the crowded table – then I have to tell him the mantelpiece is the obvious place.

[February 18]. Another dull day down in 146 Dugout. Afternoon to Arras – Town Hall like Carreg Cennin. Beautiful small white square empty. Top storey of high house ruined, cloth, armchair and a garment across it, left after shell arrived. Car to Mendicourt and back by light of star shells. Shopping at Bellevue B. E. F. canteen. Returned to find I am to go as Orderly Officer to Group 35 H.A. in Arras tomorrow.

Edward Thomas, The Diary of Edward Thomas
1 January – 8 April 1917

The Abode of Madness

We are now a long way back in a ruined village, all huddled together in a farm. We all sleep in the same room where we eat and try to live. My bed is a hammock of rabbit-wire stuck up beside a great shell-hole in the wall. Snow is deep about, and melts through the gaping roof, on to my blanket. We are wretched beyond my previous imagination – but safe.

Last night indeed I had to 'go up' with a party. We got lost in the snow. I went on ahead to scout – foolishly alone – and when, half a mile away from the party, got overtaken by

GAS

It was only tear gas from a shell, and I got safely back (to the party) in my helmet, with nothing worse than a severe fright! And a few tears. Some natural, some unnatural . . .

They want to call No Man's Land 'England' because we keep supremacy there.

It is like the eternal place of gnashing of teeth; the Slough of Despond could be contained in one of its crater-holes; the fires of Sodom and Gomorrah could not light a candle to it – to find the way to Babylon the Fallen.

It is pock-marked like a body of foulest disease and its odour is the breath of cancer . . .

No Man's Land under snow is like the face of the moon, chaotic, crater-ridden, uninhabitable, awful, the abode of madness . . .

Wilfred Owen, letter to his mother, Susan Owen, January 19, 1917,
Wilfred Owen: Collected Letters

The Universal Pervasion of Ugliness

I suppose I can endure cold, and fatigue, and the face-to-face death, as well as another; but extra for me there is the universal pervasion of *Ugliness*. Hideous landscapes, vile noises, foul language and nothing but foul, even from one's own mouth (for all are devil ridden), everything unnatural, broken, blasted; the distortion of the dead, whose unburiable bodies sit outside the dugouts all day, all night, the most execrable sights on earth. In poetry we call them the most glorious. But to sit with them all day, all night . . . and a week later to come back and find them still sitting there, in motionless groups, THAT is what saps the 'soldierly spirit' . . .

Wilfred Owen, letter to his mother, Susan Owen, February 4, 1917,
Wilfred Owen: Collected Letters

War
on the
Western Front

Trench Warfare

. . . We were ordered to relieve some troops in the advanced trench. We rode about six miles, then dismounted, leaving some men with the horses, and walked about five miles to the trenches. As we went through the first village, we got heavily shelled by the famous Black Marias; they make a noise just like an express train and burst like a clap of thunder, you hear them coming for ten seconds before they burst. It was very unpleasant, and you need to keep a hold on yourself to prevent ducking – most of the men duck.

Most of the shells hit the roofs, but one burst in the road in front of me, killing one man and wounding four or five. However, once we got out of the village they stopped, and we arrived at the trenches in the dark of the evening. We filed quietly into them and waited in the darkness. We stayed there two days and nights, being shelled most of the time. The German trenches were about 1600 yards away, with Maxim guns. They never showed their noses by daylight, and the guns were miles away. We never fired a shot all the time. They only once hit the trench, wounding two men, but about fifty shells pitched within a few yards. They set fire to a large farm a hundred yards behind us that made a glorious blaze. The Frenchmen on our right and left kept up intermittent bursts of rifle fire. This did no good and gave away the position of their trenches, so they got more shelled than we did. We have now come out and are billeted in a farm ten miles behind the trenches. We had dozens of guns behind our trenches, but they seemed to have little or no effect on keeping down the German fire. Now about tips. – Dig, never mind if the men are tired, always dig. Make trenches as narrow as possible, with no parapet if possible; dig them in groups of eight or ten men, and join up later, leave large traverses. Once you have got your deep narrow trench you can widen out the bottom, but don't hollow out too much, as a Maria shakes the ground for a hundred yards and will make the whole thing fall in. Don't allow any movement or heads to show, or any digging or going to the rear in the daytime. All that can be done at night or in the mists of morning that are heavy and last till 8 or 9am. Always carry wire and always put wire forty yards in front of the trench, not more. One trip wire will do if you have no time for more. The Germans often rush at night and the knowledge of wire gives the men confidence. Don't shoot unless you have a first-rate target, and don't ever shoot from the trenches at aeroplanes – remember that the whole thing is concealment, and then again concealment. Never give the order 'Fire' without stating the number of rounds, as otherwise you will never stop them again; you can't be too strict about this in training. On the whole I don't think gunfire is alarming, but what I see from others it has an awfully wearing effect on the nerves after a time . . .

Colwyn Philipps, letter to his parents, November 10, 1914,
Verses: Prose Fragments: Letters from the Front

Marching Song in Flanders

Laughter and song lift us along,
Over the mud and the marsh – step strong! –
Through the twisted wrack of the crying Wrong
    To the place where the black bees hum.
Tramp through Gaul to the lilt of a Call;
In many a Cause men have minded to fall,
But we have a nobler Word than all,
    The Word of a time to come.

We fight the fight of Peace;
We fight that war may cease.

Trudge the plains where Misery reigns
And life and love lie fettered in chains,
Where the bleak sky blows and the black sky rains,
    Singing beneath our breath.
Nigh and more nigh; keep the heart high!
Hush the voice and strain the eye,
All for a Dream that shall live thereby
    Come light, come dark, come death.

We fight the fight of Peace;
We fight that war may cease.

Tunnel and trench; smoke and stench;
Hail of Hell to make a man blench;
Pains that pierce, and hands that clench;
    Horrors that scream and hiss;
Bear them strong! Right the wrong!
Die in a ditch that men may live long!
Charge to the next world singing a song!
    A song! – a song of this:

We fight the fight of Peace;
We fight that war may cease.

Ypres, 1915
Eliot Crawshay-Williams

98

Second Battle of Ypres, 1915

As the darkness gives way to a grey dawn, the ground immediately about us gradually becomes visible, and behind the trench I notice some old sheets of corrugated iron lying about in the mud. Then as the light grows clearer I can see, projecting from beneath them, and sticking partly out of the half-dried mud, legs and arms and the muddy outlines of rigid bodies. Some of them are almost near enough to touch. There seems to be heaps of them, and these again offer an uninspiring sight for the men in the daytime. So before the light is too clear, Reynolds and I sneak out and do what we can to make the iron cover them more completely, and to throw odd bits of sacking and rubbish over the more prominent arms and legs and bodies which stick up from the mud. By this time it is possible to see more of the enemy trench opposite and, joining a sentry at the parapet, I find him peering intently through a small groove he has made in the top layer of sandbags.

'Anything to be seen, sentry?'

Slowly withdrawing his head he whispers: 'They're moving about there, sir. They don't seem thirty yards away, and just at the top of that hollow I can see a steel loophole, with the sky beyond it, and every time any one passes along their trench or looks through it they blot out the sky. There are other loopholes all along but you'll see this one best, sir.'

For a time I watch the loophole. When it is but momentarily darkened I know that someone passes by; when the sky is hidden for a longer time I know that someone is peering in my direction. It is a temptation to take a pot shot at that darkened loophole, but it would be folly to draw the fire of all that line of steel loopholes upon our little un-loopholed trench, especially seeing that until tonight we are isolated from our main line while they have reserves in reach.

So I turn to the sentry – a young fellow nicknamed Ginger: 'Better not fire till they open the ball, but keep a sharp lookout.'

After an active day and a busier night I am glad to find that my servant has somehow produced some hot tea and I retire beneath my piece of iron to enjoy it, with a snack of bully beef.

I have scarcely begun to eat when there is a loud bang, followed by a fusillade of bullets and I can hear bits of earth pattering down on my shelter, so I get out again and look round. The bang was obviously Ginger's opening shot. He has been unable to resist the temptation and, as I expected, the reply is coming from all directions. The bullets are raking the parapets and showering down dirt and stones upon us. Some of the men have stuck up small mirrors just above the parapet to act as periscopes, but one after another they are being shivered by the shots from the steel loopholes. But Ginger is busy, and as I go back to my breakfast I leave him bobbing up to take shots as fast as he can load, and bobbing down again before his opponents have time to sight on him.

I have barely swallowed my tea – now cold – when I hear an oath and a thud. I find it comes from Ginger. A couple of men are picking him up, and 'Nobby' Clarke is examining his head. 'He's had a narrow squeak, sir, but he's not done yet.' We find that a bullet has entered just under the peak of his cap, cut a small groove up the middle of his head and has left a neatly short tuft of his ginger hair inside the hole by which it had passed out through the top of his hat. In ten minutes he has been bound up, and the first thing he does is to start groping about for his rifle. I tell him to give it up and take a rest, but he declares he'll get the devil yet, and tries to stand up, but his legs wobble and down he sits with a bump on the fire-step. In another ten minutes however he is banging away again despite still wobbly legs, reiterating that he is not going to give the bastards rest.

Then, suddenly there comes the sound of a sliding thud from the other side of the traverse and I slip round to find two men lifting up the victim, who has gone down on his face. He breathes his last as they turn him over in their arms. He was a good steady-going fellow of about twenty-five. He had just finished his sentry turn and was standing down in the trench with his back to the parapet, stretching out his stiffened body, when a bullet entered the back of his head and came out at the front.

We cover him up in a corner under his own waterproof sheet.

Ever since Ginger started things the firing has been heavy, and it seems now that bullets rake us from all directions except the rear. At about eight o'clock there is a slight slackening and some of the men sit down while one or two begin cleaning their rifles. I go to my hole again, but not for long. I hear a commotion outside and as I come out I hear someone say: 'It's Nobby Clarke, sir, he's gone.' I find it is true. And I find, too, that when he was hit he was sitting down on the fire-step with his head about two feet below the top of the parapet. The bullet has gone in at one temple and out at the other. This clearly means that the enemy has snipers out in No Man's Land, in positions from which they can snipe into our trench. Poor Clarke lingers for an hour but never regains consciousness, and we have to put him at last beside the other fellow in the corner.

Just as soon as Clarke is laid aside there is the zip of a low bullet and a scream of pain. The youngest lad of the party is trying to crawl in from the ground behind the trench with one leg painfully trailing. We pull him in and find that the bullet has entered above the knee and torn itself out through the calf – a fearful wound. And my only authority on First Aid, Nobby Clarke, is gone. I do what I can. I hold the boy's thigh with my thumbs on the main artery till the flow is reduced, then, while someone else takes it on I get a tourniquet fixed and bind on some sort of splints. It is a tough job, and for the boy it must be terrible. But he stands it like a hero. Except for short turns in the other fire-bay to see that all is right I keep near the boy all the time. The only members of our party who can stand the strain of nursing for any length of time are one or two old hardened soldiers. One of these, I remember, used to be frequently in detention in England for drunkenness; he is a real 'hard' man, who fears neither God nor devil, an atheist he is called. Well, God made the hearts of all men. Anyway I'm glad I brought him along.

The wounded boy moans as the hours go slowly on. Then he curses and defies the enemy at the top of his voice. They shout back and there is heavy firing from across the way and a lively reply from us. But now the lad begins to cry and shout for mercy. One after another we try to calm him. At last I ask the old 'hard' to see what he can do. He goes to the lad telling him gruffly to be quiet and throwing in a few oaths. The lad responds and lapses into quietness. The old 'hard' turns away, and pretends to get ready to fire from the end of the trench, but, being near him a few moments later I see the tears running down his face. And when he recovers himself he goes back to the boy and remains, when off firing duty, the most attentive of his nurses.

Meanwhile there is scarcely any respite in the firing. Our parapets are being hit about and many glancing bullets go whining back and crash into the fir wood in the hollow. Still my sentries continue popping up and snapshooting. The enemy behind the steel loopholes must get frequently shaken up. I notice that Ginger is now lying on the fire-step and as I stoop to examine him I am told that, after carrying on for some time on groggy legs, he sat down for a rest. In a few moments he was fast asleep. So his friends threw a couple of greatcoats over him to keep him warm. He now sleeps quite peacefully despite the din.

At the end of our little trench the parapet has tied round a tree. It is about twenty-five feet high, and, although rather shop-soiled it has some branches left. At the level of the top of the parapet the trunk is nearly a foot thick, and it is a game for the enemy, when he can find nothing better, to shoot at the tree. Now and then he succeeds in cutting off another branch and cheers loudly as it drops. If it comes within reach our men pick it up and wave it with a loud counter cheer. But so many bullets have struck the trunk just above the parapet that there is now scarcely enough solid wood left to support the weight it carries.

So the morning passes. I get a hole through my greatcoat and as I take a look over the top a bullet comes through the parapet stinging my cheek with dirt. Again, as I come round from the right fire-bay to the left, one of my men jerks me down and, ping, a bullet has gone through a tin of condensed milk which was standing on the traverse just level with where my head was. The milk is scattered over me. It strikes me that if the fellow had been less prompt it would probably have been my brains, not the milk.

About three o'clock, after a period of comparative quiet, which we put down to the effects of the Teuton appetite, without any warning, there comes a shower of shells. They scream low over our heads and go crashing down into the firwood in the hollow. A pause, another burst, and they develop into rapid and incessant drum-fire. We can almost feel their breath, and as the fire quickens there is a continuous splintering and falling of trees. So directly for our position do they come, so very close behind us do they fall, and so intense is the fire that I feel it may bode an infantry attack upon our little position and I give the order to fix bayonets. The men are quick to realise what is in my mind and they send up a ringing cheer. There is a grim satisfaction in the fixing of bayonets. For long hours we have been baited, held at a disadvantage. One by one they have killed or hurt our comrades. We have seen the sufferings of that young lad, now sinking past help. And we cannot tell whether our retaliation has been effective or not. 'Come on Fritz,' is the shout and a fellow near me mutters quietly, 'I hope to God they come.'

The shelling suddenly ceases. We wait, keenly on the alert, every finger on the trigger, but keeping the glint of the bayonet, below the parapet. But we wait in vain. They are still only baiting us. After about half an hour, during which we give them occasional ironical cheers, our sentries unfix bayonets, the better to shoot. Then at last we all 'unfix'. By this time it is getting dusk and I have ready volunteers for the risky attempt to run back for help for the wounded. I select an active youngster. There is a moment of deep anxiety as he crawls over the parapet and, bending low, runs, swiftly zigzagging down the slope. A few shots are being fired, but he seems unhurt when he disappears from our sight.

I should like to send the wounded boy back, and there are plenty of volunteers for the job, but a stretcher party could not hope to get across yet, and I cannot afford so to weaken my small garrison.

Then through the gathering dusk come the company stretcher-bearers. The poor lad is lifted very gently. He seems now beyond pain. He seems in a sort of quiet delirium. As he is borne away he smiles at us and weakly waves his hand. But his smile is vacant, and far more tragic than a groan.

Ginger has lasted the rest of the day out fairly well but he is glad enough to walk behind the stretcher party, and have his head properly dressed. Presently the stretcher party returns and one after the other the dead are taken away . . .

Charles Pritchard Clayton, The Hungry One,
edited by Michael Clayton, from diaries collated in the 1920s (1978)

The Earth Was our Cruelest Enemy

When we went out into the war, spending four days in the reserve line before proceeding to the front line, a routine which was repeated week after week with nothing to break the monotony except wounds and casualties and death, we discovered one element that was strange to most of us, and one that we had not previously noticed. That was the earth. The earth beneath our heels, the water around our legs, the clumps of earth that had been built for our protection, the barren stumps of trees scattered here and there, became living beings to be distrusted and feared, so strong was their influence on our condition and our fate. To one who had been bred on the civilised, gentle earth of the poetry of Islwyn*, to encounter this earth was a shock, a savage-natured earth, a mocking, merciless earth which fed its birds and animals on the putrid flesh of our friends, friends who had been enthralled by the song of the lark above the blood of the only creatures who gave meaning to their existence. The earth was our cruelest enemy. We went to war confidently, knowing that we had men to kill, and that we had under our feet one who had always tolerated our foolishness, and one who had always received her children to sleep peacefully in her bosom after their weary days. Did we not say that all the wars of the generations were nothing but child's play on the breasts of their mother? Mockingly, she turned on us and replied that no one who violated the beauty of her green garments could escape from her vengeance; and like a hard-hearted, disillusioned prostitute, she tore us and she wounded us ten times worse that any human enemy could. Could any of us ever forget the winter nights, the bitter cold weather, the water and the ice? . . . The poison of the battlefield had contaminated the whole of creation.

And that was the hardest battle, the futile battle with the earth. The long winters filled with horrors the hearts of men who would smile at the perils of the guns. The guns shattered muscle and flesh, but the spirit could rejoice in its freedom. The earth attacked body, brain and spirit, and suppressed even the strongest will. I saw courageous men who had gone to the trenches at the Somme, strong and able-bodied and proud in spirit, return after two quiet days in February a foot shorter in stature, and with such eyes in their heads as I had never seen before, except the eyes of a rabbit caught in a snare when seeing a dog approaching. But the earth's supremacy was even more complete than that, because she had anointed us with her own malevolence. The iron sank deep into the nature of men who were once meek. I saw once, when we were returning from the line, waist-high in water, a young lad falling, and the soldier who followed immediately behind him using his face as a stepping-stone. In those days, as many were drowned as were killed, and no one would answer or notice someone who was crying out for help. We were utterly suppressed by the supremacy of the earth.

Saunders Lewis, 'Profiad Cymro yn y Fyddin: Ar Ddaear Ffrainc'
('The Experience of a Welshman in the Army: On French Soil')
(Translated from the Welsh)

* The 19th century Welsh poet Islwyn (William Thomas) was a native of Ynys-ddu, Monmouthshire.

Mother Earth

Lift gently Dai, gentleness befits his gun-shot wound in the lower bowel – go easy – easee at the slope – and mind him – wait for this one and
slippy – an' twelve inch an' all – beating up for his counter-attack and – that packet on the Aid Post.

Lower you lower you – some old cows have malhanded little bleeders for a mother's son.

Lower you lower you prize Maria Hunt, an' gammy fingered upland Gamalin – down cantcher – low – hands away me ducky – down on hands on hands down and flattened belly and face pressed and curroodle mother earth she's kind:
Pray her hide you in her deeps
she's only refuge against
this ferocious pursuer
terrible questing.
Maiden of the digged places
          let our cry come unto thee.
Mam, moder, mother of me
Mother of Christ under the tree
reduce our dimensional vulnerability to the minimum –
cover the spines of us
let us creep back dark-bellied where he can't see
don't let it.
There, there, it can't, won't hurt – nothing
shall harm my beautiful.

David Jones, *In Parenthesis*, part 7

Death of a Youth

We were practically wiped out in our section, and when the artillery stopped only 30 men were left out of 150. We had only one machine gun left, and the enemy came at us 300 strong.

In a chateau we found a dead British soldier with seventeen bayonet stabs in his body. He was carried back to let the Headquarters Staff see what the Huns did to one man.

It was at Hooge that I had what I reckon was my greatest escape. Everybody in my section of the trench was killed except Sergeant 'Jimmy' Doig, Private

Dunford (a Welsh lad of only 17-and-a-half),* and myself. We could not get back, as all the communication trenches had been blown up by the enemy's artillery. We just lay flat on our faces while shells fell all round us. For hours we crawled up and down ruined trenches among the dead trying to get to where there were some live pals.

At last, after several hours, we got to a 'safe' trench without having been scratched. The one who kept us alive was the boy Dunford. He was absolutely fearless, and when we got to the 'safe' trench – which was being shelled, of course – he said, 'Buck up, Gibbie boy; we're out of it all right.' While in this trench a bullet hit the back of my hand without hurting much, but I had another awful blow, for Dunford, the boy with a giant's heart, was shot clean through the head that same night.

Henry Alfred Gibson (originally from Cardiff; joined the 3rd Dragoon Guards from Cape Town), 'From Ypres to Loos', *Western Mail*, January 8, 1916

* Private Joe Dunford, whose parents kept the Post Office at Rhymney, was killed in June, 1915

Dedication Before Battle

Legions of better men than I
    Have died that Freedom I might have;
Shall I, because I dare nor die,
    Condemn my son to be a slave?

My life is forfeit to the past,
    No favour will I ask or give.
But, steeled in purpose to the last,
    Gladly to die if Freedom live.

Charles Pritchard Clayton

The Hour of Terror

I

I'll not go back,
   I say, I'll not go back.
Even if my superiors curse and swear,
Or have me shot at dawn, what do I care?
   I'm neither brave nor do I courage lack.

I saw the Aisne,
   The slaughter of the Aisne,
And saw the Marne where many fought and fell:
No night could ever conjure up from Hell
   Horrors such as I had encountered then.

I saw men gassed,
   O God, how they were gassed.
I saw Their blue-black faces writhe in pain,
their torn flesh covered by a crimson stain.
   Of those forced over the top, I'll be the last.

The River Neath
   (How I long to see the Neath!)
Will turn its course back inland to its source
Before a law is made by man to force
   Me back again. I'd rather welcome death.

II

His tone was tense,
   His gaze, his face were tense,
Listening to screeching shells across the sky,
As one who knew his fate, yet to defy
   That fate he urged his faith to his defence.

With grievous tone,
   With grievous heart and tone,
'Let us now pray before the Cross,' said he:
'Only God knows the ultimate mystery
   Of the final hour of pain, and God alone.'

Unflinchingly,
   He knelt, unflinchingly,
Near the makeshift altar, unafraid;
Before the image of the Cross, he prayed
   To God, and then stood up, courageously,

And daylight shone,
   Night fled, and daylight shone;
His inner struggle found an inner strength:
He looked at us and smiled; in his full length
   He stood, and went towards the trench, alone.

J. Dyfnallt Owen
(Translated from the Welsh)

Horror and Grotesque Humour

January 4, 1917

My Dear Margaret,

We have just come out from an eight-day tour in the trenches.

I can't hope to describe to you the mixture of horror and grotesque humour of this line. Nothing at all of what I have seen before of trench warfare was at all like this. In the line we held we were in shell-holes waist-high in slime, without even the semblance of a trench; dead men were as common as the living. They had died in all kinds of positions – numbers had merely drowned – until your attitude towards them became one of mingled tenderness and sympathy and humorous acceptance. One joked with them and often joined them.

No regiment goes twice in this line to come out more than a quarter strong. More than any fire, exposure or exhaustion drain the battalion. And German and English here cease their fight to join hands against the conditions. I am splendidly fit physically, mentally I suffer also from exposure. It has rained and frozen all thinking out of me . . .

Yours,
Saunders

Saunders Lewis, letter to Margaret Gilcriest,
Saunders Lewis: Letters to Margaret Gilcriest

Seventh Hell

. . . I can see no excuse for deceiving you about these last 4 days. I have suffered seventh hell.

I have not been at the front.

I have been in front of it.

I held an advanced post, that is, a 'dugout' in the middle of No Man's Land.

We had a march of 3 miles over shelled road then nearly 3 along a flooded trench. After that we came to where the trenches had been blown flat out and had to go over the top. It was of course dark, too dark, and the ground was not mud, not sloppy mud, but an octopus of sucking clay, 3, 4, and 5 feet deep, relieved only by craters full of water. Men have been known to drown in them. Many stuck in the mud & only got on by leaving their waders, equipment, and in some cases their clothes.

High explosives were dropping all around, and machine guns spluttered every few minutes. But it was so dark that even the German flares did not reveal us.

Three quarters dead, I mean each of us 3/4 dead, we reached the dugout, and relieved the wretches therein. I then had to go forth and find another dugout for a still more advanced post where I left 18 bombers. I was responsible for other posts on the left but there was a junior officer in charge.

My dugout held 25 men tight packed. Water filled it to a depth of 1 or 2 feet, leaving say 4 feet of air.

One entrance had been blown in & blocked.

So far, the other remained.

The Germans knew we were staying there and decided we shouldn't.

Those fifty hours were the agony of my happy life.

Every ten minutes on Sunday afternoon seemed an hour.

I nearly broke down and let myself drown in the water that was now slowly rising.

Towards 6 o'clock, when, I suppose, you would be going to church, the shelling grew less intense and less accurate: so that I was mercifully helped to do my duty and crawl, wade, climb and flounder over No Man's Land to visit my other post. It took me half an hour to move about 150 yards . . .

In the Platoon on my left the sentries over the dugout were blown to nothing. One of these poor fellows was my first servant whom I rejected. If I had kept him he would have lived, for servants don't do Sentry Duty. I kept my own sentries halfway down the stairs during the more terrific bombardment. In spite of this one lad was blown down and, I am afraid, blinded.

This was my only casualty.

The officer of the left Platoon has come out completely prostrated and is in hospital.

I am now as well, I suppose, as ever.

I allow myself to tell you all these things because *I am never going back to this awful post.* It is the worst the Manchesters have ever held, and we are going back for a rest.

I hear the officer who relieved me left his 3 Lewis Guns behind when he came out. (He had only 24 hours in). He will be court-martialled.

Wilfred Owen, letter to his mother, January 16, 1917,
Wilfred Owen: Collected Letters

The Battle of Arras: Easter 1917

On parade we underwent intensive training for the battle of Arras. The trenches and wood which we were to attack were reproduced for us from aeroplane photographs, so day in, day out, during six weeks of strenuous work, we traversed its length and breadth. Scarcely a contingency was unforeseen and the final capture of the wood, a very pretty piece of drill, came off in the actual event.

The men toiled at the rifle ranges, or at their bombing schools, while the officers practised revolver shooting, and pored over maps and photographs. Never was there a more concentrated effort, for in addition to purely military exercises we organised a splendid series of games and sports. My only regret was that we had no swimming bath, as it was still too cold to allow of bathing in the open. Unable to swim, I rode more miles on horseback than at any other period of my life, realising physical joy to the full. By Easter, 1917, we were as fit as fiddles.

In the evenings I lectured to the N.C.O.'s and men, or galloped off to listen to talks by Staff Officers whose rank varied from that of major to lieutenant-general. Returning from one such conference, Compton-Smith said to us, 'It would be a good stunt, if at the end of the war, all Army and Corps commanders had to attend a lecture by Private Jones. They'd learn a hell of a lot.' My only quarrel with the proposition was that I saw no reason for postponing it until the war was over. Private Jones could have told them many things which would have saved hundreds of lives and thousands of casualties. He at least would have had the sense not to proceed with an attack when all the circumstances for which it was planned had changed. Only a person sitting in safety behind his chateau door could expect troops, unsupported by a barrage and wading through snow to carry out a scheme dependent on fine weather and strong artillery support.

My mail was unusually heavy, but I could do little except reply with Field Postcards. I reserved longer answers for Janie and Dad. A letter from him contained a word which I have always treasured. It is almost too intimate for these annals, but I mention it because it illustrates his generosity, and the tie which binds us. 'Whatever happens, I shall have nothing to think of in our relationship but that which is sweet. You have never given me any pain.' During a friendship which lasted for forty years we had no misunderstandings and even the slight differences which occasionally troubled us were due to natural and inevitable divisions of loyalty. On our own fellowship no cloud or shadow ever fell.

For days I walked on air, not stopping to ask why that which made living so urgent also made it easier to die. At Serre, and later at Bullecourt and Passchendaele, I was often half-crazy with apprehension, but going up to Arras I was almost completely poised and calm. It was our brigade custom to send company commanders into every other attack, alternating battle and rest (so short were we of experienced officers), but owing to casualties the exemption due to me was impossible. On April 5th I had a long pow-wow with Brigadier-General Porter, a fine leader, Lieutenant-Colonel Compton-Smith, and Captain Don Quin, our adjutant. They decided that I should be in charge of forward operations, with A and C Companies leading the way to Devil's Wood.

In the evening I strolled through the dusk into an orchard where my men were camping. I could not help contrasting its peace with all that lay before us, for the earlier trees were in bloom and the air was touched with a hint of fugitive fragrance. Suddenly my thoughts were interrupted by a harsh, strong voice saying, 'The only good Bosche is a dead one.' The speaker stood by a brazier, talking to a group of his fellows, and as the flames shot up I could see the hate in his eyes. I knew Jones's story. He was the sole survivor of three brothers who had joined the army. 'You remember Bill,' he continued, 'a cheerier kid never left Wales, and the devils watched him shrieking on the wire at Ypres until he died. Bert was blown to hell at Loos. I'll get even with the swine yet.' With a smothered curse, which was half a sob, he turned abruptly away, hurrying off into the darkness with his sorrow. Not for worlds would I have been eavesdropping, but I had to wait a moment or two, lest any movement on my part should give rise to anxious thoughts as to how long I had been there. The group took up the story, fact and fiction rivalling each other in horror and brutality. Some of them spoke quite cheerfully of killing prisoners, but the majority protested, both on military and humanitarian grounds.

I slipped away quietly, and sauntering to my quarters found myself on the old, eternal treadmill. To butcher prisoners was to break faith, but was killing anyone more justifiable? Sleep came at last, deep and heavy, and if it brought little peace to my soul, it revived and refreshed me.

On the road to Arras the guns were howling in fury, and night and day we could hear the mutter of machine guns, high in the clouds, as our men fought their duels with German aeronauts. They were making a desperate effort to control the skies before the attack was launched. In underground cellars we rubbed shoulders with half-a-dozen other regiments, and on the night of April 7 I talked to the men of British ideals and justice, pointing out the wisdom and the rightness of taking as many prisoners as possible. Only one man remained completely sceptical. Jones told me frankly that if he came across them they were as good as dead. It was useless arguing with him, but I chatted with him for a short time and hoped that all would be well. Easter Sunday found me on a reconnaissance with my N.C.O.'s in the front line. From an observation post we could see the four lines of trenches and the wood, scarcely a tree of which remained undamaged. The position looked formidable enough, full of sinister threatenings. On the way back I ran into Lieutenant F. C. Thompson of the R.F.A. 'spotting' for his battery. He was the Latin lecturer at Cardiff when war broke out, and I had spent Boxing Day with him in Calais, on our return from leave, sharing the only bed we could obtain in a pleasant little hotel. Now we could hardly hear each other because of the roar of the guns, and after a few minutes' conversation, we had to part. It was our last meeting, as a day or two later he was killed in action. He was a very perfect gentleman.

On the morning of Easter Monday, April 9 – what a Bank Holiday – we walked into the dawn, going through the Gordons, who had taken their objective at a stride. I was too busy to feel afraid, as every now and then a runner left my side, here to hold up a hurrying section and there to hasten a little group which tended to hang back. The men swarmed over the ground at a fine pace, preferring the risk of splinters and back-bursts from our own guns to the certainty of machine-gun murder. It was a beautiful morning, with the most weird colour effects. Behind us were miles of pinpoints of flame, where our guns were firing, and in front the sunrise, and the 'golden rain' and green and red lights of the enemy, conveying their message to the artillery. Almost lying on top of the barrage, we swept through Devil's Wood without a hitch, giving the Germans no elbow room. Out of a vast dugout underneath a ruined house in the middle of the wood, eighty-three prisoners poured, and down the steps we found two machine guns ready for action. Had we allowed time for them to be mounted, they would have spelled disaster to the battalion, but as it was we captured them and their crews without loss.

Our casualties were very light, two men killed and twenty-three wounded, but until the enemy had been cleared out of Tilloy by the 37th Division, who were waiting to go through us, we had to watch for snipers from the village just beyond. One of our Lewis guns exposed a nest of them hiding behind some tumbled-down brickwork. For the time being I was happy, although my mouth was parched and dry, with a curious taste of iron on my tongue. I had a drink, lit my pipe, and began to move about seeing to the work of consolidation. We built four strong points for our Lewis-gunners and bombers, and a fifth for the Machine Gun Corps, wiring them all securely.

Then odd things began to happen. I found a poor fellow in a green uniform, obviously a hopeless case, who begged of me to put him out of his misery. Our own doctor had been killed by a shell, and even had I possessed a pellet of morphia, I could see that the man was in no condition to swallow it. Was I to kill a prisoner and at his own request? I felt I ought to – wrong though the feeling may have been – and I knew that I couldn't. His wounds were beyond description. In a moment or two kindly death solved his problem and mine. A few minutes afterwards, Jones came down the trench, pushing before him a very small German. 'What shall I do with this, sir?' he asked grimly. The question was jerked out, the harshness of the voice trying in vain to conceal the humour that danced in his eyes. I told him he'd better feed it, so without more ado he sat the little prisoner on the fire-step and plied him with biscuit and beef. All the time Jones stood over him, shouting, 'Now tell us your blasted submarines are starving us.' We gave the boy, for that is what he really was, a cigarette and sent him down to the Corps cage. A long silence ensued, broken by my question, 'Well, Jones, what about killing prisoners now?' He looked straight at me, his face set and white, but his eyes laughing still, 'Not in cold blood, sir. I couldn't do it in cold blood. Besides, he was such a kid.' So the temptation passed and the poison gas which had descended upon his soul lifted for ever.

Reaction began to set in, now that the excitement was over, and all sorts of strange ideas came into my head as I sat down on an old tree stump. An occasional shell from a long-distance gun fell on the far edge of the wood, and I could see its final passage through the air, like a cricket ball dropping to the boundary. I was filled with memories of torn and bleeding men and dying eyes that yet gleamed with hate, or quivered with fear, or were too tired to express any emotion. The one blessed thought in the whole business was that the company, for the first and last time in its fighting career, had escaped serious loss. We had been told that after taking Devil's Wood we should be relieved, but our very good fortune vetoed the proposition. I turned in with Harry Curran, and together we settled down to sleep.

During the night of April 9 a heavy snow storm surprised us, and when we stood-to in the morning the wood presented a most lovely sight to the eye, the trees and hummocks of earth all covered with a vesture of white. We had little heart for its beauty. Snow meant cold feet, and wet garments, and cooking difficulties, with movement reduced to a snail's pace in the thick and heavy mud. Happily I made a marvellous discovery. Parry, my orderly, and I were exploring a number of dugouts and underneath a pile of sacking which no one had disturbed we came across a thousand Tommies' Cookers. There were enough for all of us to have two each, and to hand over a few dozen to the stretcher-bearers for special work. The Colonel was as delighted as I at our good luck, for these little tins, with their solidified methylated spirits, guaranteed hot food and drink. What we should have done without them I do not know, as all the wood we found was wet and sodden.

Late on the afternoon of April 10, Compton-Smith sent for his company commanders, and explained that we were to attack the village of Guemappe the next morning. A heavy creeping barrage would support us, and with the King's Own and the Suffolks to lead the way through the few trenches that were left, all would be well. He was gay and confident in manner, but I detected a good deal of anxiety in his eyes. It seemed to me that he knew in his bones that it was doomed to be a rotten show. Before I went to sleep a young Swansea officer, Second Lieutenant James, reported for duty. It was his first experience of the line, so I resolved that my runners and I should go over with the platoon he was to command. I felt far sorrier for him than he did for himself, so full of pluck and energy was he at the prospect of his baptism of fire. The rest of us were utterly fed up, relief denied and another sticky job in front of us. At 2.45am on April 11 we marched up to La Chapelle de Feuchy to our assembly positions, where a considerable amount of enemy shelling made the work intensely difficult. Most of it came from 5.9s, and the German gunners kept searching. the ground in a most uncanny and uncomfortable manner. Our own reply was feeble in the extreme, and before we attacked I knew why the Colonel had looked so anxious. He must have had serious doubts from the first regarding the support we were to get. I think he had done his best to indicate the almost insuperable barriers we should be expected to overcome. Luckily the men knew nothing of all this 'theirs not to reason why, theirs but to do and die', and as I moved along our line I was amazed at their good humour and morale.

Morgan Watcyn-Williams, *From Khaki to Cloth*

The Bravest Man in France

We had a man in our platoon who was one of the most windy men I ever saw in France, and when working on the parapet at night the report of a rifle was enough to make him jump back in the trench shivering with fright: it was pitiable to see him when the enemy were shelling our line. We decided one evening to see what effect an extra drop of rum would have on him. When the rations came up to the village the Old Soldier exchanged two nosecaps for about a pint of rum (this deal had been arranged the night before) with one of the transport men. We were issued out with our rum ration in the trench, and later in the night we gave the windy one who was working on the parapet a few swigs out of the pint. His own ration never had any effect on him, but those swigs did. For the next half-hour he was the bravest man in France. He danced and yelled like a Red Indian on the warpath, shouting across to the Germans to come over and meet him halfway so that he could bayonet the bloody lot of them. We had a job to prevent him from going across and attacking the German Army single-handed.

Frank Richards, *Old Soldiers Never Die*

The Fallen Petal

It was only a little petal,
It fell from the rose you wore;
How eagerly I snatched it
As it blew across the floor.

I kept it in my pocket-book
For many and many a day:
It made me think of your sweet face
When I was far away.

Far away in the fighting line,
Where the Boys were falling fast,
I thought of you and the rose you wore
While the next breath seemed my last.

That little petal pulled me through
And out of the fire of Hell:
It seemed a charm against all ills,
Brought me back to you safe and well.

And often I think of that lovely morn
When I wished you a long farewell:
It was just as I whispered the last goodbye
That the little rose petal fell.

'T.O.M.'

The Attack

To attempt to analyse and describe one's sensations in battle is to attempt the well nigh impossible. There are moments when the brain is heated to fever pitch, and others when the work in hand demands such complete concentration that, in the revulsion that follows, all impressions are lost or fade rapidly away, only to return in after years in the dim, hazy, form of half-forgotten memories. Yet, often in tense moments, one seems to live years and indelible impressions are received which alter the whole lives and characters of men.

Of all the more interest then is the following manuscript. It is a short, thumbnail sketch of war and was written by a Welsh officer during an attack which took place some weeks ago, and under the conditions which he describes . . .

*   *   *

Our objective is gained and the fighting is dying down, but the nerve strain is still terrible, and I feel that if I do not do something to occupy my thoughts I shall be approaching madness.

I am writing down, then, what I can remember of all that has happened since marching up to the trenches 24 hours ago.

That the enemy expected our attack was apparent. Never a moment passed but a star shell flared through the night. The air was full of dust and the shells burst in lurid flame amongst the enemy's wire. I sat on the fire-step of a trench packed with men awaiting the zero hour. One lad was snoring quietly on my shoulder, another near was droning something quietly to himself. The noise and thunder around, the dark figures in the trench, gave a sense of weirdness, of power and exaltation, the beginning of the Red Fever.

The man near me stopped talking to himself and asked abruptly, 'Have you ever killed a man, Sir?' 'Yes,' I said, and then, 'Have you?' 'No! I've wounded many, but, my God! I'd rather myself be killed than take a life.'

His tense accents awakened my curiosity, and I glanced at him sharply, but he had sunk back into his reverie, his lips moving, his attitude like one who wrestles with the problems of life, and so I asked no more.

When one accepts the principle of war, thought I, wounds and death, torture and discomfort are mere incidents by the way.

The zero hour was near, and brushing aside thought, I awakened those who were asleep. Arms and bombs were examined, small details of equipment were attended to, anything was done to prevent thinking and imagination. My own feeling was one of curiosity – and confidence.

Then we were crawling, slipping over the parapet towards the enemy's trenches. Shells and flares still lit up the ground and from the east the first grey light of dawn was stealing.

I heard a shout, faintly above the roar of the shells, and instantly, it seemed, the enemy's trenches burst into a sheet of flame – flashes from machine guns and rifle. I leapt to my feet and ran heeding nothing, shouting, my whole being quivering and moving in lightning fashion, impelled by the intoxication, the lust of battle.

Some strands of wire barred my path. I dived over them, head first, into a layer of mud, at the bottom of a trench from which I rose gasping with maniacal fury. One of the enemy lay dead at my feet, and another paralysed, his features distorted with fear, was awaiting death from a man who towered above him.

I was in time to save the poor wretch's life and the action sobered me. I grew cool, calmly cool, and remembered I was to lead a bombing party down a communication trench. By good luck, I was near this trench and some of my men were with me . . . Bombs were falling around us, and we pushed slowly, yard by yard, up the trench, hurling bombs with demoniacal vigour, now darting forward and now back to escape a bursting bomb. Occasionally, we saw the faces of our enemies, and, once, I saw a face close in, like a book, as my revolver bullet hit it. In a while, we reached a place where the trench was demolished.

The shellfire raged ahead and around us, and we crawled forward in line with some infantry who were digging themselves in.

It was now broad daylight, and the musketry fire still roared from the enemy trenches a few hundred yards off. I lay panting, my chest and eyes aching, and looked along the line of men digging, digging, their entrenching tools keeping time with their palpitating hearts, groaning as they breathed. I smiled at the ludicrousness of it, and broke into a fit of laughter, when one or two stopped and regarded me nervously but soon resumed their digging . . . A trench was completed and in this way we lay exhausted. I had lifted some dead men out of the trench in order to do more digging and improve it, and was now sitting attending in a stupefied manner to two wounded men. One, shot in the neck and paralysed, was praying as he felt his life slipping, praying for his widowed mother at home. The other, shot in the stomach, clawed and bit at the ground in frightful agony, and him I dosed with morphia.

It was now late in the afternoon. I was worn out, exhausted. The blood on my clothes and hands smelt sickly in the warmth of the sun, and the sense of the futility, the terrible madness of war, welled up in me again and I lay sick – horribly sick . . . I floundered for some firm moral support to cling to and find calm. Old arguments which drove me into the Army, flit and chase in eternal procession across my brain, but reason seems blunted, turned aside, poor and feeble.

'Wounds and death are mere incidents by the way'. I remember my specious philosophising of the night before and my words come back to mock me. There is something wrong, so hellishly wrong with it all, and I am helpless, tossed about, a puny thing! I know that tomorrow I shall be calm and purposeful again, but now I want rest – rest. I want to laugh, but that spells madness. God in Heaven! Give me the clear insight to see, and the grace to follow, or take from me reason and leave me unthinking, drifting to death with the beasts of the field!

'E.C.H.', *The Welsh Outlook*, vol. v, no. 53, May 1918

Young Sassoon

We had a new Colonel, Garnett by name. I had soldiered with him abroad; he was a decent old stick but not to be compared with the colonel we had just lost. Two new officers that had just arrived seemed of a far better stamp than some that we had had during the last few months, and one named Mr Sassoon, who was wearing the ribbon of the Military Cross, was soon very popular with the men of the Company he was posted to. He had been with the First Battalion before he came to us . . .

The following morning one hundred bombers of the Battalion under the command of Mr Sassoon were sent to the Cameronians to assist in a bombing attack on the Hindenburg Trench on our right. A considerable part of it was captured but was lost again during the day when the enemy made a counter attack. During the operations Mr Sassoon was shot through the top of the shoulder. Late in the day I was conversing with an old soldier and one of the few survivors of old B Company who had taken part in the bombing raid. He said, 'God strike me pink, Dick, it would have done your eyes good to have seen young Sassoon in that bombing stunt. He put me in mind of Mr Fletcher. It was a bloody treat to see the way he took the lead. He was the best officer I have seen in the line or out since Mr Fletcher, and it's wicked how the good officers get killed or wounded and the rotten ones are still left crawling about. If he don't get the Victoria Cross for this stunt I'm a bloody Dutchman; he thoroughly earned it this morning.' This was the universal opinion of everyone who had taken part in the stunt, but the only decoration Mr Sassoon received was a decorated shoulder where the bullet went through. He hadn't been long with the Battalion, but long enough to win the respect of every man that knew him.

Frank Richards, *Old Soldiers Never Die*

Before Battle: Ypres, July 1917

'Vengeance? It is mine.' It thrills our listening ears;
'Vengeance? It is mine.' We see it warped through our fears;
'Vengeance? It is mine.' O, Lord, it is for you
To teach us what to do, what not to do.
Pray that the iron tempered in our blood
May give the blow that was long meant by Thee,
For we would guide the whirlwind –
At the helm with Thee.

D. T. Jones

From the War Diary of Thomas Richard Owen

Since I last wrote in this diary, I have been in close proximity to the Germans. And I have never been so close to being killed. That happened during the two nights of the 12th and the 13th of this month. On Monday morning, around 5am, we were shelled mercilessly for an hour-and-a-half. This was the most intense bombardment I have experienced since coming to France. The shells fell so close to us that the earth fell down like showers of snow on my back. The intensity of the bombardment made me tremble like a leaf, and at the same time I was trying to pray. My prayer was heard, and I was spared because I thanked God for strength and protection when the battle was at its most intense. Many were wounded. And when they began shelling us, I was at the time carrying a lad who had been wounded and who was groaning, and carrying him was very difficult because the trench was so narrow, and because the shells were falling so close to us, most of them blinding us. But the following night we were allowed to leave the trenches, and we were sent to a fourth trench from the reach of the enemy. Tonight we have to do some work near enemy territory . . . We have returned safely . . . I am now writing some more as I haven't written for a while, and I have nearly forgotten recent happenings. I can only say that we have had a better time of it, for about twelve days, than we had on several previous occasions. During the night, gas came over. By now we have had to go near enemy territory again, and we've had a difficult and perilous time of it, and we've lost quite a few of our lads, and many others were wounded. After those four days, we were allowed to go five miles out of the reach of the enemy, and we had nine days there.

. . . I am now writing this 300 yards from the reach of the enemy. I often see one of them, but he can't see me. They say that we will be here for four days, before we are sent to a fourth trench some two miles back, and there is talk that we are to be sent much further back, and I am writing this on July 10, 1918 . . . After the rumour that we were to be sent further back, we had to return to the trenches, near enemy territory, and the shelling gave us a hard time. We expected a shell to drop near us any minute. We had a really hard time of it, and had to face terrible dangers, for five days. We had to go back because the 2nd Battalion of the R.W.F. had to go over to capture a few prisoners, and they captured 16 and one officer and a machine gun. That was their excuse for sending us back to the trenches. Then there was talk that we were to be sent back for a rest. And while the 2nd Battalion of the R.W.F. was going over, the enemy shelled another part of the trench, thinking that we were going to invade their trenches, and that was a perilous time for us, but, mercifully, I escaped unscathed from that awful place, and I am thankful every time I survive. By now we have gone back a little distance from the Front, thinking that we are to be ordered much further back to rest, and we were to go back tonight. But then came a German push on the left and on the right of us, so that the Division which was supposed to relieve us had to go to the right to help the others to face the enemy, who was trying to overcome us, so we don't know when we will be allowed to go back for a rest. And we have to lay barbed wire near enemy territory every night, and we really deserve to be relieved, so that we can leave the noise and the dangers behind us for a little while.

The Great War diary of
Thomas Richard Owen, Anglesey,
10th Battalion South Wales Borderers
(Translated from the Welsh)

Thomas Richard Owen

119

The Last Peal
(a church in Flanders)

In peaceful times they sound the chimes
    (Afar the echoes pass),
Along each road the people strode
    To celebrate the Mass.

Now shells of fright that come by night,
    And steel that kills by day,
Sound on the square that opens there
    Where once the houses lay.

Hour after hour, the crimson flower
    Breaks into smoking leaves;
The steady spire reflects the fire,
    The very altar heaves.

None tread the path through Hell's hot wrath;
    No priests say Mass today;
No mourners come; the bells are dumb
    That tolled the souls away.

But as they fall, the roof and wall,
    The spire a drunken lurch,
The singing shells shall peal the bells
    And call the folk to church.

Oscar Lloyd

The Agile Welshmen of the Mountains

You will understand I could not write – when you think of us for days all but surrounded by the enemy. All one day (after the battle) we could not move from a small trench, though hour by hour the wounded were groaning just outside. Three stretcher-bearers who got up were hit, one after one. I had to order no one to show himself after that, but remembering my own duty, and remembering also my forefathers the agile Welshmen of the Mountains I scrambled out myself & felt an exhilaration in baffling the Machine Guns by quick bounds from cover to cover. After the shells we had been through, and the gas, bullets were like the gentle rain from heaven . . .

Wilfred Owen, letter to his mother, October 8, 1918;
Wilfred Owen: Collected Letters

'Stand-to' on Givenchy Road

It was near the end of the great German bid for victory in April 1918. We left Beuvry and passed the hamlet of Le Fresnoy and crossed the bridge over the La Bassée Canal into the village of Gorre. There we struck a route past the famous Brewery to make for the open fields and the front-line trenches.

We knew our destination was 'somewhere between Festubert and Givenchy' – a new sector to us – and, as we marched, we sang softly a popular ditty of those days. It went to the tune of a sentimental song then going strong in Blighty, about a Tulip and a Red, Red Rose. Our own exclusive lyric had pointed reference to certain gentlemen at home and ended in averring that:

> You stole our wenches
> While we were in the trenches
> Facing the angry foe;
> You were a-slacking
> While we were attacking
> The Huns on Givenchy Road.

Now, in reality, we were to know what it was like on Givenchy Road, and it was said that there was plenty of 'dirt' up in 'the doings'. The 'Pork and Beans' had broken in disorder on the left, and it was rumoured that the Germans had captured the Portuguese commissariat and were even raiding and reconnoitring in Portuguese uniforms.

The 55th Division had made a stand and held up a veritable horde of the enemy with great slaughter. Now, utterly weary, they were to be relieved, and we of the 1st Division were to hold the renewed attack of the enemy.

A part of my own company relieved a detachment of the Liverpool Scottish, and we occupied a section of the trenches almost square-shaped in form, with three sides facing a miniature salient of German troops, who surrounded us more or less in the form of a horseshoe. Our post was evidently a key position in the line.

Dead men lay about here and there; the communication trench to Headquarters – a small pillbox in the centre of the square – had partly collapsed at the sides and was sickeningly yielding underfoot with the bodies of buried men. Here and there a leg or an arm protruded from the trench side. The wire was cut in places and the gaps in the trenches, caused by trench mortar attacks, were staringly open and dangerous.

We arrived in the dark of the evening, before the moon had risen. Silently we filed into the trench at a corner of the square. A line of bare trees, tall and ghostly, marked another boundary of the line.

The Scotties trailed out with whispered greetings, and we settled down to the eternal vigil. The silence was of the dead. Not a gun fired. Not even a Very light flared. The bloated trench rats squeaked now and again and only intensified the silence.

There was nothing to do but overhaul equipment: place Mills bombs at strategic points, with slack pins ready for throwing; play cards; smoke interminable cigarettes. During the night we examined the wire and sent reconnoitring patrols into No Man's Land. They met nothing, heard nothing, saw no one, and came back scared and craving rum.

Above all we must not remain still to brood on things. For two days the silence continued, unnatural and nerve-racking. Old soldiers talked with bated breath of the horrors that were surely coming. On the evening of the third day, as we shook our limbs and set guards and patrols moving, a whispered word went round that at 'Stand-to' at dusk the Germans might attack in force.

We lined up along the trench, and gulped our rum ration and literally ached for something to happen. But the sun went down and the gloom came on, and not a sound broke the solitude. Well, it would be at 'Stand-to' at about six o'clock in the morning – a blood-chilling time.

Morning 'Stand-to' came in due course, and once more the rum went round and the whispered word of warning. A watery sun peeped through the mist and still no enemy appeared. No lark rose to greet the dawn. Not a gun hurled its load of venom. I sat down with my section of eight men and I looked at our ration of bread, bacon, and cheese. It was small enough, and God knew if we should ever get another.

'Shall we cook the whole issue?' I asked, and a nodding chorus signified assent. We lit the 'Tommy' cooker, and made a good job of the cooking, and ate a great bellyful and smoked a Woodbine at the end.

Suddenly a gun barked and a heavy explosion shook the trenches. The frantic rats squeaked and scuttled past us: men shuddered, and clattered their arms and sprang to attention.

The barrage had started. I heaved a sigh and was almost glad the suspense was over. The barrage was pitched about 40 yards short of our line of trench. Evidently it would creep to us after first smashing the wire.

I placed five men on the fire-step and fixed one man with a Lewis gun and two men to fill containers for it. We waited with livid faces. The barrage crept nearer. Now it was 30 yards, now 20 yards. We were in a hell of din and slaughter.

The trench was crumbling slowly to pieces. One of my men suddenly sank to his knees. A piece of a shell had torn at his middle and he sat down quietly to die a slow death. I shook with stark fear, but I held to my rifle and kept my place on the crumbling fire-step.

The barrage lifted again and moved nearer. The man with the wound in his side moaned at intervals, and fixed his field bandage and held his hands to it as if to hold the very life in him. His groans, coming during the briefest lulls in the shelling, were unnerving us all.

We crouched at the bottom of the trench, abject and trembling. I passed the rum bottle round and took a long swig myself. Rum numbs you at times like these. It gives you Dutch courage and a lurching contempt for danger. You die more or less decently; neither whining nor squealing – which is as it should be.

A moment later the machine gun to the right of us went up in the air and its team of men went up with it: a direct hit. The shells were dropping practically on the very brink of the trench. Now the worst had come. We were face down in the slime, with boot and finger and knee clutching and scraping for the veriest inch of cover; hiding our eyes, as we did once from childish terrors; now whimpering, now cursing, with bowels turned to water and every faculty at agonised tension.

. . . Who shall say where Providence came in? Death grinned at us and yet not a shell hit full on our dozen yards of entrenchment. Still leaping forward, the barrage blundered over us and beyond us. It left us stunned and deaf and prostrate. The dying man mercifully breathed his last in the midst of it. Still we cowered in the mud and the slime.

At nine o'clock in the morning the barrage started. It ceased as suddenly as it had begun, at exactly 11.30am. It might have been a year of time. The deadly stillness came on again but I ran among the others kicking right and left in a frenzy because I knew the attack was coming. The man would follow the machine.

Looking over the top I saw the long grey lines sweeping along 400 yards away. They were marching slowly, shoulder to shoulder, heavily weighted with picks, ammunition, and rations.

We scrambled to the fire-step. We fired madly and recklessly. The Lewis gun rattled and the two magazine fillers worked with feverish haste. It should have been horrid slaughter at the distance, for the Germans seemed to huddle together like sheep as they lurched over No Man's Land.

But there were thousands of them and our aim was hurried and bad. We fired in abandonment rather than by design. Still the grey hordes advanced. A hoarse voice shouted at the back of us. It was Sergeant Winnford: God knows how he got through to us; and he yelled, 'Retreat back to support line: you, Corporal, see them all out.'

He made for a gap in the trench. The survivors followed him. As he reached the open a stray shot, or splinter, splattered his brains out and he fell without a sound. Stupefied, the others crept through and got clear, and raced across the open land with the enemy in full cry behind. Barker was the last to crawl out. I howled at him to hurry but he was tall and lanky and dead beat. I raced at his side.

'Slip off your pack,' I shouted, as I got out of my own trappings. He did so, but he was ashen and panting. I felt a smart above my elbow and found there was blood trickling from the tips of my fingers. 'Barker, Barker!' I screamed. 'Hurry up, chum, for God's sake!' I might have saved my breath.

As I turned my head to him, and as he made a supreme effort to hasten, I saw the bullet hit the back of his tin helmet and spurt out at the front. He curled over in a heap. He was past aid.

I ran a dozen steps further. Something hit my other elbow, searing hot and smashing through, and I spun round like a top and lay once more in the slime. I thought my arm had gone. If it was death I was numb, careless and content. I sank into a dull stupor and the hordes of grey uniforms trampled over me, round me and by me, and forgot me in their own terror. They swept on and on to meet another wall of steel and flame. How many of them would see another dawn?

Presently I came fully to myself and found that my arm was still there but was bleeding profusely. Laboriously, I got my field dressing somewhere near where the blood was flowing, and I got to my knees, then to my feet in a half-blind endeavour to get somewhere, to someone . . . I staggered to meet the second wave of the advancing Germans.

Would they shoot me again as they passed me? An officer, with revolver in hand, waved me through the ranks. They parted to make a road for me. At every other step I fell with weakness and the spikes of the ground wire stabbed into my hands, my limbs, my very face, as I fell. I remember weeping like a child because I could not help falling and suffering this torture.

I cannot say how far I walked. I passed a first-aid post in an old trench, but they waved me off despairingly. They had too many to see to. Stretcher-bearers passed me, carrying a pole, with a blanket slung to it, and inside an agonised bundle of broken humanity – blood trickling and dripping from the pendulous blanket.

Eventually I simply fell into another portion of trench and there a sad-eyed, black-bearded man whispered *'Armes kind'* – meaning little child – and stripped off my tunic, leather jerkin, and cardigan, and took his own field dressing and patched up the mess of my arm. A prisoner indeed; receiving succour from a man whose countrymen I had blazed at in hate but a while ago, and from whom I had suffered this shot in my elbow.

Truly the quality of mercy is not strained. I had none of his tongue, nor he of mine, but he gave me a drink of warm coffee from a flask, and his hands were as tender as a woman's as he bandaged me.

If ever I had felt hate for the German I was cured of it now. I had had my job to do and he his. The responsibility was not ours and our fate was none of our choosing. I today; perhaps he tomorrow. But I could not stay here.

The English barrage had now started; tearing and rip-snorting along all the roads and communications. It was intended to hold up the reinforcements for the German attack. For me there was the sickening necessity of walking through the menace of our own barrage; to risk death from our own shells; to get to some place of refuge.

Three others joined me. They also had staggered from the shambles of No Man's Land, and we bled from various wounds all along that pitiless road to the rear.

How we escaped the shelling I know not. German transport wagons lumbered past us at intervals, the drivers whipping the horses to a mad gallop. Here and there dead or dying horses lay among the splintered ruins of shafts and wheels.

The very road was greasy with blood. Yet even as the horses fell the poor brutes were dragged to the side of the road and the matter-of-fact Germans whipped out knives and cut long strips of flesh from the steaming flanks. Heaps of intestines lay in the ditches.

At last a German *unter-offizier* dashed out from behind a ruined house and took charge of our little band. He took us a further short walk till we came to a large church, with the Red Cross flag flying from the tower. We were placed in a queue of men all waiting for attention to wounds. Gradually we got inside the church. May I never again see such a sight.

All along the nave improvised stretchers lay side by side and reached to the step leading to choir and chancel. Up there a dozen surgeons in ghastly stained white overalls performed operation after operation. Amputation after amputation. The smell of chloroform and ether pervaded everything. The horrible rasping sound of the silver saws grated on the ear.

Attendants carried limbs away in tall baskets. Men died before aid could get to them. Each had inexorably to wait his turn and the surgeons, with white and drawn faces, sweated and toiled silently: no time for consultations. I was attended to in my turn, and left that charnel house for the nearby prisoners' cage, where I was questioned and had my papers examined and my letters from home confiscated.

It was now nightfall. I was in a small town – La Bassée, maybe, though I had no means of knowing. Twenty-four hours previously I had 'stood-to' on the fire-step and awaited the coming of the attack. Now it was all over. There is enduring stuff in youth, and I was young and craved for life with every fibre of my being. I was not done for yet.

So I staggered among the ranks of a draft of prisoners to be entrained for the rear hospitals. We marched in columns of four to the station, and we held one another up and marched as if in a dream. They placed us in open trucks; Black Watch, South Wales Borderers, and others, and we clanked through a pitch-black night of hail, rain, and storm, through Lille and on to Tournai.

I was half delirious by then: the numbness had given place to agony, and with all of us the bitter night did its worst to finish off the work that even the shells had failed to do.

So we ended up away in high Germany, and the Army Lists posted me as 'missing'.

Thomas A. Owen, *Everyman at War*, edited by C. B. Purdom (1930)

The Somme
and
Mametz Wood
1916

July 1916: Fricourt Wood and the Somme

June 1916: we slowly continued our march southwards with not the slightest knowledge of our eventual destination, staying one, two or even three nights in small villages. It would have been in the early days of July when we approached the area of the Somme, named from the river which flowed through that region. It was evident from the terrific noise of gunfire and the continual lighting of the sky at night by Very lights that this was our destination. We knew that an offensive had developed there. Arriving and passing through Albert, much damaged by shellfire, but still functioning as a town, we were amazed to see the tall figure of the Madonna which topped the cathedral dome. As the result of shellfire, it was at horizontal right angles to the street along which we travelled. We marvelled at the angle at which it hung, looking down on us, whether in pity or enquiry, or both!

We arrived at our temporary destination. Fricourt Wood which topped a hill running west to east as we looked at it. We learned later that the front line existed here prior to the offensive, proceeded just a little way ahead in front of another wood which covered the slope right at its taking, the Cardiff City Battalion of the Welch Regiment had lost over fifty per cent of its numbers.

Fricourt Wood was relatively undamaged and our HQ was to be inside it, its width being about three hundred yards. I was still the medical corporal and had a wood-constructed bivouac in which I stored my equipment. My helper, a wonderful protective figure named Ned Williams suggested we fetch a can of water from a well he had observed at the rear edge of the wood. We had drawn a bucketful up by the windlass when we heard a peculiar and frightening sound seemingly out of the void, an increasing, terrible, screaming noise which I could not comprehend. Ned Williams swept me to the ground as he shouted, 'Keep your head down.' It was my introduction to the engines of war and destruction – an artillery shell of perhaps a little more than medium calibre.

I learned with much regret that my boss, Dr Morley, had been taken 'down the line' with some sort of infection and that a replacement had arrived, Dr Dick, a Scotsman, who told me, after dealing with the sick parade, that I had to go to the advanced divisional dressing station which was positioned a little in advance of Mametz Wood. I set off, out of Fricourt towards the Mametz valley. The ground, at that time, had not been too badly churned up. There was still a good deal of grass underfoot and to my left in the direction of the front line. Suddenly there was a terrific bang and a huge draught of air. I was frightened and looked behind me for the cause. It was plain to me what had happened. A battery of 18-pounders, dug-in and camouflaged, had fired a salvo, but I was unhurt. I continued my way along the perimeter of the wood where only two weeks previously the Cardiff City Battalion had been halved towards an area with an indicator board marked 'Bazentin-le-Petit'. There, dug into high ground, with an entrance marked with a red 'X', a field hospital (advanced). This was my destination. I entered a sandbagged passageway into a large dugout. I knew I was in the correct place by the foetid smell of men and of blood, varied by the heavy odour of anaesthetic, punctuated by plaintive and not very loud groans, moans and irregular breathing.

A young man, a doctor, both his arms bloodstained, approached me and quite cheerily asked, 'What do you want, son?' I showed him my requisition note. 'Right, sit there for a couple of minutes, I won't be long.' Two men lifted a casualty onto the table. He lifted a large piece of bloodstained gauze off the head of the man and I heard a horrible gurgling, emanating: no sign of a face; just a bloody mask. I was unaware I made any noise. But I must have, because the doctor turned to me and, patting my shoulder, said, 'Alright son, perhaps you had better wait outside. I won't be long.' The same two orderlies quickly carried out the stretcher, now with a blanket covering its burden and laid it on the ground. There followed a cheery call from the doctor, 'Come in son, I'm ready now.' He filled my bag with the necessary items, allowing me to make my way back. Ours was a Pioneer battalion and their duty was to be closely associated with the front line; digging and maintaining trenches prior to any attack; to dig jump-off trenches in advance of the front line; always at night so that when the artillery barrages opened up, they would not be holding the front line already pinpointed by them, but installed in the advance works dug for them by the Pioneers. A terrifying experience out in a muddy, shell-pocked area! Very lights ascending generally from the Bosche side. Part of the ordeal was that whilst these star shells illuminated and fell around you, still sizzling, it was sensible to remain perfectly still, which minimised the possibility of being seen and shot. In the nights that followed, that was happening to our battalion but I did not go with them. I stayed at my doctor's post and so was not engaged at that time with their work.

W. G. Bowden, *Abercynon to Flanders – and Back* (1984)

Over the Top: the Battle of the Somme

Crouching in the front trench I watch the luminous face of my watch. The two minutes before zero seem ages. Zero comes, yet the shells seem to be still right down on us. 'Time up, come along,' and we clamber up the grassy side of the trench. There is no machine-gun fire, but the flashes of our own shells seem close in our faces. I can see scarcely any men moving and I find some still crouching hard down in shell-holes. They are not to be blamed because the row is terrific now and the explosions confusing. Orders have to be roared at close range. The shorter shells temporarily blind or choke us. Gradually the main body of the leading company seem to be up and struggling and slithering along. There are certainly some short shells that fall among us and I find some of the men getting down into shell-holes again. I get annoyed and determined to stop any hiding. My language deteriorates as I yell them out of one hole after another. Now I come upon a particularly big deep hole with dark forms at the bottom of it. This is too much. I raise my revolver. 'By ——, I'm sick of this. If you don't get out and get on, I'll save the Hun some trouble.' Indeed, I feel rather like doing it, when the soft voice of an orderly protests: 'This is the Colonel, and the Battalion Headquarters, sir, just moved up.'

I do not wait to apologise but push off forward. I soon find myself alone and going straight on, as well as I can judge the direction. Suddenly the darkness on my right is broken by a succession of bomb flashes and there is much noise. There comes the voice of a man crying in terror *'Kamerad!'* and I have a glimpse of a German in a trench with his hands held high above his head while our men's bombs crash around him. I roar to the men to send him back and get on, and I get on myself. But the darkness is very deep, and I find I can see no one to right or left. Suddenly a form comes along on my left. We challenge, and I find him to be a man of our C Company. He says he has lost touch with his company so we get along together.

We have scarcely gone twenty yards on the heels of the falling shells when one of them bursts right between us and we both go down. The splinters must have thrown forward for we both struggle up again unhurt and push on, although for a moment I wonder whether we are not going faster than the shells are lifting. After pushing on another hundred yards or so without seeing any one I begin to wonder where we have got to. I feel sure we are nearly on the objective. Suddenly we become aware of voices coming from the darkness behind us on our left. Dark forms with gleaming bayonets appear and challenge. My 'Welch' brings the welcome answer 'Gloucesters.' Their platoon commander and I quickly agree that we are on our objective, and Colonel Pagan, always with his first line, joins us. He makes this to be the line of our objective. Just as I am telling him that our battalion got well away and ought to appear at any moment, more dark forms with bayonets loom up from behind and they turn out to be A Company who, to keep their direction, have carefully followed the line of a winding communication trench which was marked on our maps.

Pagan and I agree that we will set the men digging-in along the line on which we now stand, he to the left and I to the right. We seem to have got right on the top of the ridge. So I start off fixing man by man to dig himself into a hole before dawn. The men are somewhat mixed up now, but I plant them as they come, leaving the company officers to reshuffle them while the digging goes on. Coming back after stringing out the line I find Colonel Pagan looking for me. He says that the Munsters cannot hold forward to secure his left flank and that consequently he will have to fall back. This is bad. And Pritchard now comes along, and we decide that one company will take up a defensive position to secure our left flank, and that we will take up a defensive position to secure our left flank, and that we will hang on to our success.

When the dawn breaks the men on the right are sitting right along the top of the ridge but we feel very anxious lest from our left we shall be overlooked and strafed from a piece of slightly higher ground in front of the Gloucesters. But as the daylight grows we find that we can move in the open. The enemy has gone. I send a patrol forward with Sergeant-Major Flavin during the night while the digging is going on, but after following a communication trench some distance in the direction of Martinpuich they are held up by machine guns and return.

Charles Pritchard Clayton, *The Hungry One*

Mametz Wood, 1916
(From *'The Song is Theirs'*)

A knave in borrowed clothes this Spring across the sea,
trust it not . . . look there is murder here
grey behind a thorn, snare in the willow's curve
and rusty barb in the ragwort's yellow ranks.

My flesh is quick tonight: I had forgotten fear.
Love stripped me naked.

Hark to the drumbeats . . . this Drummer
hath he report I fled his parade?
Make room for me, this odour calls me
sharp to kill all fragrance.
   I have said Farewell my love.

This man, is he dead?
I had forgotten death cold hunger fury
torment and toil, leaden drag of limb
fumes of the pit grey lids and red-rimmed eyes
Fear set this face to stone
   Make room for me
   I have dallied enough.

Remembering now that I have left love
tenderness, kind touch of flesh far
in another land far in another time,
Remembering now all beauty gone
as a dream goes
     Turn back delight
     Reach not to me
This land a pockmarked harridan
brownskinned furrowed with debauchery
flaunting a raddled face greystreaked
gaunt, each empty eye a crater
where a lust burnt through

This Summer morn a mockery

Remembering this also
I have known mountains gold under the sun
I have trodden scree to bare a fern
mounted crest to meet dawn over sea
and this I know
I shall not die before her eyes
a man. A memory a legend that was life.
No more, no more.

Limbs strangely bent to mock the hurry of a start,
a hand pointing the way . . . turn not,
evil athwart the path.
They blacken in the sun, scatter of a storm now past.
A sentinel walks unseen before this wood,
flame where his footsteps fall and cloud.
He sleeps not. The acres of the sky
burn bright and a lark publishes freedom
in a land of slaves, but lo!
what butchery within this wood,
rending of flesh and red limbs crucified
on a tree?
        Is there no end to murdering of man
be he Christ or ploughman? No.
Is death a joy to hold?
These words betray.

Eyes countering mine smoulder and shine not,
say they this of me?
I am dead to all I knew before.
Is there no end to this vast continent of day?
No end but night.

Ride the great stallions of dismay
along the veins of other men?
Silence that moaning boy
let him not cry again in the dark
he hath no hurt but fear.
And in this glade hearken
answer stand-to your names.

134

They answer not,
Their names are dead as they.

> This tree stained red
> the leaves were green
> now pale as we,
> rust not of steel
> upon this green.

We have borne enough:
Let them be buried in their market-place.

Llewelyn Wyn Griffith

Crucifixion of Youth

Before the Division had attempted to capture Mametz Wood, it was known that the undergrowth in it was so dense that it was all but impossible to move through it. Through the middle of the Wood a narrow ride ran to a communication trench leading to the German main Second Line of defence in front of Bazentin, a strong trench system permitting of a quick reinforcement of the garrison of the Wood. With equal facility, the Wood could be evacuated by the enemy and shelled, as it was not part of the trench system.

My first acquaintance with the stubborn nature of the undergrowth came when I attempted to leave the main ride to escape a heavy shelling. I could not push a way through it, and I had to return to the ride. Years of neglect had turned the Wood into a formidable barrier, a mile deep. Heavy shelling of the Southern end had beaten down some of the young growth, but it had also thrown trees and large branches into a barricade. Equipment, ammunition, rolls of barbed wire, tins of food, gas helmets and rifles were lying about everywhere. There were more corpses than men, but there were worse sights than corpses. Limbs and mutilated trunks, here and there a detached head, forming splashes of red against the green leaves, and, as in advertisement of the horror of our way of life and death, and of our crucifixion of youth, one tree held in its branches a leg, with its torn flesh hanging down over a spray of leaf.

Each bursting shell reverberated in a roll of thunder echoing through the Wood, and the acid fumes lingered between the trees. The sun was shining strongly overhead, unseen by us, but felt in its effort to pierce through the curtain of leaves. After passing through that charnel house at the southern end, with its sickly air of corruption, the smell of fresh earth and of crushed bark grew into complete domination, as clean to the senses as the other was foul. So tenacious in these matters is memory that I can never encounter the smell of cut green timber without resurrecting the vision of the tree that flaunted a human limb. A message was now on its way to some quiet village in Wales, to a grey farmhouse on the slope of a hill running down to Cardigan Bay, or to a miner's cottage in a South Wales valley, a word of death, incapable, in this late century of the Christian Era, of association with this manner of killing. That the sun could shine on this mad cruelty and on the quiet peace of an upland tarn near Snowdon, at what we call the same instant of Time, threw a doubt upon all meaning in words. Death was warped from a thing of sadness into a screaming horror, not content with stealing life from its shell, but trampling in lunatic fury upon the rifled cabinet we call a corpse.

There are times when fear drops below the threshold of the mind; never beyond recall, but far enough from the instant to become a background. Moments of great exaltation, of tremendous physical exertion, when activity can dominate over all rivals in the mind, the times of exhaustion that follow these great moments; these are, as I knew from the teachings of the months gone by, occasions of release from the governance of fear. As I hurried along the ride in this nightmare wood, stepping round the bodies clustered about the shell-holes, here and there helping a wounded man to clamber over a fallen tree trunk, falling flat on my face when the whistle of an approaching shell grew into a shrieking 'YOU', aimed at my ear, to paralyse before it killed, then stumbling on again through a cloud of bitter smoke, I learned that there was another way of making fear a thing of small account.

It was life rather than death that faded away into the distance, as I grew into a state of not-thinking, not-feeling, not-seeing. I moved past trees, past other things; men passed by me, carrying other men, some crying, some cursing, some silent. They were all shadows, and I was no greater than they. Living or dead, all were unreal. Balanced uneasily on the knife-edge between utter oblivion and this temporary not-knowing, it seemed a little matter whether I were destined to go forward to death or to come back to life. Past and future were equidistant and unattainable, throwing no bridge of desire across the gap that separated me both from my remembered self and from all that I had hoped to grasp. I walked as on a mountain in a mist, seeing neither sky above nor valley beneath, lost to all sense of far or near, up or down, either in time or space. I saw no precipice, and so I feared none.

Thus it was that the passing seconds dealt a sequence of hammer-blows, at first so poignantly sharp that the mind recoiled in unbelief, but in their deadly repetition dulling the power of response and reaction into a blind acceptance of this tragedy, and in the merciful end, pounding all sensibility into an atrophy that refused to link sight to thought. A swirl of mist within me had thrown a curtain to conceal the chasm of fear, and I walked on unheeding and unexpectant.

I reached a cross-ride in the Wood where four lanes broadened into a confused patch of destruction. Fallen trees, shell-holes, a hurriedly dug trench beginning and ending in an uncertain manner, abandoned rifles, broken branches with their sagging leaves, an unopened box of ammunition, sandbags half-filled with bombs, a derelict machine gun propping up the head of an immobile figure in uniform, with a belt of ammunition drooping from the breech into a pile of red-stained earth – this is the livery of War. Shells were falling, over and short, near and wide, to show that somewhere over the hill a gunner was playing the part of blind fate for all who walked past this well-marked spot. Here, in the struggle between bursting iron and growing timber, iron had triumphed and trampled over an uneven circle some forty yards in diameter. Against the surrounding wall of thick greenery, the earth showed red and fresh, lit by the clean sunlight, and the splintered tree trunks shone with a damp whiteness, but the green curtains beyond could conceal nothing of greater horror than the disorder revealed in this clearing.

Even now, after all these years, this round ring of man-made hell bursts into my vision, elbowing into an infinity of distance the wall of my room, dwarfing into nothingness objects we call real. Blue sky above, a band of green trees, and a ploughed graveyard in which living men moved worm-like in and out of sight; three men digging a trench, thigh-deep in the red soil, digging their own graves, as it chanced, for a bursting shell turned their shelter into a tomb; two signallers crouched in a large shell-hole, waiting for a summons to move, but bearing in their patient and tired inactivity the look of dead men ready to rise at the trump of a Last Judgment.

Llewelyn Wyn Griffith, *Up to Mametz*

Death of a Brother: Private Watcyn Griffith

The Staff Officer left us, and we worked at the orders for the battalions. The enemy was shelling the Wood, searching it, as the gunners say, and there were intermittent bursts of machine-gun fire, with an occasional uneven and untidy rush of rifle fire. On our right a few bombs burst in a flat, cracking thud. At a quarter to three, while we were waiting for the hour, a sudden storm of shells passed over our heads, bursting in the Wood some two hundred yards ahead of us.

'Good God,' said the General. 'That's our artillery putting a barrage right on top of our battalion! How can we stop this? Send a runner down at once . . . send two or three by different routes . . . write the message down.'

Three men went off with the message, each by a different way, with orders to get to Queen's Nullah somehow or other. Our barrage had roused the enemy, and from every direction shells were falling in the Wood; behind us a devilish storm of noise showed that a heavy price must be paid for every attempt to leave the Wood.

The Brigadier sat on a tree trunk, head on hand, to all appearances neither seeing nor hearing the shells.

'This is the end of everything . . . sheer stupidity. I wonder if there is an order that never reached me . . . but that Staff Officer ought to have known the artillery programme for the day. And if there is another order, they ought not to have put down that barrage until they got my acknowledgement. How can we attack after our own barrage has ploughed its way through us? What good can a barrage do in a wood like this?'

At twenty past three our own artillery was still pouring shells into the wood. None of the runners had returned. Taylor sent three more to try to rescue us from this double fire, but ten minutes later we were left with no worse burden than the enemy's shelling. Reports came through from the battalions that we had suffered severely. As the afternoon drew out into the evening, we nibbled away here and there with fluctuating fortune, but at the approach of night the enemy reinforced his line and kept us from the edge while he pounded away with his artillery.

It was nearing dusk when Taylor came up to me.

'I want to have a word with you,' he said, drawing me away. 'I've got bad news for you . . .'

'What's happened to my young brother . . . is he hit?'

'You know the last message you sent out to try to stop the barrage . . . well, he was one of the runners that took it. He hasn't come back . . . He got his message through all right, and on his way back through the barrage he was hit. His mate was wounded by the shell that killed your brother . . . he told another runner to tell us.'

'My God . . . he's lying out there now, Taylor!'

'No, old man . . . he's gone.'

'Yes . . . yes, he's gone.'

'I'm sorry . . . I had to send him, you know.'

'Yes, of course . . . you had to. I can't leave this place . . . I suppose there's no doubt about his being killed?'

'None – he's out of it all now.'

So I had sent him to his death, bearing a message from my own hand, in an endeavour to save other men's brothers; three thoughts that followed one another in unending sequence, a wheel revolving within my brain, expanding until it touched the boundaries of knowing and feeling. They did not gain in truth from repetition, nor did they reach the understanding. The swirl of mist refused to move.

Llewelyn Wyn Griffith, Up to Mametz

Death of a Friend: Private Watcyn Griffith

Shelling intensified, particularly around the trees. The arrival of a monster block-buster scattered us, each seeking shelter in nearby shell-holes. Two of us made for the same shell-hole, I in front by no more than a foot, my head just downward of the rim, when a second giant exploded, stunning both of us. I had begun my slide into the hole, remaining there a few minutes. Rising to return I saw my companion lying motionless. No wounds were visible. The sole indication of injury was a tiny trickle of red in one ear. He didn't move. Concussion had killed him. Returning to the scratched-out trench I lay down in position of fire beside a machine-gunner who had been taking active defence. From a lookout a hundred yards to the front came a warning shout – 'Enemy advancing in strength a hundred yards left.' There were no more than twenty in the group to put up a defence. The officers, standing, whipped out their revolvers and we few riflemen, at the ready to fire when the target was visible. The leaders of a body of field-grey emerged. 'Hold your fire,' shouted an officer. Leading the five hundred prisoners was a grimly smiling Taffy. The counter-attack had been routed. Two outstanding incidents had occurred to break up the attack. A bombing party led by a nineteen-year-old son of a minister, Lieut. Sinnet Jones; a corporal machine-gunner, to avoid firing ineffectively through the scrub, fixed the barrel of his gun on the shoulder of a willing Private Kendall. The advancing Germans were mown down. The corporal was awarded a medal; the private earned his crown of glory. Toll for the brave Private Kendall.

The Brigade was ordered to clear the wood entirely of the enemy. Brigadier Horace S. Evans determined to accomplish this end by surprise at the point of the bayonet, without preliminary bombardment. Captain L. Wyn Griffith, acting Brigade Major, wrote a message to Division requesting this. Messages crossed. The message to Division was carried by Watcyn, my very close friend. It did not reach its destination. Watcyn was killed. He was the youngest brother of Captain Griffith. Another brother belonged to a battery supporting the brigade . . .

The Division did not cancel the bombardment. Added to the pounding German barrage was now that of our own, falling short on our own men.

Presently numbers of our own men were seen trampling to the rear, crowding the wide track. A co-signaller R. T. Evans, one of their number, called out to me – 'Come on Double Dot, Retire.' Picking up my telephone, I rose out of my shell-hole. Standing nearby was an officer pointing his revolver at his own men. He dared not fire. Was this to end in tragedy; to lose all the hard-won ground involving terrific losses? The silent officer remained silent. Suddenly the loud shout of a sergeant rang out in the wood: 'STICK IT, WELSH!' To a man they stuck it, halted, turned round. Their lines were reformed as to three lines of a square whence would come the expected attack. The order had been 'Retire two hundred yards.' The order in passing along the lines was reduced to 'Retire' . . .

Emlyn Davies, *Taffy Went to War* (1976)

Relief

Some time later, a heavy storm of shellfire drove me into a little trench where I crouched with some men to shelter. We talked in Welsh, for they were Anglesey folk; one was a young boy, and after a thunderous crash in our ears he began to cry out for his mother, in a thin boyish voice, '*Mam, mam . . .*' I woke up and pushed my way to him, fumbling in my pockets for my torch, and pulled him down to the bottom of the trench. He said that his arm was hurt. A corporal came to my assistance and we pulled off his tunic to examine his arm. He had not been hit, but he was frightened, still crying quietly. Suddenly he started again, screaming for his mother, with a wail that seemed older than the world, in the darkness of that night. The men began to mutter uneasily. We shook him, cursed at him, threatening even to kill him if he did not stop. He did not understand our words, but the shaking brought him back. He demanded his rifle and his steel helmet, and sat in the bottom of the trench to wait for the relief, talking rationally but slowly. English voices came out of the dark, enquiring for another battalion of our brigade; more men stumbled by in search of the posts they were to relieve. Our time was drawing to an end.

Llewelyn Wyn Griffith, *Up to Mametz*

Mametz Wood

Perhaps they'll cancel it.
O blow fall out the officers cantcher, like a wet afternoon
or the King's birthday.
   Or you read it again many times to see if it will come different:
you can't believe the Cup won't pass from
or they won't make a better show
in the garden.
Won't someone forbid the banns
or God himself will stay their hands.
It just can't happen in our family
even though a thousand
and ten thousand at thy right hand.

Talacryn doesn't take it like Wastebottom, he leaps up & says he's dead, a-slither
down the pale face – his limbs a-girandole
at the bottom of the nullah,
but the mechanism slackens, unfed
and he is quite still
which leaves five paces between you and the next live one to the left.
   Sidle over a bit toward where '45 Williams, and use all your lungs:
   Get ready me china-plate – but he's got it before he can hear you, but it's a
cushy one and he relaxes to the morning sun and smilingly, to wait for the bearers.

Some of yer was born wiv jam on it
clicked lucky and favoured
        pluckt brand from burning
and my darling from unicorn horn with only a minute to go, whose wet-nurse
cocked a superstitious eye to see his happy constellation through the panes.

But it isn't like that for the common run and you have no mensuration gear to
plot meandering fortune-graph nor know whether she were the Dark or the Fair
left to the grinding.

Last minute drums its taut millennium out
you can't swallow your spit
and Captain Marlowe yawns a lot
and seconds now our measuring-rods with no Duke Josue
nor conniving God
to stay the Divisional Synchronisation.

So in the fullness of time
    when pallid jurors bring the doomes
    mooring cables swipe slack-end on
barnacled piles,
and the world falls apart at the last to siren screech and screaming vertical steam
in conformity with the Company's Sailings and up to scheduled time.

As bridal arranged-paraphernalia gets tumbled – eventually
and the night empties of these relatives
if you wait long time enough
and yesterday puts on today.
    At the end of the suspense
come the shod feet
hastily or laggard
or delayed –
but anyway, no fretting of watch on the wall nor their hysteria,
can hamper nor accelerate
exact kinetics of his advent
nor make less miserable his tale to tell
    and even Mrs Chandler's tom
will stiffen one Maye Mornynge
to the ninth death.

Tunicled functionaries signify and clear-voiced heralds cry
and leg it to a safe distance:
leave fairway for the Paladins, and Roland throws a kiss –
they've nabbed his batty for the moppers-up
    and Mr Jenkins takes them over
and don't bunch on the left
for Christ's sake.

    Riders on pale horses loosed
and vials irreparably broken
an' Wat price bleedin' Glory
Glory
Glory Hallelujah
And the Royal Welsh sing:
Jesu
    lover of me soul . . . to *Aberystwyth*.
But that was on the right with
the genuine Taffies

but we are rash levied
from Islington and Hackney
and the purlieus of Walworth
flashers from Surbiton
men of the stock of Abraham
from Bromley-by-Bow
Anglo-Welsh from Queens Ferry
rosary-wallahs from Pembrey Dock
lighterman with a Norway darling
from Greenland Stairs
and two lovers from Ebury Bridge,
Bates and Coldpepper
that men called the Lily-white boys.
Fowler from Harrow and the House who'd lost his way into
this crush who was gotten in a parsonage on a maye.
Dynamite Dawes the old 'un
and Diamond Phelps his batty
from Santiago del Estero
and Bulawayo respectively,
both learned in ballistics
        and wasted on a line-mob . . .

But sweet sister death has gone debauched today and stalks on this high ground
with strumpet confidence, makes no coy veiling of her appetite but leers from
you to me with all her parts rediscovered.

    By one and one the line gaps, where her fancy will – howsoever they may
howl for their virginity
she holds them – who impinge less on space
sink limply to a heap
nourish a lesser category of being
like those other who fructify the land
like Tristram
Lamorak de Galis
Alisand le Orphelin
Beaumains who was youngest
or all of them in shaft-shade
at strait Thermopylae
or the sweet brothers Balin and Balan
embraced beneath their single monument.
    Jonathan my lovely one
on Gelboe mountain

and the young man Absalom.
White Hart transfixed in his dark lodge.
Peredur of steel arms
and he who with intention took grass of that field to be for
him the Species of Bread.
     Taillefer the maker,
and on the same day,
thirty thousand other ranks.
And in the country of Béarn – Oliver
and all the rest – so many without memento
beneath the tumuli on the high hills
and under the harvest places.

But how intolerably bright the morning is where we who are alive and remain,
walk lifted up, carried forward by an effective word.

But red horses now – blare every trump without economy, burn boat and sever
every tie every held thing goes west and tethering snapt, bolts unshot and brass
doors flung wide and you go forward, foot goes another step further.

The immediate foreground sheers up, tilts toward,
like a high wall falling.
There she breaches black perpendiculars
where the counter-barrage warms to the seventh power where
The Three Children walk under the fair morning
and the Twin Brother
and the high grass soddens through your puttees
and dew asperges the freshly dead.

There doesn't seem a soul about yet surely we walk already near his preserves;
there goes old Dawes as large as life and there is Lazarus Cohen like on field-
days, he always would have his entrenching-tool-blade-carrier hung low, jogging
on his fat arse . . .

You drop apprehensively – the sun gone out,
strange airs smite your body
and muck rains straight from heaven
and everlasting doors lift up for '02 Weavel.
   You can't see anything but sheen on drifting particles and
you move forward in your private bright cloud like
one assumed
who is borne up by an exterior volition.

You stumble on a bunch of six with Sergeant Quilter getting them out again to the proper interval, and when the chemical thick air dispels you see briefly and with great clearness what kind of a show this is.

The gentle slopes are green to remind you
of South English places, only far wider and flatter spread and grooved and harrowed criss-cross whitely and the disturbed subsoil heaped up albescent.

Across upon this undulated board of verdure chequered bright
when you look to left and right
small, drab, bundled pawns severally make effort
moved in tenuous line
and if you looked behind – the next wave came slowly, as suc-cessive surfs creep in to dissipate on flat shore;
and to your front, stretched long laterally,
and receded deeply,
the dark wood.

David Jones, *In Parenthesis*, part 7

Death of a Youth in the Battle of Mametz Wood

I had . . . in my platoon a tall clean-looking young boy with a kind open face. Some of my boys were rough and were undoubtedly built for 'dirty work' on the Bosche. But this boy was not made for war. He was tall, but straight, frail but never 'on sick'; quiet and unassuming, though by no means as pat in military movements as some of the 'fireworks' of my platoon. Some men would consider him a 'mother's boy' at first. Indeed, I myself often wished he was smarter when Generals appeared on the horizon. Sometimes a Sergeant would roughly attempt to rouse him and at the man's tone the boy would shudder and make a nervous attempt to do what was wanted.

The Sergeant-Major told me that the boy used to say his prayers in the hut each night and morning. The old man did not tell me this sneeringly but I gathered from his tone that it was hardly what he thought soldier-like. I knew, however, by the way all the men looked at this boy, that he was not considered a humbug; so that I could only say to myself at the time: 'Well, he's a jolly sight better fellow than I am.'

Before very long I asked him to become a lance corporal – to take the coveted stripe which from the description of the Sergeant-Major took so many generations to get in the regular army; with which stripe the wearer could move about men in thousands and at his will could hang, draw and quarter platoons without number.

'Now, Roberts, I'm going to recommend you for a stripe. But until you show what you can do with it we shall only put you in for "unpaid lance corporal".'

I expected, in reply, thanks, and a hope that he would be worthy of the promotion. I got instead a courteous request to be excused from taking the promotion. He did not feel he wanted to rise above the ranks.

And so it happened.

Months passed, and seeing that the lad was such an influence in the platoon, I should have made him sergeant on the spot. I asked my Company Officer to try and persuade him to accept promotion. This was done successfully by pointing out that it was his duty to the old country to render service in the way in which his officer thought he could do it best. Surely and steadily he became Corporal and afterwards Sergeant. The more experienced old soldiers used him to do more than a share of orderly work, and whenever there was something difficult on, Roberts was there. He never grumbled; he got the men along in a mysterious way which I could never understand. Officers and men saw that he was invaluable.

And trench warfare and rest, training and work, monotonously dragged on for weeks and months till we landed on the Somme.

We went into Mametz Wood. For hours and days we struggled through the dense undergrowth in search of our hidden enemy, who, after having fired at us, surrendered or bolted. On the second day we had a short pause, which I spent in collecting together the scattered remnants of the dear old boys we had trained and lived with for such a long time. It was indeed only a very small handful. We used the pause to search for some of our wounded friends. I knew that our stout stretcher-bearers could never manage to collect the wounded lying in open places for many hours, to say nothing of searching for others. So we set out to collect and take to the side of the paths the men wounded in out-of-the-way places.

We found under trees and bushes many a boy who had lost all hope of being found, and who had settled down in that desolate spot to die.

In one corner, at the foot of a tree, we found Roberts. From his wounds I could see at once that we could do nothing for him. I got down, undid his collar, took off his cap and put my hand on his clear forehead. Feeling a touch he opened his eyes, and recognising me smiled faintly, and murmured in a gentle voice, 'Captain.' In a hopeless way I tried to do something for him, but he wanted nothing. He was in terrific pain but he looked so mysteriously calm. The precious breath was getting fainter and fainter whilst his face became brighter and brighter, developing at the last a clearness that was well nigh unearthly.

Solemnly and quietly in the midst of the 'strafe' we stood there whilst passed away the soul of our friend and hero – a passing away worthy of any hero in history – something attempted – everything well done.

The only two words he murmured were '*O! Arglwydd,*'* and each word was there and then branded on my soul.

We left the place silently and solemnly for it was time to go on with the fight. But we left a sacred spot on which lay a man who was a thousand times better than we.

'G.J.', 'Some of the Royal Welsh',
The Welsh Outlook, vol. v, no. 52, April 1918

Oh, Lord

The Somme and Mametz Wood: Five Eye-witness Accounts

One terrible moment came when we were midway across No Man's Land. Without the slightest warning the ground under our feet gave way, and we seemed to sink down and down until we hardly knew what to make of it. We had rushed into a series of cunningly concealed pits that had been covered over to give the impression that the ground was solid. At once we were raked by a murderous fire, and we suffered severely. There was, however, nothing that could be described as panic. The attacking line quickly straightened itself out and dashed forward once more, the enemy concentrating on us all the time a deadly hail of bullets. We charged right up to the enemy parapet, where we were brought to a halt by a kind of stockade made of stout posts interlocked by barbed wire. There we stood for a time, a fine target for the enemy's machine-gunners and bombers. The barrier was too high to get over. Some of our chaps started tugging at the posts to break through, but they were too firmly put in for that. At last, by mounting on the backs of some of our comrades most of us were able to get across. The Huns may have been pleased to see us, but they didn't look it when we barged into them like a runaway express train. I think they were a bit surprised that we had got through so easily. They made a desperate attempt to hurl us back. We broke the back of their resistance at that point in a few minutes, and then sent them flying like mad into their reserve trenches.

Quickly making good our hold on what we had taken, we advanced to carry the reserve trenches. It was then that we realised that our first experience was only a mild purgatory, and we were now in hell itself. The place seemed alive with machine guns. I should say there was at least one gun to every man, and bullets swept across our front in streams. It was one continual downpour of lead without the slightest break. The wonder is that one of us got through to tell the tale. Somehow we managed it, and we smashed right into their reserve trenches with a soul-stirring cheer. The Huns fought like a combination of tigers and devils. They emptied grenades on us by the bucket, and turned on more machine guns. They even rushed to meet us with the bayonet, and tried to throw us back by sheer weight of numbers. I think they were mad, but Welshmen fighting for all that is dear to them can be as mad as anybody. The din and the excitement were terrible. We opened fire at almost point-blank range as the Huns dashed into us. They came to a dead stop right in front of us. Quick as lightning our commander realised what was wanted. The order to fix bayonets was given and obeyed with right good will. We recoiled a little in front of them as they resumed their onward rush, but it was only the recoil of the tiger before springing on its prey. It was glorious. We met them in one terrific shock of combat. Their line buckled up like a line of tin bayonets held out to stop a runaway train. They broke, here and there little parties made desperate efforts to hold their ground, but the main body ran as though all the devils in hell were after them. We gave them it hot with our machine guns. We sent tons of lead after them, and scores of them were shut down as they ran. It was wholesale slaughter. The little band of Huns who were too proud to run away were also too proud to surrender. They fought on, in spite of repeated calls to surrender, until every man of them was knocked out.

An unnamed Non-commissioned Officer of the South Wales Borderers, 'Huns Outflanked: Thrilling Charge by Welsh Borderers', *Western Mail*, July 15, 1916

The really lively time came that night when the Germans had a try at taking back the ground we had won in the Mametz Wood. We were ready for them, and we fairly pumped the lead into them as they came forward out of the darkness, shouting for their Kaiser, and stabbing and thrusting like madmen. Whole lines went down like ninepins, and at some places corpses were piled high enough to make a breastwork, under the protection of which the survivors were able to rest and reform their line. It was from behind one of these human breastworks that the final assault was made. Directly they sprang up we opened fire again. I never saw such beautiful work. We smashed them to bits with our first volley, and what was left of them bolted like frightened rabbits. All unknown to them other troops of ours had been working round both flanks, and just when the Huns had settled down nice and comfortable in their quarters behind their dead mates, our flanking parties got on to them. They fairly skipped with fright at the first volley, but before they could clear out our boys were into them with the bayonet . . .

That finished them for the night, but next morning the arrival of fresh troops put new life into them, and they made another attack, which was led up to by a furious bombardment. We reserved our fire until the attacking masses were close up. Then we let them have round after round of rapid. It paralysed and pulverised them. They didn't know what to fire, and cut their lines to ribbons again and again. Quickly they were redressed by the countless reserves that were being rushed up, and like madmen they swept into our trenches. We flung them out headlong in quick time, but they came back again and again, and the slaughter was absolutely sickening. In front of our position for as far as the eye could reach the ground was littered with dead and wounded. The flying Huns after their last repulse had to pick their way back over the dead bodies of their comrades, and scores of them were shot down to keep their mates company.

A Private from Merthyr Tydfil, 'Huns Outflanked:
Thrilling Charge by Welsh Borderers'

The big advance had been in progress some days when we were moved up to assist in clearing a certain wood. To our battalion and another from Wales was assigned the task of testing the strength of the enemy in the neighbourhood. We were held up about 250 yards in front of the wood by devastating shell and machine-gun fire. Heavy stuff was flying all around us, but once we got into the wood we made a desperate fight for it. It was a bigger job than we had bargained for, and the reinforcements came up just in the nick of time to save our position. I never saw such an eager lot of chaps as ours once the order to advance was given. It seemed a 'wash-out' at the start with the terrible fire which faced us, but our captain manoeuvred his men with skilfulness . . .

The Welsh boys fought like very demons through a wood which was well-nigh impregnable, and dotted here and there with cleverly concealed guns. If it had been a fair square fight it would have been all right, but the enemy was in the wood and we were outside, and our task was to drive them out. Once in the wood it was a case of everyone for himself, as it resolved itself into tree to tree fighting, as the enemy were bent upon holding the wood at all costs. The whole of the Welsh boys, however, fought with great bravery and proved themselves to be splendid fighters.

A Soldier from Bargoed, Caerphilly, 'Cleared the Wood',
Western Mail, July 18, 1916

Our battalion was moved up quietly as reinforcements. We had not proceeded 20 to 30 yards when our colonel got hit, but in spite of his injury he stuck to his post, urging his men to the attack. Directly my squad got into the wood we came across 20 to 30 Germans. Our wounded colonel urged us on with the remark, 'Get at them, Welsh: they have no heart.' No sooner said than we were on top of them with our bayonets, but the Bosches held their hands up in token of surrender. We sent them back in charge of a couple of men, but as soon as we got the other side of a tree, bombs were thrown at us from behind. I saw one of our corporals killed by a shell. I was making my way back to get my hand dressed after a gunshot wound when a shell burst near me, and in the confusion which followed I found myself back again in the wood. German dead were lying all about the place as evidence of the good executive work which the Welsh boys had done in their mad rush.

I cannot say what happened after I got back to the dressing-station, but later in the day an officer in the Royal Garrison Artillery patted me on the back and said, 'Bravo, Welsh: you have won possession of the wood at last. I have just had the news down by 'phone.' I might add that during the whole of the time we were in the wood there was terrible firing going on.

I never saw a cooler lot of men under fire than the Welsh boys, and in this connection our own Commanding Officer set a fine example, for after being wounded he continued to give us encouraging advice. In clearing the wood we took hundreds of prisoners.

A member of the Welsh Regiment, from Aberdare, 'Cleared the Wood'

I saw a German officer as we came along throw open his tunic to show us he had no weapons, and at the same time he put up his arms and shouted, 'Mercy, *Kamerade.*' I thought he was all right, but as some of our men passed a little way off he pulled a revolver from somewhere and shot at a man's head. The man was wounded, but he was able to rush at that German officer and put his bayonet through him. I saw one German prisoner in our uniform. He must have taken it off one of our prisoners or a dead man. Several times we saw the Germans killing German prisoners with machine-gun fire.

Private J. Evans of the Royal Welsh Fusiliers, from Treorchy, 'Cleared the Wood'

After the Battle of Mametz Wood

The next two days we spent in bivouacs outside Mametz Wood. We were in fighting kit and felt cold at night, so I went into the wood to find German overcoats to use as blankets. It was full of dead Prussian Guards Reserve, big men, and dead Royal Welch and South Wales Borderers of the New Army battalions, little men. Not a single tree in the wood remained unbroken. I collected my overcoats, and came away as quickly as I could, climbing through the wreckage of green branches. Going and coming, by the only possible route, I passed by the bloated and stinking corpse of a German with his back propped against a tree. He had a green face, spectacles, close-shaven hair; black blood was dripping from the nose and beard. I came across two other unforgettable corpses: a man of the South Wales Borderers and one of the Lehr Regiment had succeeded in bayoneting each other simultaneously. A survivor of the fighting told me later that he had seen a young soldier of the Fourteenth Royal Welch bayoneting a German in parade-ground style, automatically exclaiming: 'In, out, on guard!'

Robert Graves, *Goodbye to All That*

The Capture of Mametz Wood

We did not ask whether the reward were equal to the sacrifice; it may be that there is no equality in such matters, that war is the very negation of all value. Confined as we were in a world governed by a force operating ruthlessly in one direction, there was a wall on either side of our path. All that could happen to us was, at the whim of this force, a quicker or slower progress along our narrow alley, lacking knowledge of our destination, impotent to control our motion. We could not know whether our destination would prove to be our Destiny, nor was it given to us to glance over the walls at other ways of climbing the hill. This is not to say that our attitude was one of fatalism; when one may not look to the right and left, there still remains another dimension. If resistance were of no avail, non-acceptance sprang up within us all as a natural reaction against the method of our employment. It was not so much that we admitted our inability to gauge the need for such a task; we did not even doubt that the capture of Mametz Wood was an indispensable operation, we imagined no Evil Fate choosing us as a weapon.

It would be untrue to suggest that our discontent rose up against the existence of a Battle of the Somme, or that we rebelled inwardly at the likelihood of another experience of this nature. There was no discussion about the relative

151

merits of rival methods of attack or of alternative fronts. Although our lives were the letters that went to its spelling, the word 'Strategy' was never on our lips. We held no opinion on such high matters, but the generosity with which we disclaimed knowledge of so large a territory of the world of soldiering heightened the confidence, amounting almost to arrogance, of our condemnation of certain practices then in high favour with our superiors.

To every one of us it was bitterly clear that wars could not be won by piling up corpses in front of machine guns. Shellfire was inevitable, and its dangers were fair risks of war, but when one line of men had failed to satiate the hunger of machine guns, there was nothing inevitable in sending forth another wave to destruction. The argument was not vitiated by isolated instances of success here and there, at a price never quoted. Nor indeed was there anything of the inevitable in a constant failure to link up the loose threads of intention scattered over the battlefield, an omission that was made catastrophically evident to us in the gap that divorced artillery support from infantry action.

These were the thoughts that built up a weight of dissatisfaction, dragging at our heels day and night, clogging all power to eliminate the needless tortures of battle. All war was bad, but the thinking of our masters made it worse: wrong was in the saddle, all the world over. If we had devoted our lives to the study of war, this inward revolt against the method of our governance in the field might have risen clear of vagueness into a definite plea for another way of war-thinking, but we were neither civilians nor soldiers. We had lost the layman's power of judging between the rival theories of experts, without capturing the acquiescent confidence of a soldier. All the counsel we could give amounted to little more than a cry of 'Not thus . . . not thus.'

Added to the burden of fatigue and grief, we were governed by a dark feeling of personal failure. Mametz Wood was taken, but not by us, it seemed; we were the rejected of Destiny, men whose services were not required. The dead were the chosen, and Fate had forgotten us in its eager clutching at the men who fell; they were the richer prize. They captured Mametz Wood, and in it they lie.

Llewelyn Wyn Griffith, *Up to Mametz*

The Battle of Mametz Wood

All through our night-watches came urgent dispatches
    To get ourselves ready as soon as we could;
The order was given: 'The foe must be driven
    Away from his lair in the depth of the wood.'

The darkness ascended and daylight descended,
    And the strangest day dawned on us there as we stood,
And on that strange morning we awaited the warning,
    The word to advance and capture the wood.

Our officers shouted: 'The foe must be routed,
    You Welsh must be brave,' and we all understood;
'Pray, as the storm gathers, to the God of your fathers;
    You must fight unto death – you must capture the wood.'

And the lads started singing a hymn that went ringing
    Around the whole trench, as the singing was good;
And it was the finest, and, yes, the divinest,
    Singing yet heard, before taking the wood.

The bloodshed was endless, the slaughter relentless,
    But we fought on as hard as anyone could;
The foe was defeated, but our ranks were depleted,
    Leaving many a grave at the edge of the wood.

Anonymous
(Translated from the Welsh)

The Aid Post Mametz

Every time I looked towards that gully through which came the communication trench, I could see a bearer-party with its burden huddled up on the stretcher. These parties were endless: it became the most natural thing in the world to see them lined against the burnt brown grass and the chalky upturned soil.

In front of us was a battery of six-inch navals, a few yards behind us four monster 9.2in. howitzers. Around us were guns in rows, guns in bunches, and isolated monster guns. Guns cracked like whips, guns roared, guns thudded; there were guns everywhere, seemingly in thousands.

We were stationed in a hollow amongst them all – an Advanced Collecting Station for wounded, and it is of the wounded I would speak – not of the Johnsons that dropped on the road and the ridge behind us, on Minden Post, on the ruins of Carnoy way back on the right, and on what remained of Mametz to the left. They were wonderful – these wounded. It was as if cheerfulness had infected almost all of them. It is difficult to understand how broken men can still be cheerful – but they were.

One of our first cases was a 'walking case' – a bit of shrapnel in his jaw, a 'pickelhaube' on his head, and a cheerful grin on his face. The effect was extremely ludicrous. He *would* talk. The charge of the Swanseas was the greatest thing of the war. The Sergeant was safe, but Dai Thomas – Dai had stopped a big one. Dai was his pal and (he paled) Dai's wife had to be told, for before going over the top, Dai had asked him to write . . . Dai had seemed to know . . . Yes, Dai's wife had to be told!

Machine-gun wounds poured in (they were not men; they were wounds), clean wounds, and for the most part easily healed – kill or cure wounds – a fine 'blighty' or eternity. Then came the shell wounds – hideous and ghastly wounds – wounds which depressed our souls.

Risking the observation of the enemy, we got a kitchen going, and our cooks slaved preparing 'dixies' of hot tea, cocoa and soup. No restaurant ever did such a trade, ever pleased and satisfied its customers as that field kitchen did. From the communication trench they flowed in, more and more of them, and yet more. We laid them in rows in bivouacs of huge tarpaulins. The worse cases we took direct to the Dressing Station.

They were ravenous; they gulped hot tea with shining eyes, and asked for more. 'Ah, that's good,' was the invariable remark, 'Never tasted anything so good! Three days – nothing to eat only iron rations. May I have another, please?' It was pleasure, incomparable pleasure, to attend to their needs. They were so appreciative, so grateful, so cheerful. Then a cigarette while their dressings were renewed or rearranged, and they took their turn to be carried by Welshmen over the old 'No Man's Land' with its tangles of wire and shell-holes, to the Big Advanced Dressing Station.

Cheerfully they waited in the bivouac, some quietly enjoying the rest, others relating and comparing their experiences and inquiring after their friends. It was my duty to arrange their transport. Never once was a murmur against my decisions; they trusted the Red Cross implicitly. One – wounded in the thigh I remembered distinctly – waited fully half an hour for his turn, and when it came asked, 'Are you sure, Quarter, there isn't one worse than me? I can wait all right.'

Oblivious of the inferno about them, some of them slept on their muddy stretchers: slept a sleep of utter exhaustion.

Wounded even unto death, the Welsh officers' first thoughts were for their men. They proved themselves British gentlemen, and I was proud to be of the same race, to speak their tongue and to be able to succour them.

As we tended what were once fine, manly, beautiful human bodies, we thought of the horror, the frightfulness of this ghastly thing that had overwhelmed our world. Our world – it seemed an age since we lived in it – was fair, joyous and beautiful. Our world – and we smiled – our world was now a hollow in a Hell of mangled, torn bodies. '*Pan na fydd rhyfel mwyach*'* – the words came from my old world to my brain. And what I heard as a meaningless, void phrase, became a passionate yearning – '*Pan na fydd rhyfel mwyach.*'

There was little time for reflection for the communication trench continued to pour forth its stream of maimed, mutilated men. As one party of exhausted bearers laid their burden down, I saw a man rush forward with a basin of soup, and lift the blanket from the motionless form. It had no face! He laid the blanket gently back, and threw himself on the ground and burst into tears of pity for the form still pitifully alive. Again I saw the old vicar in his old world pulpit droning '*Pan na fydd rhyfel mwyach.*'

Towards noon, when the attack upon the wood was developing, and the stream was greater than ever, two lads, with whom I had played in my boyhood in that faraway village upon a Welsh hill, were brought in. They had joined a Glamorgan Battalion which was winning its laurels in this attack; one was a corporal, the other a machine-gunner. They saw me, and for a short two minutes we recreated that old world of ours. 'Do you remember that . . . Do you remember how . . .' Yes, I would write to their people at the first opportunity. They were both fine 'blighties', and would be as right as rain after a few months in the old country. 'Thanks. Goodbye. Good luck.'

Standing beside a row of stretchers, I heard a voice whispering huskily 'Buck up, Coll.!' I turned and saw ——, a close college friend of mine. Once more was the old world recreated. That last night in Coll., when after the Farewell Smoker he had come to my room, was relived. Why hadn't I written? Why hadn't he

* *When war shall be no more*

written? He had married, and there was a child. Thank God, he would see them soon. 'Goodbye. All good luck.' He too would soon be fit.

Through the afternoon we toiled like slaves. Evening came, and about seven o'clock I suddenly felt hungry. I had had no food since that morning. Some bully beef and bread – food hitherto despised – proved *appetising*. Hot tea completed the meal. There was blood on the rim of the cup. What did it matter? Nothing mattered.

As evening wore on our patients became fewer, and for the first time the bivouacs were empty. Climbing over the ridge with the O.C., I watched the German 'evening hate' and our guns reply. Over Mametz, and Fricourt Wood, the Johnsons burst persistently, seeking, sometimes not in vain, the British batteries and British men. A steel-blue sky, with a hand of red in the West, provided a fitting background for the bursting shells and the blinding flash of the guns.

Through the twilight, the ration parties stole up the communication trench bearing provisions for their comrades lost to sight in the darkness of the wood. Suddenly the Bosches shelled the communication trench and the crest of the ridge before us, judging with exactness the time when the ration parties would cross. Very soon we were busy again, Transport Men, Pioneers and Engineers were brought in. The bearers were again treading by the light of a faint moon the devious and dangerous track to the Advanced Dressing Station.

Relieved of my work at the Aid Post, I joined the bearer parties. All through the night we toiled, bearing our stretcher-burdens across the shell-pocked ground. We toiled, silent but dogged, until arms, neck, and legs were one combined ache. We toiled until our hands were blistering and bleeding. As if in a dream, we crossed and recrossed that ground. We would have sold our souls for one hour's rest on the ground, in the mud, anywhere; but still the wounded came in to the Aid Post, and still we bore them to the Advanced Dressing Station. We were just one little link in the chain which bound Mametz to England, and we did not break.

Near the Dressing Station, there was a battery of guns to the left of the path, and their blinding flashes and nerve-racking crashing continued every few minutes throughout the night. The air was filled with hissing serpents, crackling whip lashes, and trains roaring through tunnels. The 9.2 on the right shook the ground, and our burdens groaned as the shiver embraced them. The blinding glare of the navals lit up our path momentarily, and the twilight became darkness after the flash.

I helped to carry a big Sergeant-Major – a thigh wound. He had 'taken it' in the charge at daybreak, and had lain for sixteen hours in a shell-hole. His chief anxiety was that he was too heavy for us: he weighed sixteen stone. We assured him that we could easily manage. He was proud of the boys. He had trained them, and d——, they were a credit to the Army. There was not a better battalion in the whole British Army than his – the 41st – the 'better death than shame' boys. They were d—— fine soldiers. We begged him to lie still and not tire himself. He was all right. Before we reached the Dressing Station he insisted upon our sharing the contents of his water-bottle, still three-parts full of weak rum and water. He had not thought much of the Red Cross fellows before, but by d——, he was glad to know us; he insisted upon shaking our hands. 'Any of you home in "Blighty", just call upon me at Pantyffynnon. I keep the "Red Cow" there, and there's a welcome and a feed for any of you who cares to come.'

Our exhaustion caused us to forget everything but our wounded. We no longer heard the guns; we ceased to see their flashes and to heed the tremors of the earth. We were consumed by a longing for rest, but no one fell out. New batches of wounded found us with a new energy – and we toiled on.

The darkness in the East became grey, and a new day dawned on our world. For a second there was a hush – a strange expectancy. No gun was heard. Then all at once the iron chorus opened again, belching death into the German lines . . . Another day! Numbed, faltering, exhausted, we 'carried on'. That well-worn phrase henceforth bore a more pregnant, a fuller meaning.

During a pause in the work, I watched absently, impersonally, the Johnsons falling on the road behind us. A motor cyclist came along, and a Johnson fell in front and another behind him. I calculated idly that he would not be hit. He rode on unharmed. An ambulance followed him. An ominous whistle, and a shell burst near the vehicle, hiding it in a cloud of smoke. In a detached manner, I thought that the ambulance was hit. No, it emerged safely from the cloud. I was not glad. Had it disappeared, it would have caused me no sorrow. These things were our world. They were not to be deplored; they were the ordinary affairs of our life.

All day long the stream of wounded flowed into and through our Aid Post – at times almost submerging it. There was little rest from toil. One wound detached itself from the others and became an entity – a man, no a boy – a boy of eighteen, lying white and still on his stretcher. I looked again: his feet had been blown off. A stretcher party took him immediately to the Dressing Station, and there I saw him later. He was one of many very still forms wrapped in their blankets, lying on a green strip of secluded ground. I went up and looked at him. He was just a boy – just on the threshold of life. And now he was dead – and all the glorious possibilities latent in him dead with him.

Through the day we toiled, treading and retreading that path between the Aid Post and the Advanced Dressing Station. The supply of 'wounds' was constant, unceasing. Then night came – night with its kaleidoscopic display of devil's fireworks. Exhaustion had become a habit, and we worked as automatons work.

But with night came relief, and we trod heavily the shell-pitted road to Fricourt. Past that row of monster guns, past the battalions coming into the line in the night, past ammunition limbers bearing food for the ever hungry cannon, we reeled rather than marched along. On the right the Germans were shelling Fricourt Wood, and the bursting of the shells among the ragged trees sounded eerie and hollow. Reaching the transport, we found a lorry awaiting us, and we climbed in, some of us falling asleep in spite of its jolting progress. The billets reached, every man flung himself down on the bricked floor and slept.

And through the night the man who had seen that faceless form stirred restlessly, and moaned in his sleep.

Fred Ambrose, *With the Welsh*

An Omen of Death

During one spell in the line at Hulloch, Dann and I came out of our little dugout, which was about fifteen yards behind the front-line trench, to clean our rifles and bayonets. We were just about to begin when there appeared, on the back of the trench we were in, the largest rat that I ever saw in my life. It was jet black and was looking intently at Dann, who threw a clod of earth at it but missed, and it didn't even attempt to dodge it. I threw a clod at it then; it sprung out of the way, but not far, and began staring at Dann again. This got on Dann's nerves; he threw another clod but missed again, and it never even flinched. I had my bayonet fixed and made a lunge at it; it sprung out of the way for me all right, but had another intent look at Dann before it disappeared over the top. I would have shot it, for I had a round in the breach, but we were not allowed to fire over the top to the rear of us for fear of hitting men in the support trench; one or two men had been hit in this way by men shooting at rats, and orders were very strict regarding it. Dann had gone very pale; I asked him if he was ill. He said that he wasn't but the rat had made him feel queer. I burst out laughing. He said: 'It's all right, you laughing, but I know my number is up. You saw how that rat never even flinched when I threw at it, and I saw something besides that you didn't see or you wouldn't be laughing at me. Mark my words, when I do go West that rat will be close by.' I told him not to talk so wet and that we may be a hundred miles from this part of the front in a week's time. He said: 'That don't matter: if it's two hundred miles off or a thousand, that rat will still be knocking around when I go West.' Dann was a very brave and cheery fellow, but from that day he was a changed man . . .

We arrived on the Somme by a six days march from the railhead, and early in the morning of July 15 passed through Fricourt, where our First Battalion had broken through on July 1, and arrived at the end of Mametz Wood which had been captured some days before by the 38th Welsh Division which included four of our new service battalions. The enemy had been sending over tear gas and the valley was thick with it. It smelt like strong onions which made our eyes and noses run very badly; we were soon coughing, sneezing and cursing. We rested in shell-holes, the ground all around us being thick with dead of the troops who had been attacking Mametz Wood. The fighting was going on about three-quarters of a mile ahead of us.

Dann, a young signaller named Thomas, and I, were posted to A Company. The three of us were dozing when Thomas gave a shout: a spent bullet with sufficient force to penetrate had hit him in the knee – our first casualty on the Somme. Dann said: 'I don't suppose it will be my luck to get hit with a spent bullet; it will be one at short range through the pound or a twelve-inch shell all on my own.' I replied, as usual, that he would be damned lucky if he stopped either, and that he couldn't be able to grouse much afterwards. 'You're right enough about that, Dick,' he said. A few hours later the Battalion moved around the corner of the wood, the Company occupying a shallow trench which was only knee-deep. The first officer casualty on the Somme was the lieutenant who got the M.C. for shouting: 'We'll have to surrender. They've got behind us.' Hammer Lane was next to this officer, deepening the trench, when a very small bit of shrapnel ricocheted off his shovel and hit the officer in the foot. He began to holler like mad and the Colonel who was not far off rushed up and wanted to know if he was badly hit. Lane answered: 'No, sir. He's making a lot of bloody row over nothing at all.' The Colonel told Lane to shut up and never speak of an officer in that way again. Lane told me later in the day that if the officer had had his bloody belly ripped open he could not have made more row than what he did . . .

Enemy shells were now coming over and a lot of spent machine-gun bullets were zipping about. He [Dann] sat on the back of a trench writing his quick-firers when – zip! – and he rolled over, clutching his neck. Then a terrified look came in his face as he pointed one hand behind me. I turned and just behind me on the back of the trench saw the huge black rat that we had seen in Hulloch. It was looking straight past me at Dann. I was paralysed myself for a moment, and without looking at me it turned and disappeared in a shell-hole behind. I turned around and instantly flattened myself on the bottom of the trench, a fraction of a second before a shell burst behind me. I picked myself up amid a shower of dirt and clods and looked at Dann, but he was dead. The spent bullet had sufficient force to penetrate his neck and touch the spinal column. And there by his side, also dead, was the large rat: the explosion of the shell had blown it up

159

and it had dropped by the side of him. I seized hold of its tail and swung it back in the shell-hole it had been blown from. I was getting the creeps. Although Mametz Wood was, I daresay, over fifty miles as the crow flies from Hulloch, I had no doubt in my own mind that it was the same rat what we had seen in the latter place. It was the only weird experience I had during the whole of the War.

Frank Richards, *Old Soldiers Never Die*

War
on the
Eastern Front

On board the *Essequibo* en route to Salonika. Albert Evans Jones (Cynan) sits on the left of the front row.

The Death of Rupert Brooke

When we returned to Port Said, A Company was full, commanded by Freyberg, with Nelson second, the four platoons being led by Johnny Dodge and myself, Charles and Rupert, in that order. Seldom can two neighbouring platoons of the Army, New or Old, have been more notably led. No sooner were we complete, no sooner had Charles begun to apply his troop-leading lore to his naval bipeds, and to fill the camp with his superb parade voice, than we were reduced. The day after we came back from Cairo, I got a touch of the sun, which began as a violent headache and then shifted the scene of its ravages downwards, and retired sick to the Casino Hotel. Two days later I was joined by Rupert, who had the same complaint but worse, with high fever; he was put in my room because the hotel was full, and because I thought I was well, but I relapsed slightly and in the end we shared that room for a week, completely starved (with one or two adventures in eggs and the little sham soles of the Mediterranean, which brought about relapse and repentance), and weak as kittens, disabilities which did not prevent me from enjoying it greatly. This enjoyment was perhaps not diminished by the thought of the windswept camp, where one of our stokers remarked that the continual absorption of particles of sand was rapidly forming in his interior a tombstone, the removal of which would, he felt, present a problem . . .

Rupert and I were trundled on board the *Grantully Castle* when the battalion pushed off rather hastily about April 11, this time meaning business. Our protestations of fitness were true in my case but not in Rupert's, although after two or three days in his cabin he began to get up and go about, officially well but really pulled down. On this voyage the Hood had the *Grantully* to themselves, which vastly improved every one's temper and enjoyment. It further enabled a rearrangement of tables in the dining-saloon, and a table was formed consisting of Charles, Rupert, Arthur Asquith, Denis Browne, Cleg Kelly, Johnny Dodge, and myself, under the presidency of one of the ship's officers, who was occasionally, I think, a little surprised at our conversation. I subsequently happened to hear that this table was known to the others as 'the Latin Club' . . .

We all read *Duffer's Drift*, we painted our holsters green to go with our webbing – green as our war experience – we were convinced that the campaign would most unfortunately be ended in a month by the R. N. D. occupying the entire Gallipoli peninsula and setting its foot on the neck of the Turks; we were very wise indeed. But always, whatever the matter in hand, Charles and Rupert delighted each other and the rest of us; they also walked on deck together, and I suspect talked of less hilarious and more permanently significant things . . . and about April 17 we anchored in the southern bay of Scyros, that smelt to heaven of thyme.

Here, next day, Charles and I wandered all over the south half of the island in brilliant sunshine and sweet smelling air: we were fed on milk and goat's cheese by a magnificent islander – whom we identified with Eumæus – in his completely Homeric steading, were rowed back to our ship by another sturdy Greek fisherman and his still sturdier wife, and were greeted over the ship's side with slight sarcasm by Rupert, who had taken our watches and suffered endless boredom to enable us to overstay our scheduled time without dire consequences. Here we floundered about on precipitous perfumed hillsides packed with spring flowers and sharp stones, in the throes of Battalion and Divisional Field Days more bewildering, unexpected, and exhausting than any we had previously dreed on the Dorsetshire downs, till Rupert, who would not be left behind, felt tired and went to bed early while we still sat and smoked and talked after dinner. Here, one day after, we knew that the germ of pneumonia had attacked him, weak as he was, in the lip, and I was frightened to see him so motionless and fevered just before he was shifted – lowered over the side in a couch from the *Grantully* to a French hospital ship – and here, after one day more, Charles commanded the burial-party and I the firing-party, when we buried him among the olives of Scyros the night before we sailed for the Peninsula.

Patrick Shaw-Stewart, letter to Ronald Knox, April 1915,
Patrick Shaw-Stewart, edited by Ronald Knox (1920)

Rupert Brooke

He was a delicious companion, full of good jokes and perfect at other people's. He held the most violent and truculent opinions, and with the gentlest manner you ever saw. I think he had drawn in his horns and abandoned his insolence (as some others of us have tried to do) for the war, in order to live happily with queer hotch-potchy brother officers. He will be a great legend now and have a great fame: it is encouraging to know that his poetry is good enough to stand on its own merits: a soldier-poet's death casting a lustre over fairly but not very good poetry would have been awful, wouldn't it?

Patrick Shaw-Stewart, letter to Ronald Knox, June 2, 1915,
Patrick Shaw-Stewart

I Saw a Man this Morning

I saw a man this morning
   Who did not wish to die:
I ask, and cannot answer,
   If otherwise wish I.

Fair broke the day this morning
   Against the Dardanelles;
The breeze blew soft, the morn's cheeks
   Were cold as cold seashells.

But other shells are waiting
   Across the Aegean sea,
Shrapnel and high explosive,
   Shells and hells for me.

O hell of ships and cities,
   Hell of men like me,
Fatal second Helen,
   Why must I follow thee?

Achilles came to Troyland
   And I to Chersonese:
He turned from wrath to battle,
   And I from three days' peace.

Was it so hard, Achilles,
   So very hard to die?
Thou knowest and I know not –
   So much the happier I.

I will go back this morning
   From Imbros over the sea;
Stand in the trench, Achilles,
   Flame-capped, and shout for me.

Patrick Shaw-Stewart

A Night Advance

It's wonderful how people dig in these circumstances (we expected to be attacked, but the Turks were too great mugs) – I myself dug briskly for half an hour, at the end of which my hand was covered with blisters, so I walked up and down the line instead, asking the men why the hell they didn't dig quicker. We expected the day to reveal the Turks about twice as far off as it actually did, so we all were both surprised and pleased to find where we had quite accidentally got to. My section finished up opposite two heaps of very dead Turks (that element is to my mind the worst in war) and I was moved to head a party of volunteers to bury them at dawn; but they began to fire at us before we had properly finished, so we had to let them continue to remind us of their presence all day.

Patrick Shaw-Stewart, letter to Ronald Knox, June 2, 1915,
Patrick Shaw-Stewart

The Dardanelles: Evacuation of the Peninsula

Tonight, I can now say without indiscretion, is the historic night, not altogether glorious, but so far very adroit, of our disappearance from the Peninsula. It's pretty sad when you think of what it has cost us, but since they got German ammunition through, the shelling has been tiresome, and I am quite persuaded that it's the only thing to do. Only the French guns remain (of the French), and the French C.O. and I have been walking up and down looking unconcerned and smelling the breeze (in case it should develop), and burning anything we think the Turks would enjoy or be able to use. I have burnt some queer things, including a bowler hat.

Well, I have certainly seen the campaign of the Dardanelles – the beginning, the end, and all the middle. I am lucky to be walking off it, but I mustn't speak too soon, as they are shelling the beach from the region of Troy, and I have got to get on to the *River Clyde* somehow in an hour or two. Meanwhile, I am hanging on to the telephone, which my signallers are itching to dismantle.

All day we have been looking at the weather in terror in case the wind should rise, but, thank the Lord, it is still only a gentle breeze. It takes one back to that other night, in April, when we waited on the ship and listened to the terrific bombardment at the landing – now it is just the opposite. I am waiting on shore and it is as quiet as the grave, except when the batteries from Asia send us an occasional shot. If they had any idea of what we are up to they would simply make hay of the beaches, and it's rather satisfactory to feel we are cheating them, and they will wake up in the morning and find us gone.

But, on the whole, it's nothing to be proud of for the British Army or the French either – nine months here, and pretty heavy losses, and now nothing for it but to clear out.

I wonder what next?

Patrick Shaw-Stewart, letter to Ronald Knox, January 8, 1916,
Patrick Shaw-Stewart

A Welsh Nurse in Salonika

I am very happy despite everything . . . It is strange when you come down to the bedrock of matters how few things are really necessary to one's happiness. At first we had no butter, margarine, or even dripping, and the bread was sour. Fresh milk is unknown; it is all condemned. We dine (!) in a draughty tent, sit on wooden benches, and drink out of enamelled mugs, but are we downhearted? No! We are the first English (and Welsh) hospital staff out here. The Canadians came out a few weeks before us.

I have been under fire twice. The first time I was walking with three others on the hill some distance from the camp. We looked up, saw an aeroplane, and waved our handkerchiefs, thinking it was a French one. The next thing we heard was a 'whizz', and then we saw a bomb fall just a field away. Three more aeroplanes came, and more bombs fell. Then our guns thundered, and after a time the machines flew away. No one was hurt, and I am glad to say we were not a bit frightened.

A few days ago a whole crowd of them came, and this time they dropped bombs on our camp though we fly the Red Cross flag. One fell within a yard of me, but, fortunately, it did not explode, but buried itself in the soft earth. There was absolutely no panic, and no damage was done in the camp, beyond a few holes made in the ground. Our enemies are brave, are they not, to make war thus on helpless men and defenceless women?

We are told that several men in England are working for peace – peace at any price. Surely not! I wish I had one of the peace party here.

It is nearly 4am, and I am sitting in a tent. Outside the wind is blowing with a violence that threatens to bring the tent down about my ears. In a corner a tiny oil stove seems to intensify the coldness of the room. Two small candles try – unsuccessfully – to lighten the gloom. Shortly I must start again on my round and visit nearly 50 tents in the rain and cold. It is not pleasant, but think of the soldiers! Don't you think that we out here and you, the folks at home who are watching and praying, have paid too high a price to have peace at any cost? We must beat them to their knees and then – peace.

Salonika is to us still a city of mystery. We are not allowed one yard beyond the camp.

Nurse M. Jones, 'In a City of Mystery:
Welsh Nurse's Story of the Salonika Air Raids',
letter to John Rowland, Cardiff, *Western Mail,* January 29, 1916

Extracts from an Officer's War Diary

March 7, 1916

Orders were given that we were leaving camp at 6pm for an all-night march, and all our kits had to be carried.

One day's rations were issued, which consisted of one tin bully, four biscuits, one bottle water, no tea or cocoa. The water on no account was to be touched unless orders given.

Paraded at 6pm. Orders: no leaving ranks, no talking or smoking, if anyone falls out must be left behind, and do the best he could. It was a lovely night, and we were directed by a searchlight from the river.

Nobody knew what was going to happen, or where we were bound for.

10pm. First halt, and a much-needed one, especially carrying all kit.

10.15pm. Started again, and marched until 4am, and when halt was given, all fell down and went fast asleep.

5am. I was sent for by the Colonel and gave orders that latrines had to be dug. Arrangements were made and put men on duty.

9am. Orders were given to march and away we went. An aeroplane came over and gave us the order. We marched until 2pm, and then made another halt. We were told that was the place for a dressing station, so made all arrangements.

4pm. Oh, my God! What's happened? The noise of guns and rifles is terrible!

The attack had started. The infantry were going on splendidly. Bullets were dropping all around us, but the excitement was too much. At last, the Cavalry came dashing along and we knew that we were advancing.

Orders came that we had to advance, so we packed everything up and dreamt of being in Kut the following day.

10pm. Settled down again, but so hungry and thirsty, but wounded were arriving and must be attended to. Working all night attending to wounded until 5am, and then I sat down and fell asleep. Noise of guns began to get worse, and seemed to be getting nearer. We were asking everybody for news and couldn't get any and had no idea of what was happening. Graves had to be dug for the dead – then orders were given to parade at 9am for a retreat.

It was heartbreaking, so I dashed up a small hill to see if I could see what was really happening. I could see the Turks quite plainly rushing about, and our men retiring as quickly as possible.

Again the Taube came over and dropped bombs all amongst us, but even the wounded didn't realise the danger, and it was impossible to do anything for them.

Everything was ready to retreat and Colonel Sloane came dashing up on his horse, and said I was to be in charge of all waiting cases, and if any man fell out he was to be left.

Still hungry and thirsty, hadn't tasted food for two days, and water bottle empty. My feet ached and were bleeding, but still I had to go on.

Shells were dropping around us, but thank goodness, no one was hurt.

One o'clock: our first halt, and we had only done about 4 miles. Seemed more like 40 miles. The wounded were in an awful state, and were begging for water, but still, we had none. On and on until 7pm, and then we reached Orah, a distance of 22 miles. The sights of boats helped us along, otherwise am sure we would never have reached it. On the march, one of our batteries halted and turned round and fired into the enemy, and one of the Infantry Rgts. took up a fresh position, and held the enemy for 12 hours before reinforcements arrived.

On reaching Orah, I was greeted by several medical officers who gave me tea and biscuit.

As the convoy came along, an officer who had received a wound in the leg, but had managed to march all day, looked across to me with hunger written on his face. I rushed across with some tea, but he refused it and asked for bread. I gave the tea to some wounded soldiers and rushed back to camp and got some bread and butter. When I gave it to him, he thanked me ever so much, and said it was the first bit of food for three days.

Our day's work had not finished, but had to attend to the wounded which numbered over 600 and that was only one Field Ambulance.

About one in the morning, I lay down in the open and tried to sleep, but it was useless, and by 5 o'clock my Indian sepoy got up and made me some tea. So far had not had any rations for 3 days, and my stomach was like a lump of lead.

I made enquiries about ration, but could not get any satisfaction.

At 9 o'clock a message came for me from A.D.M.S., and I had to go immediately, a distance of 3 miles. The Colonel thanked me for all the good work I had done and said I must be knocked up, but was sorry that our Field Ambulance must go up again that afternoon.

I must have looked very sad, and had a beard of 4 days' growth. He took pity on me and got me transferred to 113th Indian Field Ambulance.

It was a day of rejoicing, for my luck changed, and I met my good friend, Sergt Kelly. A tent was given us, and how pleased I was to have a roof over my head.

We started well by having an excellent feed – curry and stewed pears; seemed almost too good to eat – and a most delightful sleep in the afternoon. Tea was served at 6 o'clock, and a good drop of tea, but just as we were enjoying it a shell came over and burst right over our heads. 'Mercy, what's that?' – and a dash for helmets when small pieces came through the tent.

The major started rushing about and said 'Everybody in their tents!' I was ordered to rush across to my men who were at the other end of camp, and found all three tents empty. Two men were sitting round a fire making tea, and didn't care if 30 shells came over. Well, of course, orders must be obeyed, and after some great deal of talking, I got them in the tents when another one burst and a large piece flew right by my head, so near that I felt the draught. I dropped into the tents for a minute, and the Indians wanted me to stay, but I said, 'No, if I am to be killed I will with an Englishman.' I dashed across to my tent and frightened poor Sergeant Kelly. He said I was as white as a ghost and the wet was pouring off me.

A wireless message was sent to say they were shelling a hospital, and the reply came, 'Shift in 24 hours.' That, of course, meant more work. However, we slept the night peacefully, and prepared for a new home.

March 11, 1916

Removed to new quarters at Orah. Boiling hot day and very little water. Got attached to new officer, Capt. Kapur, and did the sanitation on water side.

Fixed up 3 large destructions for burning all manure in area. Disinfected malalias in various places as several cases of smallpox had broken out.

March 12, 1916

Taking men out for duty in the morning, and a Taube came over and dropped bombs but no one hurt. Doing duties until March 18.

March 19, 1916

Orders given at 11am for going up lines. Everything ready and started at 2pm. Word was given that a mail had arrived, so I rushed to a field p.o. to find that 4 letters were waiting me, the first I had received since being up the lines.

Arrived at Camp Suma at 7pm, put up tents and made ourselves comfortable for the night.

March 20, 1916

Oh dear, how ill I was feeling and as weak as a kitten.

Went out with Capt. Street to the wells to pick up kits only about one mile from the tents.

Came back and was too ill to go out.

March 21, 1916

Reported myself with dysentery and was inoculated and told to rest. However, the work had to be done, so it was impossible to rest.

March 25, 1916

Orders came along, and I had to go with Capt. Sweet in the trenches to attend to the Connaught Rangers.

March 28, 1916

We marched about 11 miles during the heat of the day, and immediately went on duty. An attack was in progress, so had plenty of wounded to attend to. Our supply of bandages had finished so only had first field dressings.

This went on for 5 days during which time we hardly had any rest, and sleep was almost impossible. Our rations consisted of bully beef, biscuits and water. It was impossible to make tea, as fires were quite out of the question.

March 31, 1916

Returned to 113th I.F.A. and found out I had been reported as missing. Capt. Sweet had no business to claim me, and as he had done so he hadn't reported it.

April 1, 1916

Returned to Camp Suma and decided to have a rest.

Every day we were shelled, but nothing seriously happened.

April 4, 1916

Orders were given to shift and we paraded at 4pm. Major Bradley was in charge and led the four field ambulances.

Unfortunately, he lost his way, and went too much to the right, and we were observed by the enemy who intended giving us a very warm time. They sent over about 42 shells (shrapnel), and we had to lie in the open. This lasted about 3 hours, but, fortunately, no damage was done to us, but one of our batteries close by fared badly.

At last we started again, and at last got to Thorneo Mullah. Orders were given that no lights or fires, so again we had to go without tea. After placing the transport into position, we settled down for the night, slept with all clothes on and in the open; at 1 o'clock, Major Bradley came along and said all transport must go back at once, otherwise at sunrise the enemy would observe and we should draw fire.

So off we started, pitch dark, and only the stars to guide us.

After going about one hour, one of the garries broke down, and we were stranded on the desert, afraid that the Arabs would attack us.

At last everything in working order, so off we started.

Could not find the place given so decide to put up for the night. Slept on garry and was very tired.

April 5, 1916

4am. What's happening? Terrific fire and the bursting of shells, like the lights of the West End of London, and the smoke like a thick fog. The great bombardment had started, and such a wonderful light. This lasted about 4 hours, and then the Infantry started.

One gun came along and the men begged for water, said they hadn't any for 2 days. They had sent over one thousand shells and were taking up a new position.

6pm. Orders came, and we had to return to Thorneo Mullah, and got there about 8 pm.

We were provided with dugouts, so had a real good sleep.

April 6, 1916

All going well and the attack still on. I had to go into the trenches with Capt. Kapur to attend to 47th Sikhs. The work was very hard as such a large number were wounded.

April 7, 1916

At 7am a shell came over and killed Capt. Kapur who was only 3 yards away. I rushed to him, but it was too late and carried him to the Aid Post. Sent word to the Headquarters that he was killed, and to send someone to give me assistance, but it did not arrive for at least 18 hours, during which time I had to do all first aid myself.

April 12, 1916

Returned to Thornea Mullah and very glad. Found that 2 officers and 3 Sub. Asst. Surgeons had been killed, and generally speaking, our ambulance had had a very rough time.

April 13, 1916

Was sent out with Sergt Underhill to find some dead horses which had been reported. We were about 3 miles from camp when suddenly shells began to drop – discovered the Arabs were attacking. We rushed back to find they were all ready to retire, but fortunately, one of our batteries turned their guns on them, and the 34th Sikhs went out and made them retire.

April 14, 1916

Returned to Sandy Ridge, all with a very downhearted feeling, as our second attempt to relieve Kut had failed.

The heat was now intense, and quite impossible to be out during daytime.

April 15, 1916

At Sandy Ridge and intend making ourselves comfortable. Quite close to the River Tigris, so we could clean all our clothing and have a bath.

Went out with Sergt Kelly and inspected some of the Old Turkish trenches, also saw a lot of prisoners making incinerators. Called at the Field p.o. only to find no letters for me.

April 17, 1916

Another attack had started, and I was ordered up to the 1st Aid Post with Capt. Sweet. The shellfire was terrible and we lived in fear. At midnight we were ordered to return, and very pleased to.

On arriving at field ambulance, they were overrun with wounded, and we had to set to and help.

April 18, 1916

Attack still on and over 600 cases passed through our hands.

Bandages, splints, &c had run out, and we got about 30 Indians working making bandages, and as fast as they were made, so they were used, and in many case men's shirts were torn, and used as bandages. One poor chap was brought in with a shrapnel wound in the foot and 12 bayonet wounds in the body. He remained perfectly still whilst being dressed, but begged for water. The Major said No; however, I just managed to give him some when the Officer wasn't looking.

The next few days were very quiet, only a shell dropping occasionally.

April 18, 1916

Cholera has started and we had to erect a separate hospital.

Capt. Wells was in charge and I had to attend to all the water and disinfect all garries.

I was feeling very ill at the time, but it was impossible to give up. Cholera was still getting worse, and we were losing about 80 per cent. It was a terrible job, as food stuff was so scarce.

April 28, 1916

The Sanitary sections arrived and I was only too glad and some of them could relieve me.

Walker took over my job at the Cholera Camp and I went on Water duties at Headquarters.

We were heavily shelled and had to retire for the night in dugouts.

All day we could see large volumes of smoke in the direction of Kut and couldn't understand what it all meant.

Our guns were very busy continually firing.

April 29, 1916

We received the bad news of the fall of Kut and took it very badly. Everybody was walking with head down and not a smile. It was a terrible blow to our General, but he had done all that was possible and if only we could have got the necessary reinforcements we should have been able to relieve Kut. But there's one great thing to consider: If only the Turks had known what few men we had, they could have driven us right back.

Great praise should be given to the Manchesters and Connaught Rangers, who fought like men and suffered every hardship.

For several days our work was of general routine and just attended to wounded and sick cases that were coming in.

The cholera was still very bad and required a great deal of attention.

I had been relieved of the duties by Walker and unfortunately he was not strong enough to carry on and was very soon taken ill. He was transferred to No. 8 Field Ambulance where he received medical treatment.

May 2, 1916

Headquarters shifted to Abu Ruhman about 2 miles away. I was instructed to attend twice daily, early morn and evening, to inspect the drinking and if necessary medically treat same and do the ordinary sanitation. This was done until May 10, when I was instructed to attend the 1st Manchesters in the trenches and do disinfection.

Had to go about six miles, and what with sun and dust it was unbearable.

On the way back next day I came across one of the R.E. lying in the open hopelessly ill. He had been lying there for hours waiting for assistance, and had lost his dispatches and revolver.

Helped him along to 1st Aid Post and discovered he had cholera.

Returned to 113th I.F. Ambulance 9.30pm.

War Diary of Lieutenant Edwin Evan Jones,
in possession of his great-nephew, Dr Robert Griffith Jones

After the Battle of Qatia, April 23, 1916

The Turk came to Oghratina, where a few months before he had dealt hardly with our yeomanry. He came past Oghratina. Then my Battery was sent for at an hour's notice. In the early dawn of a late July day we marched forward to Romani. Hot and weary we arrived six hours later, an hour before we were expected. But we were there. The Turk was almost within gunfire.

And then we waited again. One day. Two days. Still the Turk came on, building, digging, strengthening. On the third day we were allowed to have a shot at him. Two days before we had been visited by some enemy planes, and sustained our first casualty . . . We were inclined to hit back. It is dull and irritating work lying down to be bombed, without the chance of firing in return. So we went forth joyfully.

Out under the smooth yellow crest of Katib Gannit we marched rattling along, with our pedrails making a noise like dozens of machine guns in action. Down across the scrub-speckled desert into Qatia, there to meet the General of our new Brigade.

He and I rode out to the old Qatia battlefield to reconnoitre. Our ride made me shudder. A battlefield must always be shudderful. This was a peculiar one. The Turks had been left in possession, the dead had been buried, and little crosses showed their number. But the horses lay in long withered heaps, just where they had been shot in their picketing lines (it had been a surprise). They were now dry, almost smell-less things, with the scorched flesh and skin peeling off their skulls and bones. And there were other relics, odd, pathetic evidences of the sudden and murderous and fatal onslaught. The site of the tents was shown by tins, and fragments of clothing, and notebooks and papers. A topee lay derelict and decaying. A pack of cards was scattered here and there. It was not difficult to construct the scene: the peaceful camp, the quick alarm, the desperate resistance, the eventual doom. It was all strangely and horribly easy. The place was full of dead and of their ghosts and memories.

Eliot Crawshay-Williams, *Leaves from an Officer's Notebook*

175

By the Old Caravan Road

On a day,
   A far-off day,
Baby Jesus
   Passed this way.
Mary mother
   Trod this road
With her heavenly
   Human load.
Jesus must have
   Rested here
At Romani
   By the *bir*;
By the *bir*
   His baby hand
Tossed in play
   The yellow sand . . .

By the *bir*
   The yellow sand
Sullied lies
   On every hand;
Red with blood;
   Black, brown, and blue,
Where the shells
   Death-dealing flew . . .

If now Jesus
   Passed this way
What do *you* think
   He would say?

Eliot Crawshay-Williams

June in Egypt, 1916

June! – and, here,
Quivering heat,
Shimmering sand,
An aching land
Of sun's beat
And straggling, sere,
Wizened scrub;
Of mile on mile
Of nothingness
Scorched by the stress
Of some most vile
Beelzebub.
In this hell
Humankind
(You and I)
Live (and die)
Bent in mind
On killing well . . .
Over away
Across the plain
Of baking sand,
In an alien land
Ripe to be slain,
Ready to slay,
Other men
(Like you and me)
Scorch and endure,
Plan and procure,
Incessantly,
To kill again . . .
June, here;
This year.

June! – and there
The grasses stand
Green and tall,
And cuckoos call,
By Overstrand –
By Mundesley, where
The air breathes sweet
Of crisp dry turf
(O! wine-like smell
I love so well)
And salt from the surf;
Where lovers meet,
As I and a maid
(Divine with youth,
In her eyes
The light that cries
A splendid truth –
Unafraid)
Met long ago
(Before this hell)
Met, and loved,
Loved, and proved
Love was well,
Long, long ago . . .
June, there:
Yester year.

El Quantara, 1916

Eliot Crawshay-Williams

The Battlefield of Komani

The Turks still held to Wellington Edge firmly, and as daylight came the sputtering of the rifles became more intense, while, since we were only about fifteen hundred yards from the ridge, bullets were about. The C.E.A. was lying on the sand-dune which sheltered us to the southward, and when day made observation possible I went up to him and watched the battle.

We could at once see that the Turk's case was hopeless. He had clung to his position through the night; but now his time had come. With our glasses we could plainly see the individual Turks under their tiny hillocks of sand, and they were in a sad plight. For not only were they threatened frontally, from our direction. From the west also our troops were closing in on them, and even from the east they were under fire. Consequently, they knew not from what quarter to seek protection or cover, and we could see them moving desperately round as bullets came from a fresh source. It could not last long.

It did not last long. As we watched, a Turk came out and hoisted something on a stick, some kind of a rude flag. Others followed him. Turks oozed out of their cover all over the ridge. The firing dried up as if by magic. Our troops rushed up the hill. The fight was over.

In a little, dense columns of prisoners were forming on the hilltop. Telling the Battery or, rather, the Batteries, for we were in company with another E.H.A. Battery to follow, we pushed on to the scene of surrender. I was to have my first sight of a battlefield, uncleared, fresh after action.

First we came on the prisoners, sturdy, good-looking fellows most of them; but famished and athirst. Poor devils! I thought. Half a water-bottleful of water distributed among some particularly parched-looking prisoners helped to show my feelings to them; for my Arabic produced no impression on them. They were very grateful, smiled thankfully, saluted, and joined the ranks of their comrades, to be marched off under an escort with fixed bayonets. There were several columns of prisoner Turks, and little bunches of stragglers kept coming in. Our infantry were radiant.

At the top of the hill I suddenly came on a trench. In it I saw some Turks. At least, they had been Turks. Rifles, accoutrements, ammunition, were everywhere, and among them these shattered bits of humanity. I did not feel sick; I felt just infinitely pitiful, infinitely disgusted with the world. And this was the line of trenches I had been firing on yesterday.

I gazed on a man lying huddled at my feet, half his skull shot away by shrapnel. 'You killed him,' I said softly to myself. Another lay face upwards with a grim set smile. (Death is not beautiful; death is not peaceful; death is horrible and revolting and awful.) 'You killed him,' I said. Yet another was on his side, his head a mass of blood and flies. He was in a scooped depression in the sand, a half-prepared grave. As I looked at this corpse, to my utter horror it slowly and feebly raised a hand, and mechanically tried to brush away the crowding, obscene swarm of flies. I shuddered, and shouted to a Medical Officer nearby:

'This chap's alive. Can't you do anything for him?'

The M.O. came up and looked at him sadly.

'No. He's practically dead.'

'Put a bullet in his head,' I begged.

But that could not be done.

In that moment on the battlefield of Komani I felt surge up within me a fierce tide of bitterness against a world that could work such things. And then a despairing pity for all of us, blind struggling human beings that blunder on so miserably, each in his own way, towards, no doubt, some distant end. 'Judge not,' not 'that ye be not judged' (that is a low and selfish motive), but because no man can tell what allowances should be made.

Still, it is difficult not to judge on a battlefield (or in a slum, for the matter of that).

And a bit of judging does good sometimes. So perhaps judge but with pity.

Eliot Crawshay-Williams, *Leaves from an Officer's Notebook*

Aerial Attack

We had only come in the night before. The camp was a dump of baggage. Only a tent here and there had risen from the débris, like sparse mushrooms. The Officers' Mess consisted of a heap of stores, a couple of shapeless white bundles, a trestle table covered with breakfast things, and some upturned boxes for seats.

The C.O. had just finished giving us his usual breakfast resumé of the situation as it presented itself to him. This happens during the porridge. The bacon was appearing, when about 700 yards to the north there was a cloud of black smoke and 'Cramp!'

I looked at it. Six-inch shell, I said to myself, a little surprised; for we hadn't known of any six-inch guns, though we suspected them. Just as I was thinking this 'Swish-sh-sh-sh-sh-sh! Cramp' and another cloud of black smoke half-way between us and the first. Then I knew what it was. There was no time to do much. The next would be on or near us.

I jumped up.

'Get down! Lie down!' I shouted over to the men's tents, where they were all clustering round breakfasts. And I threw myself flat on my face. Then I turned to look up. Yes, there he was, straight overhead. And at the same moment once again 'Swish-sh-sh-sh-sh-sh!' . . .

179

During that interminable period in which a heavy body was whistling down from the aeroplane overhead, I had time to think quite a lot. Of course I thought the bomb was coming straight for the middle of my back. One always does. Then I thought of the line of the other two bombs. Yes, it was dead on us. Then I thought of the wind, blowing from the north-west. But it blew the same for the others. No! It would come . . . 'Sh-sh! CRAMP!'

I got up.

The next one would fall farther on. The cloud of black smoke puffed up, this time from just beyond the men's cookhouse.

'Get to the horse lines!' I yelled. 'Take the horses and scatter! He may come back.' And indeed he did come back.

The tiny speck up above wheeled about gracefully, like some silver gnat in the blue. Then he came steadily, slowly, over us. He seemed to hover. I swear he did. I looked up expectant. I listened. But there was no 'swish-sh-sh!' For an endless age he was above us. Then he was clearly past us. And then 'Cramp! cramp! cramp!' and great puffs of black smoke from down by railhead.

After that, silence, and our silver gnat had disappeared into space.

A long whistle, and from their dispersed stations the men came slowly in. Battery life was the same again. But not quite yet. For two men came hurrying up, supporting between them another.

''E's 'it, sir,' they panted. 'Be'ind, sir!'

A splinter from one of the bombs had gone through his breeches and just scratched him on the back of the thigh. Shock more than injury had made him go under for the moment. When we left him in the shade of a tent, after dressing the place, he went off to show his wound round.

But he was our first casualty.

And he will get a gold stripe on his left sleeve.

Eliot Crawshay-Williams, *Leaves from an Officer's Notebook*

Failure to Blow Up a Train

Blowing up trains was an exact science when done deliberately, by a sufficient party, with machine guns in position. If scrambled at it might become dangerous. The difficulty this time was that the available gunners were Indians; who, though good men fed, were only half-men in cold and hunger. I did not propose to drag them off without rations on an adventure which might take a week. There was no cruelty in starving Arabs; they would not die of a few days' fasting, and would fight as well as ever on empty stomachs; while, if things got too difficult, there were the riding-camels to kill and eat: but the Indians, though Moslems, refused camel-flesh on principle.

. . . At dawn, with the unfit of the Arabs, the Indians moved away for Azrak, miserably. They had started up country with me in hope of a really military enterprise, and first had seen the muddled bridge, and now were losing this prospective train. It was hard on them; and to soften the blow with honour I asked Wood to accompany them. He agreed, after argument, for their sakes; but it proved a wise move for himself, as a sickness which had been troubling him began to show the early signs of pneumonia.

The balance of us, some sixty men, turned back towards the railway. None of them knew the country, so I led them to Minifir, where, with Zaal, we had made havoc in the spring. The re-curved hilltop was an excellent observation post, camp, grazing ground and way of retreat, and we sat there in our old place till sunset, shivering and staring out over the immense plain which stretched map-like to the clouded peaks of Jebel Druse, with Um el Jemal and her sister-villages like ink-smudges on it through the rain.

In the first dusk we walked down to lay the mine. The rebuilt culvert of kilometre 172 seemed still the fittest place. While we stood by it there came a rumbling, and through the gathering darkness and mist a train suddenly appeared round the northern curve, only two hundred yards away. We scurried under the long arch and heard it roll overhead. This was annoying; but when the course was clear again, we fell to burying the charge. The evening was bitterly cold, with drifts of rain blowing down the valley.

The arch was solid masonry, of four metres span, and stood over a shingle water-bed which took its rise on our hilltop. The winter rains had cut this into a channel four feet deep, narrow and winding, which served us as an admirable approach till within three hundred yards of the line. There the gully widened out and ran straight towards the culvert, open to the sight of anyone upon the rails.

We hid the explosive carefully on the crown of the arch, deeper than usual, beneath a tie, so that the patrols would not feel its jelly softness under their feet. The wires were taken down the bank into the shingle bed of the watercourse, where concealment was quick; and up it as far as they would reach. Unfortunately, this was only sixty yards, for there had been difficulty in Egypt over insulated cable and no more had been available when our expedition started. Sixty yards was plenty for the bridge, but little for a train: however, the ends happened to coincide with a little bush about ten inches high, on the edge of the watercourse, and we buried them beside this very convenient mark. It was impossible to leave them joined up to the exploder in the proper way, since the spot was evident to the permanent-way patrols as they made their rounds.

Owing to the mud the job took longer than usual, and it was very nearly dawn before we finished. I waited under the draughty arch till day broke, wet and dismal, and then I went over the whole area of disturbance, spending another half-hour in effacing its every mark, scattering leaves and dead grass over it, and watering down the broken mud from a shallow rain-pool near. Then they waved to me that the first patrol was coming, and I went up to join the others.

Before I had reached them they came tearing down into their prearranged places, lining the watercourse and spurs each side. A train was coming from the north. Hamud, Feisal's long slave, had the exploder; but before he reached me a short train of closed box-wagons rushed by at speed. The rainstorms on the plain and the thick morning had hidden it from the eyes of our watchman until too late. This second failure saddened us further and Ali began to say that nothing would come right this trip. Such a statement held risk as prelude of the discovery of an evil eye present; so, to divert attention, I suggested new watching posts be sent far out, one to the ruins on the north, one to the great cairn of the southern crest.

The rest, having no breakfast, were to pretend not to be hungry. They all enjoyed doing this, and for a while we sat cheerfully in the rain, huddling against one another for warmth behind a breastwork of our streaming camels. The moisture made the animals' hair curl up like a fleece, so that they looked queerly dishevelled. When the rain paused, which it did frequently, a cold moaning wind searched out the unprotected parts of us very thoroughly. After a time we found our wetted shirts clammy and comfortless things. We had nothing to eat, nothing to do and nowhere to sit except on wet rock, wet grass or mud. However, this persistent weather kept reminding me that it would delay Allenby's advance on Jerusalem, and rob him of his great possibility. So large a misfortune to our lion was a half-encouragement for the mice. We would be partners into next year.

In the best circumstances, waiting for action was hard. Today it was beastly. Even enemy patrols stumbled along without care, perfunctorily, against the rain. At last, near noon, in a snatch of fine weather, the watchmen on the south peak flagged their cloaks wildly in signal of a train. We reached our positions in an instant, for we had squatted the late hours on our heels in a streaming ditch near the line, so as not to miss another chance. The Arabs took cover properly. I looked back at their ambush from my firing point, and saw nothing but the grey hillsides.

I could not hear the train coming, but trusted, and knelt ready for perhaps half an hour, when the suspense became intolerable, and I signalled to know what was up. They sent down to say it was coming very slowly, and was an enormously long train. Our appetites stiffened. The longer it was the more would be the loot. Then came word that it had stopped. It moved again.

Finally, near one o'clock, I heard it panting. The locomotive was evidently defective (all these wood-fired trains were bad), and the heavy load on the up-gradient was proving too much for its capacity. I crouched behind my bush, while it crawled slowly into view past the south cutting, and along the bank above my head towards the culvert. The first ten trucks were open trucks, crowded with troops. However, once again it was too late to choose, so when the engine was squarely over the mine I pushed down the handle of the exploder. Nothing happened. I sawed it up and down four times.

Still nothing happened; and I realised that it had gone out of order, and that I was kneeling on a naked bank, with a Turkish troop train crawling past fifty yards away. The bush, which had seemed a foot high, shrank smaller than a fig-leaf; and I felt myself the most distinct object in the countryside. Behind me was an open valley for two hundred yards to the cover where my Arabs were waiting and wondering what I was at. It was impossible to make a bolt for it, or the Turks would step off the train and finish us. If I sat still, there might be just a hope of my being ignored as a casual Beduin.

So there I sat, counting for sheer life, while eighteen open trucks, three box-wagons, and three officers' coaches dragged by. The engine panted slower and slower, and I thought every moment that it would break down. The troops took no great notice of me, but the officers were interested, and came out to the little platforms at the ends of their carriages, pointing and staring. I waved back at them, grinning nervously, and feeling an improbable shepherd in my Meccan dress, with its twisted golden circlet about my head. Perhaps the mud-stains, the wet and their ignorance made me accepted. The end of the brake van slowly disappeared into the cutting on the north.

As it went, I jumped up, buried my wires, snatched hold of the wretched exploder, and went like a rabbit uphill into safety. There I took breath and looked back to see that the train had finally stuck. It waited, about five hundred yards beyond the mine, for nearly an hour to get up a head of steam, while an officers' patrol came back and searched, very carefully, the ground where I had been seen sitting. However the wires were properly hidden: they found nothing: the engine plucked up heart again, and away they went.

T. E. Lawrence, *Seven Pillars of Wisdom* (1935)

Experiences of a Stretcher-bearer in Macedonia

We had all hoped that we could remain together as a Welsh Company of one heart and one soul, and that the bond which had been forged between us at Sheffield and Llandrindod Wells would continue on the battlefields.

But the value of such a fellowship was incomprehensible to the English military mind. The old close-knit company was broken up, and we were scattered throughout Macedonia and France, and transferred to English units which had already been on the battlefields – some went to the Struma Valley, some to the Lake Doiran region, some to the Vardar and others to Monastir, and others were scattered between the various hospitals of the Balkans.

Thus I became, with a few others from the old company, a member of the 86th Field Ambulance on the banks of the Struma River, opposite the artillery guns of Fort Rupel, in the mighty mountains that guarded the narrow gorge between Macedonia and Bulgaria. I remember the first night of enemy bombardment. A small band of us, under the command of our Captain-doctor, had occupied an old cowshed outside the village of Bairacli-Djoumaza and had turned it into an Advanced Dressing Station, and we had thrown a blanket over the entrance to conceal our candlelight. Presently, after the artillery guns on both sides had ceased firing, our infantrymen surged forward to attack, and the enemy's bullets began splattering through the tiles on the roof. Soon the inevitable cry came from outside, 'Stretcher-bearers, Stretcher-bearers.'

'Herbie' was the first to be sent outside, a dependable, quiet lad from Cardiganshire, and at the time almost a monoglot Welsh-speaker, at least as far as expressing himself in English was concerned, although he could understand commands in English well enough. He was ordered to follow the Greek from Cyprus who was in charge of the two mules which were strapped to the stretchers used to carry the casualties. Herbie was to attend to the wounds and the Greek was to lead the mules. When Herbie raised the blanket at the entrance for a second as he went outside, we could see flashes of light penetrating the darkness. We knew that it was like hell itself outside, and we feared for his safety. Three minutes later Herbie's head popped back inside the cowshed, past the blanket, and he seemed to be in a state of extreme agitation. The Captain thought that he was afraid, and he started cursing him eloquently, accusing him of cowardice. 'No!' Herbie shouted, 'Stop, man. The driver was ask me to come to tell you one bloody *mul* is dead, we want another.' Who could blame him for thinking that no English sentence in the army could be complete without that adjective? What else had he heard?

Another mule was supplied and Herbie patiently went back to his task; and like many of us, he carried casualties to the Advanced Dressing Station throughout that terrible night, and during the following day. That day stands out in my memory for two reasons. First, because I came across an old bed-ridden Greek woman who had been left in the loft of a farmhouse on the edge of the village. The rest of the family had fled when the great battle commenced. She was trembling with fear, but was too crippled by arthritis to be able to get up. We carried her from there on a stretcher, and she was conveyed by a two-mule ambulance to one of the army hospitals. As this strange procession was carrying the old woman on a stretcher through the village, a Bulgarian soldier, who had been frightened out of his wits by the noise of the bombardment, emerged from the cellar of one of the houses. 'Come on, Johnny,' I said to him, and he was all smiles as he followed the stretcher like a lamb. That was the only time that our unit of the R.A.M.C. took a prisoner. The poor man showered his captors with gifts, to express his gratitude.

The 86th was an old Territorial Field Ambulance, and most of its members knew each other at home, because they all came from the same region, Tyneside, and they spoke their own peculiar English dialect. When we joined them, they were very prejudicial towards us, on account of two reasons: first, because we were not old soldiers, and, therefore, not as experienced as they were, and, second, because most of us were Welshmen and college students. This prejudice would manifest itself in little unfair and unworthy minor incidents. For example, we always had to deal with the dirtiest, the hardest and the most perilous tasks, and to complain was in vain. But this prejudice towards us was carried to its extreme on one occasion, when food was being dished out in the kitchen, and some of the Welsh lads could not restrain themselves any longer from grumbling and complaining to the cooks.

That night, after drinking his rum ration, topped by other drinks, one of the fat cooks came up to the Welshmen's tent, to wreak his vengeance on us. He started raging and raving outside the tent, boasting that he could beat six 'bloody Welshmen' at the same time. 'Take no notice of him, lads,' I said, 'he's had too much rum do drink.' The fact that we were so quiet inside made him even more furious, and he started kicking the iron hooks out of the ground, and the tent started to collapse. 'Oh, damn,' my friend Iestyn said, 'this is too much to bear,' and he popped his head through the entrance and shouted to the fat cook in English: 'Hey, you, there's no need for six Welshmen to settle your problem. I'll be out myself in a second, just wait till I get my boots on.' 'Very brave,' I thought, 'but suicide, undoubtedly.'

Soon we had all followed Iestyn outside, and when a rumour circulated around the camp that there was to be a fight, the Tyneside soldiers poured out of their tents. A makeshift boxing ring was formed under the full moon of Macedonia, and two empty rum jars were procured, to be knocked together and used as a bell. Our slim, red-headed lad looked so slight in contrast to the fat, foul-mouthed cook, and should one of the cook's heavy blows have landed on the little Welshman during the first round, he would have been history; but he had quick-stepped to the right or to the left, and, consequently, his opponent had wasted the strength of his muscular arms on punching nothing but air. I could see immediately, as I watched Iestyn's feet dancing elegantly, that this wasn't the first time he had been in a boxing ring. It was a delight to see the subtle and skilful movements of his feet and head as he dodged his opponent's punches, and the skirmish soon began to turn into a comic spectacle as far as the onlookers were concerned, but not to the furious challenger. By the third round he was out of breath, and by the fourth he was completely exhausted, and it was then so easy for Iestyn to dance into the ring and floor him with a straight uppercut under the chin. He fell flat on his back and remained in that position for much longer than the official count of ten! And fair play to the Tynesiders, they enthusiastically cheered the winner. The cook returned to the kitchen, assisted by two of his friends, like a dog with its tail between its legs.

When we settled back into our beds once again, I said, 'Iestyn bach, you didn't learn to box like that in Trefeca College.'

'True enough,' he said. 'You see, before I started preaching, I was one of Freddie Welsh's sparring-partners. And tonight the old tricks all came back to me.'

During parade the following morning, Iestyn was ordered to report to the Orderly Room, where he was to appear before our Colonel. 'Here we go again,' said some of the Welsh lads, 'an Englishman starts making mischief and a Welshman gets punished for it.'

But not this time. When Iestyn returned, after telling the whole story to the Colonel (including his gymnasium experiences with Freddie Welsh), he had three stripes on his sleeve. The Colonel had promoted him to drill-sergeant, and he was instructed to take charge of the whole Company's physical exercises. A message was sent to Base requesting a supply of gymnasium equipment and boxing gloves, and an official boxing club was established. It was at that club that I and many others were taught 'the noble art of self-defence'. And from then on, the Welsh lads were left alone.

A. E. Jones (Cynan), *Hunangofiant Cynan: Maes y Gad*
('Cynan's Memoirs: On the Battlefield'), *Barn*, no. 101, March 1971
(Translated from the Welsh)

Flies

I can scarcely trust myself to write about the flies. One tends to lose control. I have seen men almost go off their heads under the actual infliction of flies. I have heard them address the flies with a concentrated fury of hatred and disgust of which I had never suspected them capable. I have seen others gradually, day by day, give up the struggle and resign themselves to be crawled on. I have felt myself that, if I had an enemy deserving of the uttermost agony and torture, I would desire him to be cursed with flies. And the most horrible, the most maddening part of it is that all the time you hate, and loathe, and rave, the flies are not only generally immune, but also serenely unconscious and uncaring. You cannot communicate your feelings to the fly. Even if you kill it, blasting it with curses as you do so, it merely perishes an innocent and surprised victim of an unknown sudden doom. There is no sense of sin, of just retribution, of defeat. And there are millions more. No; flies are essentially a subject for calm, comprehensive, scientific treatment. That is what they ought to get, and generally don't. We ought to be able to deal with flies, even in Egypt. We fail miserably to do so. All our efforts, even when we make them, are wretched little palliatives, at which the fly, were he actually a vindictive enemy instead of a simple example of a natural law, would justifiably jeer. He beats us. Hopelessly.

He should not beat us. He is not only one of the minor horrors of war; he is one of the major perils of existence. He is a loathsome, scavenging carrier of dirt and disease. He is the embodiment of all that is insanitary. Where the fly is, science and sanitation have failed and are defeated.

Of course, he is the camp follower of filth. Filth is his habitation, his food, his *raison d'être*. He has his place in the world, and that place is filth. So long as there is filth there will be flies. And when science and sanitation say, 'No more filth,' they will also say, 'No more flies.' Until that day the fly not only will live: he will have a right to live. He is the scavenger of filth; he is Nature's means of dealing with filth. And until Science instead of Nature attends to the business of dealing with filth, the fly will remain, filth's most obedient humble servant.

People's food and noses and eyes and bald heads are only side-issues in a fly's life; his real business is with unutterable disgustingnesses. That is why, when I feel his little tender tentacles tickling my eyelids, I shudder and feel sick. That is why, when, as is a custom with these Oriental flies, he will not go away when flapped at, but darts in persistently and with devilish swiftness until at last he attains my lips, I could shriek with hatred and horror. That is why, when I see him crawling in his battalions over the bread, the meat, the sugar, drowned in the milk, buried alive in the jam, I hate food and cannot eat. That is why, when I see a little native child, its eyes wide open, with a ring of flies crawling round their edges, sucking of their moisture, hanging in their lashes, I feel ill with horror and disgust. That is why, when I think of all these things, I could rise up and curse our scientists, who know all and give the world no relief.

Eliot Crawshay-Williams, *Leaves from an Officer's Notebook*

To a Fly

Pestilent creature,
    Foul, with your shy
Soft-clinging feet, your
    Myriad eye,
Where have you been? and
    What saw you there? . . .
'Fat men and lean, and
    Dark men and fair.'
Where were you spying? . . .
    'Over the hill;
Dead men and dying;
    Quick men and still.'
Loathsome, unclean thing,
    Soil not my food,
Get gone! obscene thing,
    Sucker of blood! . . .
'Fool! do you chide me?
    Grudge me supplies?
Man will provide me,
    Man, the all-wise!'

Eliot Crawshay-Williams

Method and Organisation

We are now Australians. Our organisation is scattered over Egypt, I mean our particular branch of the Australians, the Anzac Mounted Division and we find ourselves occupying the position we have occupied since the beginning of the war (except at Alexandria), that of a single R.H.A. Battery with a Mounted Brigade. We are fortunate. Most Mounted Brigades have had their horses taken away, and their artillery, in fact if not in name, has become field artillery.

Our General and our Staff are quite a change. Bluff, breezy, downright, capable, with a horror of red tape, official correspondence, boards, and other War Office indispensables, they generally manage to 'get there'. I am pretty sure they would 'get there' in battle. And, after all (though my knees tremble a little in writing this), to 'get there' in battle is the chief end of a soldier, whatever some may think. Not that I would depreciate for a moment the value of method and organisation. One of the marvels and excellences of this war is the way method and organisation enable our armies to live and move and have their being over the face of this earth. The fact that the gigantic machine works, that the stream of rations and forage does not run dry and men and beasts starve, that Regiments and Batteries and Divisions are transferred from England to Egypt, from India to Mesopotamia, from East Africa to France, that 'the wheels go round' ceaselessly, regularly, all of this is a wonder and a credit. No doubt it might be better. No doubt there might be more precision and less avoidable discomfort, more forethought and less haste. No doubt there is muddle and incompetence and heart-rending waste. No doubt a race of administrative geniuses would run the machine with fewer checks and jolts and screeches. But it moves. And great is the pride with which we may legitimately watch its movement. After this war we shall have done one great thing: we shall have fought it.

Eliot Crawshay-Williams, *Leaves from an Officer's Notebook*

The Price too High

Seeing a regiment march in from the desert brings home the miracle of our daily life. At Alexandria I watched, one day, a battalion come in from the western front. Dusty, mahogany-faced, weary, ill-kempt, they filed past in a long thin stream of fours. No glittering badges to show who they were, no cheery singing, no jokes or laughter: only this long procession of haggard men men who had 'had enough'. But they were alive, they were healthy. They had been out in the desert weeks, months, and they had lived. Their means of life and health had

189

been brought to them day by day; they had suffered, no doubt, and endured. But they had lived, and fought, and come back most of them. And all over the world that was going on, is going on, day by day. A marvellous machine! a wonderful triumph, despite all minor defects! For the major point is it works.

To me, at least, the chief redeeming features of war are the strengthening of the comradeship of men, the widening of the boundaries of the individual life by travel and experience, and the development of the organising faculties of the State. But the price is too high. And the price is unnecessary. We need burn no houses to get our roast pig.

Eliot Crawshay-Williams, *Leaves from an Officer's Notebook*

The Conqueror

The whirling moons go on their way;
    The swirling tides for ever run;
There is no magic that can stay
    The ceaseless circling of the sun.
The desert sun, the Eastern moon
    Age after age have looked upon
Man's little strife; these shores are strewn
    With spoil of generations gone.
Abram and Joseph slow did pace
    With loose-limbed camels and their gear;
Today a less untrammelled race
    Brings but a few more playthings here.
O you whose iron heel bestrides
    The ancient pathways of the plain,
The sun and moon, the unwearying tides,
    The silent desert shall remain,
When you have found forgotten graves
Beneath the sand, beneath the waves.

Eliot Crawshay-Williams

Noon brought a fresh care. Through my powerful glasses we saw a hundred Turkish soldiers issue from Mudowwara Station and make straight across the sandy plain towards our place. They were coming very slowly, and no doubt unwillingly, for sorrow at losing their beloved midday sleep: but at their very worst marching and temper they could hardly take more than two hours before they reached us.

We began to pack up, preparatory to moving off, having decided to leave the mine and its leads in place on chance that the Turks might not find them, and we be able to return and take advantage of all the careful work. We sent a messenger to our covering party on the south, that they should meet us farther up, near those scarred rocks which served as screen for our pasturing camels.

Just as he had gone, the watchman cried out that smoke in clouds was rising from Hallat Ammar. Zaal and I rushed uphill and saw by its shape and volume that indeed there must be a train waiting in that station. As we were trying to see it over the hill, suddenly it moved out in our direction. We yelled to the Arabs to get into position as quick as possible, and there came a wild scramble over sand and rock. Stokes and Lewis, being booted, could not win the race; but they came well up, their pains and dysentery forgotten.

The men with rifles posted themselves in a long line behind the spur running from the guns past the exploder to the mouth of the valley. From it they would fire directly into the derailed carriages at less than one hundred and fifty yards, whereas the ranges for the Stokes and Lewis guns were about three hundred yards. An Arab stood up on high behind the guns and shouted to us what the train was doing – a necessary precaution, for if it carried troops and detrained them behind our ridge we should have to face about like a flash and retire fighting up the valley for our lives. Fortunately it held on at all the speed the two locomotives could make on wood fuel.

It drew near where we had been reported, and opened random fire into the desert. I could hear the racket coming, as I sat on my hillock by the bridge to give the signal to Salem, who danced round the exploder on his knees, crying with excitement, and calling urgently on God to make him fruitful. The Turkish fire sounded heavy, and I wondered with how many men we were going to have affair, and if the mine would be advantage enough for our eighty fellows to equal them. It would have been better if the first electrical experiment had been simpler.

However, at that moment the engines, looking very big, rocked with screaming whistles into view around the bend. Behind them followed ten box-wagons, crowded with rifle-muzzles at the windows and doors; and in little sandbag nests on the roofs Turks precariously held on, to shoot at us. I had not thought of two engines, and on the moment decided to fire the charge under the second, so that however little the mine's effect, the uninjured engine should not be able to uncouple and drag the carriages away.

Accordingly, when the front 'driver' of the second engine was on the bridge, I raised my hand to Salem. There followed a terrific roar, and the line vanished from sight behind a spouting column of black dust and smoke a hundred feet high and wide. Out of the darkness came shattering crashes and long, loud metallic clangings of ripped steel, with many lumps of iron and plate; while one entire wheel of a locomotive whirled up suddenly black out of the cloud against the sky, and sailed musically over our heads to fall slowly and heavily into the desert behind. Except for the flight of these, there succeeded a deathly silence, with no cry of men or rifle-shot, as the now grey mist of the explosion drifted from the line towards us, and over our ridge until it was lost in the hills.

In the lull, I ran southward to join the sergeants. Salem picked up his rifle and charged out into the murk. Before I had climbed to the guns the hollow was alive with shots, and with the brown figures of the Beduin leaping forward to grips with the enemy. I looked round to see what was happening so quickly, and saw the train stationary and dismembered along the track, with its wagon sides jumping under the bullets which riddled them, while Turks were falling out from the far doors to gain the shelter of the railway embankment.

As I watched, our machine guns chattered out over my head, and the long rows of Turks on the carriage roofs rolled over, and were swept off the top like bales of cotton before the furious shower of bullets which stormed along the roofs and splashed clouds of yellow chips from the planking. The dominant position of the guns had been an advantage to us so far.

When I reached Stokes and Lewis, the engagement had taken another turn. The remaining Turks had got behind the bank, here about eleven feet high, and from cover of the wheels were firing point-blank at the Beduin twenty yards away across the sand-filled dip. The enemy in the crescent of the curving line were secure from the machine guns; but Stokes slipped in his first shell, and after a few seconds there came a crash as it burst beyond the train in the desert.

He touched the elevating screw, and his second shot fell just by the trucks in the deep hollow below the bridge where the Turks were taking refuge. It made a shambles of the place. The survivors of the group broke out in a panic across the desert, throwing away their rifles and equipment as they ran. This was the opportunity of the Lewis gunners. The sergeant grimly traversed with drum after drum, till the open sand was littered with bodies. Mushagraf, the Sherari boy behind the second gun, saw the battle over, threw aside his weapon with a yell, and dashed down at speed with his rifle to join the others who were beginning, like wild beasts, to tear open the carriages and fall to plunder. It had taken nearly ten minutes.

I looked up-line through my glasses and saw the Mudowwara patrol breaking back uncertainly towards the railway to meet the train-fugitives running their fastest northward. I looked south, to see our thirty men cantering their camels neck and neck in our direction to share the spoils. The Turks there, seeing them go, began to move after them with infinite precaution, firing volleys. Evidently we had a half-hour respite, and then a double threat against us.

I ran down to the ruins to see what the mine had done. The bridge was gone; and into its gap was fallen the front wagon, which had been filled with sick. The smash had killed all but three or four and had rolled dead and dying into a bleeding heap against the splintered end. One of those yet alive deliriously cried out the word 'Typhus'. So I wedged shut the door, and left them there, alone.

Succeeding wagons were derailed and smashed: some had frames irreparably buckled. The second engine was a blanched pile of smoking iron. Its driving wheels had been blown upward, taking away the side of the fire-box. Cab and tender were twisted into strips, among the piled stones of the bridge abutment. It would never run again. The front engine had got off better: though heavily derailed and lying half-over, with the cab burst, yet its steam was at pressure, and driving-gear intact.

Our greatest object was to destroy locomotives, and I had kept in my arms a box of gun-cotton with fuse and detonator ready fixed, to make sure such a case. I now put them in position on the outside cylinder. On the boiler would have been better, but the sizzling steam made me fear a general explosion which would sweep across my men (swarming like ants over the booty) with a blast of jagged fragments. Yet they would not finish their looting before the Turks came. So I lit the fuse, and in the half-minute of its burning drove the plunderers a little back, with difficulty. Then the charge burst, blowing the cylinder to smithers, and the axle too. At the moment I was distressed with uncertainty whether the damage were enough; but the Turks, later, found the engine beyond use and broke it up.

The valley was a weird sight. The Arabs, gone raving mad, were rushing about at top speed bareheaded and half naked, screaming, shooting into the air, clawing one another nail and fist, while they burst open trucks and staggered back and forward with immense bales, which they ripped by the railside, and tossed through, smashing what they did not want. The train had been packed with refugees and sick men, volunteers for boat-service on the Euphrates, and families of Turkish officers returning to Damascus.

There were scores of carpets spread about; dozens of mattresses and flowered quilts; blankets in heaps, clothes for men and women in full variety; clocks, cooking pots, food, ornaments and weapons. To one side stood thirty or forty hysterical women, unveiled, tearing their clothes and hair; shrieking themselves distracted. The Arabs without regard to them went on wrecking the household goods; looting their absolute fill. Camels had become common property. Each man frantically loaded the nearest with what it could carry and shooed it westward into the void, while he turned to his next fancy.

Seeing me tolerably unemployed, the women rushed, and caught at me with howls for mercy. I assured them that all was going well: but they would not get away till some husbands delivered me. These knocked their wives off and seized my feet in a very agony of terror of instant death. A Turk so broken down was a nasty spectacle: I kicked them off as well as I could with bare feet, and finally broke free.

Next a group of Austrians, officers and non-commissioned officers, appealed to me quietly in Turkish for quarter. I replied with my halting German; whereupon one, in English, begged a doctor for his wounds. We had none: not that it mattered, for he was mortally hurt and dying. I told them the Turks would return in an hour and care for them. But he was dead before that, as were most of the others (instructors in the new Skoda mountain howitzers supplied to Turkey for the Hejaz war), because some dispute broke out between them and my own bodyguard, and one of them fired a pistol shot at young Rahail. My infuriated men cut them down, all but two or three, before I could return to interfere.

So far as could be seen in the excitement, our side had suffered no loss. Among the ninety military prisoners were five Egyptian soldiers, in their underclothes. They knew me, and explained that in a night raid of Davenport's, near Wadi Ais, they had been cut off by the Turks and captured. They told me something of Davenport's work: of his continual pegging away in Abdulla's sector, which was kept alive by him for month after month, without any of the encouragement lent to us by success and local enthusiasm. His best helpers were such stolid infantrymen as these, whom I made lead the prisoners away to our appointed rallying place at the salt rocks.

T. E. Lawrence, *Seven Pillars of Wisdom*

The Sandbag

Now the uses of the sandbag are peculiar and diverse;
From the making of a mountain to the patching of a purse;
But in order to do homage to the things that it can do
Some uses of the sandbag I will briefly sing to you.
Well, of course, you get behind it when the bullets first appear,
And by shortening your trajectory it may lengthen your career,
While, if you are a gunner, you will find it rarely fail
To help you shoot with certainty, when placed beneath the trail.
Next, should you be a horseman and your nosebag go astray,
A sandbag (if a broad one) will contain the corn and hay;
And as for picketing, if there's no other way to do it,
Fill a sandbag, dig it in a bit, and tie your headrope to it.
Suppose you're on the desert and your *topee* comes to grief,
Gets trodden on by horses, or is collared by a thief,
Then, to save yourself appearing in the weekly lists as 'dead',
Take the sandbag from the saddle and dispose it round your head.
Mess secretaries, if they be full of cunning and address,
Will employ the sandbag lavishly in furnishing the Mess,
Such little things as sofas and (uneasy) easy chairs
Are simple of construction with sandbags placed in layers,
While a comfortable pathway from the tent of the C.O.
Is made by laying sandbags on the desert in a row.
Your unit wants a letter-box – procure a post and nail
And hang a sandbag on it to accommodate the mail;
Precisely similar concerns, if scattered here and there,
Will prevent stray tins and garbage from appearing everywhere,
Thus improving at a single stroke the aspect of the place
And the language of the Colonel (which is sometimes a disgrace).
Now it often may occur when you're on service in the field
That you travel in a cattle-truck (whose contours do not yield),
So if you've any sentiments *re:* sitting down next day
You will take upon such voyages a sandbag full of hay.
In private use the sandbag does much miscellaneous duty,
Props your pole, keeps down your tentpegs – and if England, Home and Beauty
Deigns to scribble you a letter, and that Ariel of war,
The Postal Service, gives it up – say in a month or more –
And (such a thing does happen) by some curious mishap
You cannot answer it at once, why, then the little chap
(The sandbag, understand, I mean, and not the precious letter)

Will make a writing-table drawer – and none will make it better.
Moreover, if you want a mat, a tablecloth, or rug,
A dirty-clothes-bag, or, maybe, your tent needs making snug,
If you are hard up for a stand to put your basin on,
Why, take a sandbag (or a few) – your difficulty's gone!
Indeed if I survive this war, whatever track I hit
I'll see to it a sandbag shall be found among my kit;
And when I go to Heaven, where, from what the prophet sings,
The furniture is scanty and the clothing mostly wings,
I shall bring my little sandbag and, if such a thing's allowed,
Put it down to keep the damp out when I'm sitting on a cloud;
Or if by any accident I take the downward turning
(Like the girl in the Cinema), and 'the question becomes burning',
Then in Hades with my sandbag (full of sand) I will appear,
And set it on the coolest coal that happens to be near.

Eliot Crawshay-Williams

War at Sea

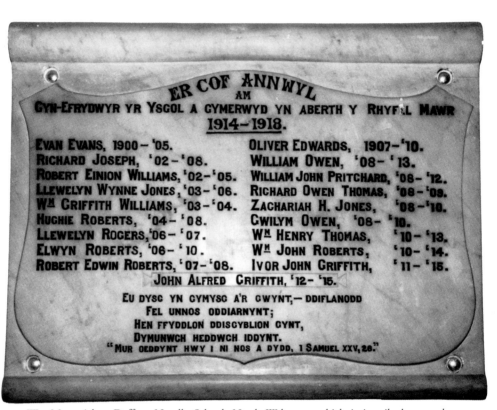

ER COF ANNWYL
AM
GYN-EFRYDWYR YR YSGOL A GYMERWYD YN ABERTH Y RHYFEL MAWR
1914-1918.

EVAN EVANS, 1900 – '05.	OLIVER EDWARDS, 1907 – '10.
RICHARD JOSEPH, '02 – '08.	WILLIAM OWEN, '08 – '13.
ROBERT EINION WILLIAMS, '02 – '05.	WILLIAM JOHN PRITCHARD, '08 – '12.
LLEWELYN WYNNE JONES, '03 – '06.	RICHARD OWEN THOMAS, '08 – '09.
Wᴹ GRIFFITH WILLIAMS, '03 – '04.	ZACHARIAH H. JONES, '08 – '10.
HUGHIE ROBERTS, '04 – '08.	GWILYM OWEN, '08 – '10.
LLEWELYN ROGERS, '06 – '07.	Wᴹ HENRY THOMAS, '10 – '13.
ELWYN ROBERTS, '06 – '10.	Wᴹ JOHN ROBERTS, '10 – '14.
ROBERT EDWIN ROBERTS, '07 – '08.	IVOR JOHN GRIFFITH, '11 – '15.

JOHN ALFRED GRIFFITH, '12 – '15.

EU DYSG YN GYMYSG A'R GWYNT, — DDIFLANODD
FEL UNNOS ODDIARNYNT;
HEN FFYDDLON DDISGYBLION GYNT,
DYMUNWCH HEDDWCH IDDYNT.
"MUR OEDDYNT HWY I NI NOS A DYDD, 1 SAMUEL XXV, 26."

War Memorial at Dyffryn Nantlle School, North Wales, on which is inscribed an *englyn* to commemorate former pupils of the school who fell in the Great War

Torpedo Fear
Somewhere off the Coast of Portugal, February 15, 1916

We move sedately on in the midst of a great blue plate of rippling water. The sun plays down with a warmth which begins to be of the South. Long slow-moving mounds of water, a hundred yards apart and as high as a good sandhill, come inexorably after us, overtake us, and pass on ahead. A cloud of gulls hovers incessantly over the stern and in our wake. The sky is blue above, with an edge of faint clouds round the far circle of the horizon. There is just a gentle breeze, warm and mellow. A soft tranquillity pervades everything, and we should be thoroughly complacent were it not for the lurking, drone-like thought which cannot help but lie at the bottom of every mind. For it is an unpleasant fact that the better the weather is for us the better it also is for the submarine. Up in a sort of crow's nest a native is always watching. A ship's officer, too, on the bridge has his eyes skinned. Various military persons, officers and others, are also supposed to be assisting in spotting any twinkle or ripple of a periscope. But I am told that it is practically unheard of for a stationary submerged submarine to be detected. There is only a shaft like a walking stick, perhaps the momentary glitter of the sun on metal (it might be a wave), and then, when you have gone well by the waiting monster (so that you cannot ram her), the quick rush of a torpedo going fifty miles an hour, thirty seconds suspense, and then down in four minutes (average). The hole in the ship's hull is about 20 by 30 feet, I hear.

That is when they wait for you; they see you afar off, and unostentatiously creep to a point near which you will pass. When you sink, there is really no time for boats (and even if there were, we have only boats for one-third of our crew and passengers). So, unless some boat is in sight that's all. And, supposing there be a boat in sight, maybe they will have to consider the risk to their own safety in coming to pick you up. So it can scarcely be wondered at if that uncomfortable uncertainty prowls about at the back of everyone's mind, even on such a sunny day as this.

I wouldn't write like this if I did not know that by the time ('if and when', in fact) you get this we all shall be past the danger. And if you don't get it – well, then it doesn't matter, either.

Eliot Crawshay-Williams, *Leaves from an Officer's Notebook*

The Sinking of the HMS Tara

We were making for Sollum, an Egyptian port on the border of Egypt and Tripoli. The ship was torpedoed on the starboard side of the engine at about 10.10am in the morning and sank about seven minutes later. Three boats managed to get clear of the ship, and 93 out of 104 ship's crew were landed by the German submarine U.35 at Port Sulieman, a creek about 20 miles to the westward of Sullom. The torpedo was reported by the look-out man in the crow's nest, who saw it coming towards [the ship]. The helm was put over but as the ship was only travelling seven-and-a-half knots per hour she refused to answer her helm, as the torpedo struck the ship on starboard side, probably disabling the starboard engine and dynamo, also killing the hands in the engine room at the time, also three men who were in their cabins about the engine room. One of the ship's lifeboats on top deck was blown away with the explosion. The submarine was seen some distance away, and nine rounds were fired at her, but all missed the target. I was in bed when the accident occurred, and got out on deck when I heard the report of the gun, so I got to the starboard side, but couldn't see a soul there, so came [to] the port side and saw two lifeboats clear of the ship, and the small boat in the water, getting ready to get clear, so I managed to get aboard of her, before [she] left, but when we were clear of the ship, we found that we had no oars in the boat, and the plug was out of her . . .

We then got some oars from the other boats, and then proceeded to rescue one of the firemen who had fallen overboard. We were able to see [the] ship, sinking, she went down by the stern, about 8 miles from the shore. After the ship disappeared, the submarine appeared on surface a few minutes later, and trained his gun on us, and went right through the wreckage, but never attempted to pick anyone out of the water, leaving that to us in the boats to do. He was now flying the German flag, and when he saw that we were all in the boats, he made some of us get on deck of the submarine, so [as] to lighten the boats, and started [to] tow [them] towards Tripoli. A good look-out was kept by them all the time until we were nearing the shore. He let go the three boats that he was towing and told them to stop there. Then he took the German flag down and hoisted the Turkish flag and proceeded up the creek, and made arrange[ments] with the Turkish authority there to take us and make us prisoners. We were given water and biscuits [by] the crew of the submarine, and one of the men [who] was naked was given an old overhaul pants. We were met by the Turkish officers and several Senussi soldiers, who looked very savage, and probably we would have been killed there only for Nouri Pasha and his officers.

Jackson the cook was found dead in the sea, and was picked up by one of the boats, and brought with us ashore. We were left sitting on the rocks for some hours, as they hadn't decided where to put us, and at about 5pm we were told to walk some little distance up the beach. Here we dug the grave for the cook as best as we could, and [he] was buried there that evening, Captain Tanner saying as much of the burial service [as he] could. We then cover[ed] him, and formed a cross over him with one of the oars of the boat. After we had found who was missing we were told to do the best of it for the night, but later on two rotten tents arrived, and we manage[d] to get into them, huddled together. We received a goat that night which was killed, and roasted whole, also some water and one hard biscuit each.

David John Davies, engineer on the HMS *Tara*,
War Diary, entry for November 5, 1915;
diary kept at Anglesey County Record Office

Death of a Crew Member

November 13. Great hopes of early release, but we are all disappointed. A new Officer, a German named Osman Bey, arrived. He told us to make a list [of] six months' provisions from Alexandria. I don't [know] whether these stores were sent or not, but we didn't receive any of them. Wm Thomas quarter-master['s] leg taken off by a pair of ordinary scissors, promised to remove him to hospital at Alexandria on the following day, but he died at 11.30pm.

November 14 *Sunday*. We buried Wm. Thomas at 8.30 in the morning. The burial service was held by Capt. Tanner, and the hymn sung was 'I pitch my tent a day's march nearer home'. Everybody sad and weeping. English and Welsh hymns sung in the evening by the whole crew, everybody feeling very lonely and quiet.

Diary of David John Davies, entries for November 13/14, 1915

Tortured by Arabs

Terrible ordeal of Welsh Sailors

The crew of the *Tara*, who were rescued from the Senussi Arabs by the Duke of Westminster, were all Holyhead men. Previous to undertaking naval patrol duty they manned the *Hibernia* on the Holyhead-Dublin route.

Within the past few days the surviving members of the *Tara*'s crew have arrived in England, and are now in hospital recovering from the effects of the exposure and hardships they underwent whilst in the hands of the Arabs.

Interviewed on Sunday by a *Western Mail* reporter, they said:– 'Our ship was torpedoed by a submarine on the morning of Guy Fawkes' Day. The weapon struck the *Tara* by her engine room and killed the eleven men who were there, though all the others below managed to escape. So badly was the ship hurt that she began to settle very quickly, and sank in about six minutes.

'Some of us jumped into the sea, others took to the boats, which had been smartly lowered, and the latter picked up the men who were swimming. Some of these were quite exhausted, and the ship's cook died in the boat.'

In Hands of Arabs

'After she had sunk the *Tara*, the submarine came and towed us to land at the entrance to a sort of ravine, where a party of Senussi Arabs who were waiting made us prisoners. Although many of us were wet through and it was bitingly cold, the Arabs gave us no fresh clothing, but left us to sleep on the ground in the open air throughout the night, and we were chilled to the marrow.

'The Arabs gave us one small goat to divide amongst the 92 of us. It was all the meat we had from them. Afterwards our food consisted of about a handful of rice per man per day. After a day or two we were moved into the interior and partly lodged in some appallingly dirty caves in the rock. Those of us who could not get into these were forced to sleep in the open all night without any covering beyond the scanty clothing we had left the ship in. One of our men had broken a leg, and for days suffered great pain. At last a Turkish surgeon who was with our captors amputated the broken leg with a pair of scissors, giving the patient nothing to ease the pain, and the poor fellow died soon after this primitive operation had been performed upon him.

Twelve Days' March

'Leaving our cave dwellings, the Arabs marched us for twelve days and nights through the desert, giving us only a little rice and hardly any water, until we were almost dropping from exhaustion. We were promised a good Christmas, but got nothing except some snails and green stuff.

'By this time dysentery had broken out amongst us, and we suffered from it so terribly that four of our party died. Worse still, we were starving, our rice ration, always absurdly insufficient, having been reduced to almost nothing. Some of us were beaten with thonged whips because we could not understand what the Arabs said to us.

'Between starvation, ill-treatment, and continual exposure to the cold without sufficient clothing, we were almost at the end of our endurance when rescue came. The arrival of the duke's motor-car party was quite a surprise. It came in the afternoon of St Patrick's Day, and we were so worn out that we broke down and cried for joy.'

Arrival at Holyhead

Members of the Crew Get a Royal Welcome

Scenes of extraordinary enthusiasm were witnessed at Holyhead on Sunday night, on the occasion of the arrival home of nine officers and forty members of the crew of the *Tara*.

Thousands of people had gathered in and around the railway station and the men made their appearance to the accompaniment of frantic cheering.

As the train steamed in, a choir assembled on the platform sang Welsh hymns and patriotic airs, but the effect of the music was lost in the tumultuous cheering which rent the air.

The men seemed dazed at the greatness of the welcome extended to them.

Western Mail, April 24, 1916

A Lusitania Survivor

I unhooked my skirt so that it should come straight off and not impede me in the water. The list on the ship soon got worse again, and, indeed, became very bad. Presently the doctor said he thought we had better jump into the sea. I followed him, feeling frightened at the idea of jumping so far (it was, I believe, some sixty feet normally from 'A' deck to the sea), and telling myself how ridiculous I was to have physical fear of the jump when we stood in such grave danger as we did. I think others must have had the same fear, for a little crowd stood hesitating on the brink and kept me back. And then, suddenly, I saw that the water had come over on to the deck. We were not, as I had thought, sixty feet above the sea; we were already under the sea. I saw the water green just about up to my knees. I do not remember its coming up further; that must all have happened in a second. The ship sank and I was sucked right down with her.

The next thing I can remember was being deep down under the water. It was very dark, nearly black. I fought to come up. I was terrified of being caught on some part of the ship and kept down. That was the worst moment of terror, the only moment of acute terror, that I knew. My wrist did catch on a rope. I was scarcely aware of it at the time, but I have the mark on me to this day. At first I swallowed a lot of water; then I remembered that I had read that one should not swallow water, so I shut my mouth. Something bothered me in my right hand and prevented me striking out with it; I discovered that it was the lifebelt I had been holding for my father. As I reached the surface I grasped a little bit of board, quite thin, a few inches wide and perhaps two or three feet long. I thought this was keeping me afloat. I was wrong. My most excellent lifebelt was doing that. But everything that happened after I had been submerged was a little misty and vague; I was slightly stupefied from then on.

When I came to the surface I found that I formed part of a large, round, floating island composed of people and débris of all sorts, lying so close together that at first there was not very much water noticeable in between. People, boats, hencoops, chairs, rafts, boards and goodness knows what besides, all floating cheek by jowl. A man with a white face and yellow moustache came and held on to the other end of my board. I did not quite like it, for I felt it was not large enough for two, but I did not feel justified in objecting. Every now and again he would try and move round towards my end of the board. This frightened me; I scarcely knew why at the time (I was probably quite right to be frightened; it is likely enough that he wanted to hold on to me). I summoned up my strength – to speak was an effort – and told him to go back to his own end, so that we might keep the board properly balanced. He said nothing and just meekly went back. After a while I noticed that he had disappeared.

Margaret Haig Thomas, *This Was My World* (1933)

The Fallen

'Going West'
(Army euphemism for dying)

I've seen the graves among the trees that used to shade Le Gheer,
The cemeteries that lie around the billets in the rear,
The little mounds beside the trench, the cross upon the wall,
The corpses out in No Man's Land (they lie there as they fall).

The bodies keep the Flanders clay, the chalk pits of the South;
The eyes are closed with heavy earth, there's dust upon the mouth;
The poppies flame above them, but they do not heed the dance
Of English flowers that cover them upon the fields of France.

At night I stare out in the dusk, until I'm almost blind,
And shadows steal along the trench, and fill my empty mind.
With murmuring ghosts who haunt it till the visions disappear,
Of lads who lie in Flanders, but whose hearts are far from here.

A wind blows from the East at dawn, the sunrise holds the sky,
We stand to arms so silently we hear the souls go by.
They fill the air, and clamour past upon the Western breeze;
They shake the branches as they pass, and ruffle up the seas.

The moor and mountain call to them, they know their ancient rocks,
The green fields of the valley lands are rich for them with flocks.
They'll make the sunlight warm for us, and meet us in the rain,
'Gone West' in many an alien land, they all come west again.

Oscar Lloyd

Spring Offensive

Halted against the shade of a last hill,
They fed, and eased of pack-loads, were at ease;
And leaning on the nearest chest or knees
Carelessly slept.
                    But many there stood still
To face the stark, blank sky beyond the ridge,
Knowing their feet had come to the end of the world.
Marvelling they stood, and watched the long grass swirled
By the May breeze, murmurous with wasp and midge;
For though the summer oozed into their veins
Like an injected drug for their bodies' pains,
Sharp on their souls hung the imminent ridge of grass,
Fearfully flashed the sky's mysterious glass.

Hour after hour they ponder the warm field
And the far valley behind where the buttercups
Had blessed with gold their slow boots coming up,
Where even the little brambles would not yield,
But clutched and clung to them like sorrowing arms;
[All that strange day] they breathe like trees unstirred,

Till like a cold gust thrills the little word
At which each body and its soul begird
And tighten them for battle. No alarms
Of bugles, no high flags, no clamorous haste –
Only a lift and flare of eyes that faced
The sun, like a friend with whom their love is done.
O larger shone that smile against the sun –
Mightier than his whose bounty these have spurned.

So, soon they topped the hill, and raced together
Over an open stretch of herb and heather
Exposed. And instantly the whole sky burned
With fury against them; earth set sudden cups
In thousands for their blood; and the green slope
Chasmed and steepened sheer to infinite space.

Of them who running on that last high place
Breasted even the rapture of bullets, or went up
On the hot blast and fury of hell's upsurge,
Or plunged and fell away past this world's verge,
Some say God caught them even before they fell.

But what say such as from existence's brink
Ventured but drave too swift to sink,
The few who rushed in the body to enter hell,
And there out-fiending all its fiends and flames
With superhuman inhumanities,
Long-famous glories, immemorial shames –
And crawling slowly back, have by degrees
Regained cool peaceful air in wonder –
Why speak they not of comrades that went under?

Wilfred Owen

To R. J. Ford
May 9, 1915

What had he not beheld? Far Texas plains;
The Afric veldt; and where the mango tree
And palm bend under weight of tropic rains;
The burning suns of India; every sea
That rolls between the continents – all these
He knew and trod: and then those steadfast eyes
Which faced a score of battles unafraid
Saw, through the sudden mist, God's Paradise:
And seeing it he entered, as he prayed.

J. L. P.

Late Captain Ford
Touching Tribute at Cardiff Memorial Service

A service was held at St Margaret's Church, Roath, Cardiff, on Tuesday, in memory of Captain Richard Jellard Ford, of the 2nd Worcester Regiment, who fell in action in Flanders on May 9. Captain Ford, who was the younger son of the late Alderman Thomas Ford, a former mayor of Swansea, and brother of Major Ford, of Swansea, married the eldest daughter of Mr. P. H. Coward, of Cardiff.

A large gathering of relatives and friends attended the service, which was conducted by Canon Beck. On the altar steps a cross was laid bearing the following inscription: 'In memory of a gallant officer from a sincere friend.' At the entrance of the chancel a cross of laurels and two laurel wreaths from relatives and friends were placed.

In an impressive sermon Canon Beck referred to prayer as one of the most powerful weapons of the spiritual kingdom. Had we during the course of this appalling war used this mighty weapon as we ought? If only Christian people had prayed as we ought, how many of those horrors of war, which to some of us were an abiding nightmare, might have been spared us? How much nearer might peace at that moment be . . . Deliberately he offered his life in the service of King and country, and there they got the great redeeming feature of war, the one bright beam of light which transformed and transfigured all the darkness. It was the eager, willing spirit of self-sacrifice even unto death. What a glorious ending to this life – to die for others! And this eager spirit of self-sacrifice in the case of Captain Ford was enriched by a splendid courage, for was he not the possessor of that coveted decoration, the Military Cross? Yet, this brave officer, this distinguished soldier, was not ashamed to own himself a Christian worshipper – it seemed but yesterday that he was worshipping in that very church.

Western Mail, May 19, 1915

A. R. P.
(Killed in action, July 21, 1917)

Bright-eyed, I knew him, great with youth;
Intrepid, sanguine, going on
To days when mine should all be done.
This day, I'm told the bitter truth,
Yet cannot think it, first or last,
That he has fallen while we march
Toward the morning's open arch.
Rather let us believe he passed
Into that deathless firmament
Beyond our day and cloudy skies,
Where youth and age are well content,
And morning light, and young men's eyes
Resume the thoughts we read in his:
High hopes, mysterious happiness.

Ernest Rhys

A Private

This ploughman dead in battle slept out of doors
Many a frozen night, and merrily
Answered staid drinkers, good bedmen, and all bores:
'At Mrs Greenland's Hawthorn Bush,' said he,
'I slept.' None knew which bush. Above the town,
Beyond 'The Drover', a hundred spot the down
In Wiltshire. And where now at last he sleeps
More sound in France – that, too, he secret keeps.

Edward Thomas

Dead Man's Joy

What if the Spirit should
Lie prisoned in the loam
Oppressed by weight of stones and earth
In its last home?

They bury deep in England;
They bury light in France.
I would be buried where my bones
Would shiver to a fairy's dance.

So that the green sod turning,
Some jolly farmer's boy
Might find my bones a-ploughing
And shout for very joy.

And I, my spirit free,
Would wander back to England;
So bury me light in France:
They bury too deep in England.

Hywel Davies

My other friend is Captain Graves, our present Commanding Officer. He is better known perhaps as 'Robert Graves', poet and as (also genial), author of 'Fairies and Fusileers', a book of poems recently published by Heinemann. He is Irish, but living at Harlech, and serving in a Welsh regiment, of which he is very proud, he makes far more use of Welsh 'material' than of the Irish. He scatters his oaths profusely, and has, to my opinion, a peculiar 'Georgian' genius which will certainly bear fruit. He is twenty-three years of age, has lost one lung in France, and recites his poetry with a sort of half-gasp which is very effective. He has really written some good things, and those which are unprinted (one too obscene to be printable as yet) are better still.

Hywel Davies, letter to Ivor Lewis, 20 November, 1918;
letter kept at the National Library of Wales, Aberystwyth

My Captain

I have not grieved, though he be dead.
Bending over him in death
Something he gave me as he fled –
Something from his dying breath
That lingers with me still:
A firmer faith, a more enduring creed,
A resignation to the greater need,
The larger will.
And dead, not to me lost
So utterly. The slow dawn wakes;
A hundred broken lights are tossed
From dewy grass, and trees, and far lakes.
And from the great heart's cove there breaks
A thought, intuitive and dim,
That he is of all things, all things of him.

I have not grieved, though he be dead,
For dying, he hath purged my fear.
Content to follow where he led,
I tremble not – he stands so near.

Hywel Davies

In Memoriam*

His sacrifice was not in vain, his face
    In our minds will remain,
    Although he left a bloodstain
    On Germany's iron fist of pain.

Hedd Wyn
(Translated from the Welsh)

* The original poem is in traditional 'englyn' form

213

The Fallen

Cold, still and stark –
A temple with its sacred lights gone dark,
A mansion whence the dweller hath ta'en flight
Into unknown, mysterious, pathless night –
He lies; a hero fallen for the cause that *he*
    Believed was right.

If khaki-clad or grey,
Ask not. 'He fell' is all we need to say.
His comrades who passed on and left him there
Could only breathe one brief goodbye. No care
Could they bestow on him who fell. To fall
    Was his sole share.

And on the hill
He fell, there yet he lies, cold, stark and still –
    But in the night
When all was calm, and silent stars shone bright,
Methought I saw a figure by his side –
A mother's figure, who shed tears and sighed.
But mother's sighs and tears could not into
    Those eyes bring light.

Can all that War,
Or Peace, may bring, bring back to her
A recompense that will tenth-part outweigh
Her burning tears, her sorrow night and day?
What gains can fill her emptiness, or charm
    Her grief away?

Vain powers on high,
The while ye talk and argue, heroes die!

Harry W. Jones

The Funeral

Tonight, we buried him with many others
In distant France, whose alien soil now smothers
His face; here he will lie forever, under
The branches of her vinetrees, and the thunder
Of guns no longer will disturb his peace,
He'll hear no more the rustling of the breeze.
Soon by his grave, the primrose's yellow flower
Will show that love defeats all might and power;
Soon from the trenches buttercups will come;
Where bullets whistled once, the bees will hum.
Lovers will walk through fields that once were red,
The lark will sing where shells wailed overhead.
Where poison gas once lingered on the breeze
Flowers will fill with fragrance fields of peace.
Where shrapnel once rained down in scattered showers
Only the hail of May will beat on flowers.
The sharp-edged bayonet buried deep in clay
Will pose no threat to children as they play.
Only the blue forget-me-nots will tell
Tomorrow of the trenches and their hell:
And yet, though nature will her scars conceal,
The scar within my heart will never heal.

I stood at night to watch his resting place,
The night of Victory, the night of peace,
Asking so many questions, but my sad words
Were stolen by the wind, and went unheard.

A. E. Jones (Cynan)
(Translated from the Welsh)

K.G.H.F. Killed in Action

Les hommes sont tous condamnés à mort avec des sursis indéfinis.

Victor Hugo

He is coming back from Furlough,
    From sunlight fields of Leave,
For his wandering hours are ended
    (The time of his reprieve).

He has put by life and its Mufti,
    Forsaken civil ways
That some of us follow for beauty
    And some of us for praise.

There is oil on the bolt of his rifle,
    Buttons are burnished bright,
And the glint of the brasswork pierces
    The gloom of nearing night.

Far-heard is the sentry's challenge,
    And brief the words he speaks,
For the password's easy of finding
    To the Billet which he seeks.

He will come to the grim old Guardroom,
    Approach with steady breath,
And hand his pass to the Sergeant
    Who guards the gates of Death.

He'll march right in to Attention,
    Buoyant and unafraid;
Fall in, when the bugle calls him
    To the ultimate Parade.

Oscar Lloyd

Behind the Trenches at Festubert

A straggling burial ground, unfenced, unmown,
　　Unconsecrated save by those who sleep
In scattered rows or casual graves alone –
　　Such careless rendezvous with Death they keep!

Their name and deed a simple cross records
　　That shows its shadow on each bare, rough mound;
And e'en to some its deathless rite affords
　　Who *nameless* lie in this lone, foreign ground.

But, like the fancy of some 'uncouth rhyme'
　　Show *here* the touch of some old comrade's hand:
Or that quaint custom which, in olden time,
　　Left with the warrior dead his shield and brand:

For on two crosses nigh the trenches' track
　　Hang the Glengarry caps of two who fell
In the grim strife of three long summers back,
　　And won the honour which these crosses spell.

They hang awry and limp – shorn of the pride
　　That matched the spirits proud and debonair,
Just for remembrance left of those who died –
　　And a new green doth hide the tartan fair.

*　　　　*　　　　*

And Fancy pictures some wild Highland glen
　　With two thatched cots beside a singing burn
Where two boys to the stature grew of men
　　And from one dawn's red maze did not return.

Private Alfred Jenkins

Goliath and David*
(For D.C.T., killed at Fricourt, March 1916)

Once an earlier David took
Smooth pebbles from the brook;
Out between the lines he went
To that one-sided tournament,
A shepherd boy who stood out fine
And young to fight a Philistine
Clad all in brazen mail. He swears
That he's killed lions, he's killed bears,
And those that scorn the God of Zion
Shall perish so like bear and lion.
But . . . the historian of that fight
Had not the heart to tell it right.

Striding within javelin range
Goliath marvels at this strange
Goodly-faced boy so proud of strength.
David's clear eye measures the length;
With hand thrust back, he cramps one knee,
Poises a moment thoughtfully,
And hurls with a long vengeful swing.
The pebble, humming from the sling
Like a wild bee, flies a sure line
For the forehead of the Philistine;
Then . . . but there comes a brazen clink
And quicker than a man can think
Goliath's shield parries each cast.

* 'D.C.T.' was David Cuthbert Thomas, the son of a clergyman from the rural parish of Llanedi in Carmarthenshire. He was educated at Christ's College, Brecon. He joined the 1st Royal Welsh Fusiliers at the age of twenty, and became one of Siegfried Sassoon's closest and most intimate friends; it has been suggested that Sassoon was physically attracted to him. David Thomas is portrayed as 'Dick Tiltwood' in Sassoon's *Memoirs of a Fox-hunting Man*. Out working with a wiring-party on the evening of March 18, 1916, he was wounded in the throat by a stray bullet, and died a few hours later. Sassoon reacted to Thomas's death with overwhelming grief and profound anger. His death stimulated Sassoon to write his best war poems. David Cuthbert Thomas is 'Soldier David' in Sassoon's poem, 'A Letter Home', and another poem by Sassoon, 'The Last Meeting', was also written in memory of his friend.

Clang! clang! and clang! was David's last
Scorn blazes in the Giant's eye,
Towering unhurt six cubits high.
Says foolish David, 'Damn your shield!
And damn my sling! but I'll not yield.'

He takes his staff of Mamre oak,
A knotted shepherd-staff that's broke
The skull of many a wolf and fox
Come filching lambs from Jesse's flocks.
Loud laughs Goliath, and that laugh
Can scatter chariots like blown chaff
To rout: but, David, calm and brave,
Holds his ground, for God will save.
Steel crosses wood, a flash, and oh!
Shame for Beauty's overthrow!
(God's eyes are dim, His ears are shut.)
One cruel backhand sabre cut –
'I'm hit! I'm killed!' young David cries,
Throws blindly forward, chokes . . . and dies.
And look, spike-helmeted, grey, grim,
Goliath straddles over him.

Robert Graves

Killed in Action
(Edward Thomas)

Happy the man whose home is still
   In Nature's green and peaceful ways;
To wake and hear the birds so loud,
   That scream for joy to see the sun
Is shouldering past a sullen cloud.

And we have known those days, when we
   Would wait to hear the cuckoo first;
When you and I, with thoughtful mind,
   Would help a bird to hide her nest,
For fear of other hands less kind.

But thou, my friend, art lying dead:
   War, with its hell-born childishness,
Has claimed thy life, with many more:
   The man that loved this England well,
And never left it once before.

W. H. Davies

To S. A.

I loved you, so I drew these tides of men into my hands
            and wrote my will across the sky in stars
To earn you Freedom, the seven-pillared worthy house,
               that your eyes might be shining for me

                             When we came.

Death seemed my servant on the road, till we were near
                     and saw you waiting:
When you smiled, and in sorrowful envy he outran me
                    and took you apart:
                         Into his quietness.

Love, the way-weary, groped to your body, our brief wage
                     ours for the moment
Before earth's soft hand explored your shape, and the blind
                 worms grew fat upon
                         Your substance.

Men prayed me that I set our work, the inviolate house,
                  as a memory of you.
But for fit monument I shattered it, unfinished: and now
The little things creep out to patch themselves hovels
                     in the marred shadow
                     Of your gift.

                             T. E. Lawrence

To One Who Fell in Early Youth

'And so,' they say, 'think of his merry ways,
His laughing eyes that never filled with tears,
Though fired with passion, never drooped with fears;
The memory of his smiles for ever stays.'
They know not how he loved the long warm Mays,
And talked of joys to come along the years,
As we together walked beside the meres.
'Tis I who know the love of those long days!
Though June is here, for me the days are sad;
So frail and fair a life he gave away,
Who freely gave, and joined the Great Array.
And now I sit and look with vacant stare,
And think of long warm Mays and joys we had;
All these to me are now but comfort bare.

'M. J. L.'

Lost in France: Jo's Requiem

He had the ploughman's strength
in the grasp of his hand.
He could see a crow
three miles away,
and the trout beneath the stone.
He could hear the green oats growing,
and the south-west wind make rain.
He could hear the wheel upon the hill
when it left the level road.
He could make a gate, and dig a pit,
And plough as straight as stone can fall.
And he is dead.

Ernest Rhys

A Legend of Ypres

Before the throne the spirits of the slain
    With a loud voice importunately cried,
    'O Lord of Hosts, whose name be glorified,
Scarce may the line one onslaught more sustain
Wanting our help. Let it not be in vain,
    Not all in vain, O God, that we have died.'
    And smiling on them our good Lord replied,
'Begone then, foolish ones, and fight again.'

Our eyes were holden, that we saw them not;
    Disheartened foes beheld – our prisoners said –
Behind us massed, a mighty host indeed,
Where no host was. On comrades unforgot
    We thought, and knew that all those valiant dead
Forwent their rest to save us at our need.

Elinor Jenkins

The Unknown Grave

Wait here, and see this grave marked with a cross
    Carved crudely without either craft or care
    From an old wooden box. Stars nightly stare
On hundreds such, which emphasise our loss.
Whoever here lies, his soul did soar,
    Encircled by a light of pure love,
    Back to the One who gave that soul, above
The malice of an age made mad by war.

Here, perhaps, was buried at close of day
    The heart of an English mother, or the lapse
    Of faith of a lass from Anglesey, perhaps;
And if it was a German (who can say?),
The cloth of blood erases from the slate
Of history every outrage. Stand and wait.

A. E. Jones (Cynan)
(Translated from the Welsh)

In Memoriam

(R. G. Popkin, killed in action, September 27, 1918)

You loved the sunshine and a cloudless sky,
The light and gladness of a summer day;
You knew no winter, but it seemed your way
Would ever through the lands of summer lie
Where faith is strong, and hope can never die.
Men meeting you would smile, and passing say
'Who cares for storms, what if the skies be grey?
We caught his laughter as we passed him by.'

Now night has come for me and never more
We'll watch a golden sunset from the shore
Or tramp the heath and hear the curlews' cries.
You live in summer still, for you have won
The glory of a never setting sun,
The beauty of eternal, cloudless skies.

E. Williams-David

Died on Active Service

Along a hard and stony track
    On a bright day in June,
With forward eyes and aching back
He marched beneath a heavy pack
    To a thin mouth-organ tune.

While other men contrived to fling
    Their packs, unseen, away,
He would not cast a single thing
But called upon his mates to sing,
    While he contrived to play.

They felt the better for the tune,
    It forced their feet along,
And on that blazing day in June
He marched from early morn till noon;
    They thought him tough and strong.

The music ceased, the player swayed,
    They lifted him aside.
With others quitting he had stayed,
While others faltered he had played,
    And in his tracks had died.

Charles Pritchard Clayton

Longing

(In Memory of W. E. J., a friend and a fellow-chaplain)

Springtime buds along the meadows, hedges flowering white in May;
Thorns concealed by flowers' beauty: still my heart grieves night and day.

August bees are murmuring softly, summer birds sing in the sky:
In my heart the guns of Flanders will still roar until I die.

The scythe reaps the corn of Autumn, branches under apples bend;
When a flower falls prematurely, is God's purpose at an end?

Christmas mirth around the fireplace, children laughing in the glow;
Far away my friend lies under a plain cross in rain and snow.

A. E. Jones (Cynan)
(Translated from the Welsh)

Happy Warriors

Clear came the call; they leapt to arms and died
 As in old days the heroes prayed to do;
Great though our sorrow, greater yet our pride,
 O, gallant hearts, in you.

Surely they sleep content, our valiant dead,
 Fallen untimely in the savage strife;
They have but followed whither duty led,
 To find a fuller life.

Who, then, are we to grudge the bitter price
 Of this, our land, inviolate through the years,
Or mar the splendour of their sacrifice
 That is too high for tears?

God grant we fall not at the test – that when
 We take, mayhap, our places in the fray,
Come life, come death, to quit ourselves like men,
 The peers of such as they.

Arthur Lewis Jenkins

Promising Poet Killed Whilst Flying

On New Year's Day the news reached London that Arthur Lewis Jenkins, the eldest son of the late Sir John Lewis Jenkins, K.C.S.I., some time vice-president of the Indian Viceroy's Council, had been killed in an accident while flying at Ripon, in Yorkshire. So has ended a career full of the most brilliant promise.

Sir John Lewis Jenkins was one of the strong men of the Indian Civil Service. A pure-bred Welshman, the son of the late County Councillor James Jenkins, of Llangadock, Carmarthenshire, he was marked out by birth and early training for dealing in a conciliatory and statesman-like way with 'native problems'. It was he, more than any other one man, who was responsible for the transference of the capital from Calcutta to Delhi. He was cut down suddenly six years ago in the full vigour of his manhood. He was married to a daughter of Sir Arthur Trevor, K.C.S.I., by whom he had seven children, one of whom, Elinor Jenkins, published a successful book of 'poems' last year.

Arthur Jenkins won a scholarship at Marlborough College, of which in due course he became head boy. Later on he took an open classical scholarship at Balliol College, Oxford, and it was his intention, but for the outbreak of war, to enter the Indian Civil Service. Obtaining a commission in September, 1914, he was sent out with his regiment to India, and afterwards to Aden. While there he wrote a charming little poem on 'Arabia', which appeared in 'Punch'. He saw some little service, which he thus commemorated:–

> Sharp rattling fights at peep of day,
>   Machine guns searching scrub and plain,
> Red lances questing for the prey,
>   And shrapnel puffs that melt again:
> Swift shifting stroke and counter-stroke,
>   Advance unhurrying and sure,
> Until the stubborn foeman broke –
>   These are the memories that endure.

From Aden he proceeded to Egypt, where he joined the Flying Corps. A few months ago he came back to this country, and he would have gone to the Western front shortly. Though only 25 years of age, he had already shown great promise of a distinguished career. Tall, handsome, of vigorous frame and remarkable appearance, he was a figure that attracted attention in any assembly . . . Today the young singer lies in Richmond churchyard, and he, too, like the other gallant hearts that have gone before him, has found 'a fuller life'.

Western Mail, January 3, 1918

Hedd Wyn*

I

The sad poet lies under alien soil
    In silence forever;
   His two hands too still to stir,
   Eyes that can see no longer.

Your lifetime is now over, your brief life
    By your flame made brighter;
   Your dust untimely interred,
   Your roving done forever.

The moon shines gently tonight; as it seeps
    Trawsfynydd in moonlight
   You lie still, your eyes closed tight,
   Still by a trench in starlight.

You trod on Trawsfynydd's marshland, on rock
    And bracken and peatland;
   You loved to roam your homeland,
   Now you lie in a foreign land.

II

Brothers, remember in earnest the lad,
    When the moon shines brightest:
   Sadder it was than sadness
   To lay the frail poet to rest.

To send a lad so tender from his hearth,
    From his home, was bitter,
   To have his body interred
   In alien soil was crueller.

Leaving labour and furrow, leaving streams,
    Mountain pastures also;
   Leaving day, leaving meadow,
   Leaving woods where green leaves grow.

* The original poem is in traditional 'englyn' form

Pining for its companion, the Chair waits,
     Alone and forsaken,
     In peace and with compassion
     For one who will never return.

R. Williams Parry
(Translated from the Welsh)

Unveiling ceremony of the Hedd Wyn Memorial, Trawsfynydd, North Wales, August 11, 1923.

R. Williams Parry

The Home Front

Ellis Humphrey Evans (Hedd Wyn) and his sister, Mary

War

Why must I live in this grim age,
    When, to a far horizon, God
Has ebbed away, and man, with rage,
    Now wields the sceptre and the rod?

Man raised his sword, once God had gone,
    To slay his brother, and the roar
Of battlefields now casts upon
    Our homes the shadow of the war.

The harps to which we sang are hung
    On willow boughs, and their refrain
Drowned by the anguish of the young
    Whose blood is mingled with the rain.

Hedd Wyn
(Translated from the Welsh)

In Time of War

As I go walking down the street
Many's the lad and lass I meet;
There's many a soldier I see pass,
And every soldier has his lass.

But when I saw the others there,
The women that black mourning wear,
'Judged by the looks of these,' I said,
'The lads those lassies court are dead.'

W. H. Davies

233

The Cherry Trees

The cherry trees bend over and are shedding,
On the old road where all that passed are dead,
Their petals, strewing the grass as for a wedding
This early May morn when there is none to wed.

Edward Thomas

To Mother

Can I make my feeble art
Show the burning of my heart?
Five-and-twenty years of schooling
Since you bore me, weak and puling,
Every day and every hour
I have battened on your power,
   While you taught of life the whole;
You my Best Beloved and nighest,
You who ever claimed the highest
   Was the one and only goal.
Often weary, often ailing,
Never for a moment failing,
Always cheering, always propping,
Often checking, sometimes stopping,
When the sands of life seemed sliding
You were helping, you were guiding –
   Claimed for me the glorious role;
You my loved one and no other,
You my only lovely Mother,
You the pilot of my soul.

Colwyn Philipps

As the Team's Head-Brass

As the team's head-brass flashed out on the turn
The lovers disappeared into the wood.
I sat among the boughs of the fallen elm
That strewed the angle of the fallow, and
Watched the plough narrowing a yellow square
Of charlock. Every time the horses turned
Instead of treading me down, the ploughman leaned
Upon the handles to say or ask a word,
About the weather, next about the war.
Scraping the share he faced towards the wood,
And screwed along the furrow till the brass flashed
Once more.
    The blizzard felled the elm whose crest
I sat in, by a woodpecker's round hole,
The ploughman said. 'When will they take it away?'
'When the war's over.' So the talk began –
One minute and an interval of ten,
A minute more and the same interval.
'Have you been out?' 'No.' 'And don't want to, perhaps?'
'If I could only come back again, I should.
I could spare an arm. I shouldn't want to lose
A leg. If I should lose my head, why, so,
I should want nothing more . . . Have many gone
From here?' 'Yes.' 'Many lost?' 'Yes, a good few.
Only two teams work on the farm this year.
One of my mates is dead. The second day
In France they killed him. It was back in March,
The very night of the blizzard, too. Now if
He had stayed here we should have moved the tree.'
'And I should not have sat here. Everything
Would have been different. For it would have been
Another world.' 'Ay, and a better, though
If we could see all all might seem good.' Then
The lovers came out of the wood again:
The horses started and for the last time
I watched the clods crumble and topple over
After the ploughshare and the stumbling team.

Edward Thomas

235

Mater Mea

Should I be laid to rest, nameless and deep,
    Beneath the moon, in some far unknown grave,
Wistfully at close of day, my friend would keep
    Alive the memory of his friend, who gave
His life for others. Poets would lament,
    With gentle elegies and sorrowful rhyme,
The death of one whose passion was unspent,
    Whose song was silenced long before its time.
But there is one who could not be consoled
    By her son's glory, weeping, in misery,
All night for those two hands lying still and cold
    On a still bosom, across the storm-tossed sea,
Calling through the gruelling night on the Son of God
And on her own son through a foreign clod.

R. Williams Parry
(Translated from the Welsh)

The Birds of Steel

This apple tree, that once was green,
    Is now a thousand flowers in one!
And, with their bags strapped to their thighs,
    There's many a bee that comes for sweets,
To stretch each bag to its full size.

And when the night has grown a moon,
    And I lie half-asleep in bed,
I hear those bees again – ah no,
    It is the birds of steel instead,
Seeking their innocent prey below.

Man-ridden birds of steel, unseen,
    That come to drop their murdering lime
On any child or harmless thing
    Before the early morning time:
Up, nearer to God, they fly and sing.

W. H. Davies

236

The Lonely Battle of Women

Shortly before eight o'clock in the morning the boat train steamed out of Victoria station, leaving Wyn standing on the platform, one of many women fighting each a lonely battle against a distant peril. Some were to know defeat, others triumph, but none was to escape the rack of doubt and suspense. I cannot tell her tale of that day; the return to an empty room, the quiet packing of a bag, and the cruel sight of other women looking into their husbands' eyes. I saw no beauty in the Kentish orchards that had delighted my eyes but ten days ago, and the flowering hedges were a mockery. If I survived the dangers of war I might once again come home on leave, but many months would have to pass. The 'life' of an infantry officer at the front in those days was very short; it worked out to a mathematical average of a few weeks, fatal or non-fatal wounds came quickly to a junior officer in a line regiment. I had seen many men come and go, and there was little comfort in the prospect before me. There were many officers on the train who were obviously better placed than I – some wonderful difference had raised them to the Staff, but I could see no endowment of mine that could ever serve to take me across the gap that divided the brains of the army from its brawn. My lot was pitched in the mud, and the less I longed for the fleshpots, the better would I be able to eat my bully beef and tinned jam. I had met but few of these higher creatures, nor had I tested their mettle, so that it was easy to hold to a belief that my path would never cross their orbit of revolution round that mysterious centre where war was governed. Thus I thought at the time, but destiny was to take me into their midst and to make me one of them, after a close and painful realising of their human limitations.

Llewelyn Wyn Griffith, *Up to Mametz*

Written in an Album

Some we know tonight are treading
    Europe's fields of mud,
Where the enemy is shedding
    French and British blood.

Others we once knew are sleeping
    Under foreign clay,
Where the breeze is always weeping,
    Weeping night and day.

All life's paths twist and meander
    Like the nightwind's sway;
Where they will lead us to wander
    Only God can say.

Hedd Wyn
(Translated from the Welsh)

In Memoriam (Easter, 1915)

The flowers left thick at nightfall in the wood
This Eastertide call into mind the men,
Now far from home, who, with their sweethearts, should
Have gathered them and will do never again.

Edward Thomas

The Pity of It

When memory of Prussian foulness fails,
    One thing will keep its fame
    Of cruelty and shame –
The strike in Wales.

Eliot Crawshay-Williams

The Black Spot

We have no claim to the stars
    Nor the sad-faced moon of night
Nor the golden cloud that immerses
    Itself in celestial light.

We only have a right to exist
    On earth in its vast devastation,
And it's only man's strife that destroys
    The glory of God's creation.

Hedd Wyn
(Translated from the Welsh)

The Messenger

They fling their gladness high in air,
The mad little woodland throng,
As they seek to mesh the rays of dawn
In their tangled web of song.

They trill till the grove is one shivering joy,
Setting the leaves a-dance;
They cannot have heard of the bitterness
In the moaning trenches of France.

And who will deny them their hour of bliss?
Sing, though the whole world grieves!
Too soon will the cuckoo cross the waves
With the bruised news to the leaves.

Wil Ifan (William Evans)

A Song of the Welsh
St David's Day, 1916

There is a race in an island place that rose in the morning gleam
And made its sword of an olden song, its armour out of a dream:
And its warriors died in a stubborn pride that recked no price of tears,
But followed the call of the singing sword that rang athwart the years.

And the eyes of a nation's hope grew bright, like roses out of the dawn,
But ever the dark of the shadow fell and the twilight came forlorn,
For the feet of the iron legions pressed where Menai sobbed and sighed,
And the Saxons came in a roaring flame, and Arthur swooned and died.

Then rose a host from out of the foam, and a tyrant out of the sea,
And harried the race of the singing sword with the hounds of Normandy,
Till the quarry turned, their arrows burned, and their lances thrust and leapt
At Evesham grey in the bitter day when the soul of Montfort slept.

And the men of the sword went far abroad when France was a blaze of spears,
And the longbow's dirge was a crimson surge at Crécy and Poitiers.
But over a sunless road they trod when Glendower brake his shield,
Till the song of the sword rang loud and clear in the crash of Bosworth Field.

Then, lo! afar, from Corsica the ravening eagles sped,
From the Midland Sea to Muscovy where the trampled snows were red,
And the song of the sword came calling wild, and Picton's henchmen flew
From Badajos through Quatre Bras to the crown of Waterloo.

And now, through the plains that the nations spoil, the new-flung legions came.
Their path was a torrent of broken men, their feet were a scorching flame,
But the men of the sword were linked with Gods and neither spell nor truce
Could stem the spate from the Marne's locked gate to the red, red wrath of Loos.

          *   *   *

Their sword is made of an olden song, their armour out of a dream,
They have seen in the rills of a thousand hills the sword of the lightning gleam.
Their dream is the soul of man unbound from birth to eternity,
And the song of the sword is a sounding chant of the pæan of liberty.

And the land they love and the land they made and the place men know them by
Is a land where a tree is a singing thing and the wind a lullaby,
Where the mists are white in the morning light as a maiden's bridal veil
In a home that is ever the harp of song and legend and fairy tale.

A. G. Prys-Jones

Death of a Son, Death of a Brother

Military Intelligence Office Cairo
4.6.15

I haven't written since I got your wire as I was waiting for details. Today I got father's two letters. They are very comfortable reading:– and I hope that when I die there will be nothing more to regret. The only thing I feel a little is, that there was no need surely to go into mourning for him? I cannot see any cause at all – in any case to die for one's country is a sort of privilege: Mother & you will find it more painful & harder to live for it, than he did to die: but I think that at this time it is one's duty to show no signs that would distress others: and to appear bereaved is surely under this condemnation.

So please, keep a brave face to the world: we cannot all go fighting: but we can do that, which is in the same kind.

Military Intelligence Office Cairo
[Undated]

Poor dear mother,

I got your letter this morning, & it has grieved me very much. You *will* never never understand any of us after we are grown up a little. *Don't* you ever feel that we love you without our telling you so? – I feel such a contemptible worm for having to write this way about things. If you only knew that if one thinks deeply about anything one would rather die than say anything about it. You know men do nearly all die laughing, because they know death is very terrible, & a thing to be forgotten till after it has come.

There, put that aside, & bear a brave face to the world about Frank. In a time of such fearful stress in our country it is one's duty to watch very carefully lest one of the weaker ones be offended: and you know we were always the stronger, & if they see you broken down they will all grow fearful about their ones at the front.

Frank's last letter is a very fine one, & leaves no regret behind it.

Out here we do nothing. There is an official inertia against which one is very powerless. But I don't think we are going to have to wait much longer.

I didn't go to say goodbye to Frank because he would rather I didn't, & I knew there was little chance of my seeing him again; in which case we were better without a parting.

> T. E. Lawrence, letters to his parents (following the death of his brother Frank, who had been serving in France as a second lieutenant of the 1st Gloucesters, killed by shellfire on May 9, 1915, aged 22), *Lawrence of Arabia: The Selected Letters*, edited by Malcolm Brown (2007)

Welsh Poet Exempted
Dr Parry Williams' Appeal Succeeds

Dr Parry Williams, who has on two occasions achieved the distinction of winning both the chair and the crown at the Welsh National Eisteddfod, appealed to the Carnarvonshire Tribunal on Tuesday. The Glaslyn Local Tribunal had refused exemption on the chairman's casting vote. Appellant, who is on the teaching staff at Aberystwyth University College, appealed on conscientious grounds, and pleaded that he was doing work of national importance at the college. The appeal, which was heard privately, was allowed.

> *Western Mail,* April 26, 1916

Meditations
in
Time of War

The original wooden cross that was used to mark Hedd Wyn's grave in Artillery Wood Cemetery, Boesinghe, Belgium

No One Cares Less Than I

'No one cares less than I,
Nobody knows but God,
Whether I am destined to lie
Under a foreign clod,'
Were the words I made to the bugle call in the morning.

But laughing, storming, scorning,
Only the bugles know
What the bugles say in the morning,
And they do not care, when they blow
The call that I heard and made words to early this morning.

Edward Thomas

A Soldier's Testament

If I come to die
    In this inhuman strife,
I grudge it not, if I
    By laying down my life,
Do aught at all to bring
    A day of charity,
When pride of lord or king
    Un-powerful shall be
To spend the nation's store,
    To spill the people's blood;
Whereafter evermore
    Humanity's full flood
Untroubled on shall roll
    In a rich tide of peace,
And the world's wondrous soul
    Uncrucified increase.
But if my life be given
    Merely that lords and kings
May say: 'We well have striven!
    See! where our banner flings
Its folds upon the breeze
    (Thanks, noble sirs, to you!);
See! how the lands and seas
    Have changed their pristine hue.'
If after I am dead
    On goes the same old game,
With monarchs seeing red
    And ministers aflame,
And nations drowning deep
    In quarrels not their own,
And peoples called to reap
    The woes they have not sown . . .
If all we who are slain
    Have died, despite our hope,
Only to twist again
    The old kaleidoscope –
Why then, by God! we're sold!
    Cheated and wronged! betrayed!

Our youth and lives and gold
   Wasted – the homes we'd made
Shattered – in folly blind,
   By treachery and spite,
By cowardice of mind
   And little men and light! . . .
If there be none to build
   Out of this ruined world
The temple we have willed
   With our flag there unfurled,
If rainbow none there shine
   Across these skies of woe,
If seed of yours and mine
   Through this same hell must go,
Then may my soul and those
   Of all who died in vain
(Be they of friends or foes)
   Rise and come back again
From peace that knows no end,
   From faith that knows no doubt,
To haunt and sear and rend
   The men that sent us out.

                                        Eliot Crawshay-Williams

247

To the Nations

Let us get on with things!
Out of the way with this hampering war!
This idle, senseless waste of time!
Are there not a million evils unremedied?
Are there not men starving?
Women prostitute?
Children in misery?
Is not the mass ignorant?
Are not the rich indolent?
Is justice done?
Wins merit reward?
Has the worker the wage of his toil?
Mankind, lives it well,
In beautiful cities,
In wide streets,
Healthy houses?
Is disease conquered?
Are men and women strong, lovely, wise?
And art . . .
Music . . .
Is there no more to do that we should kill one another?

Come! to our work!
Out of the way with this pestilent war!
Let us get on with things!

Eliot Crawshay-Williams

War

There are very few people who will defend war as such; and certainly I have found that no one will who has been in battle. But there is an appreciable number of sincere and otherwise humane persons who profess to find in war experience some strange perfecting influence not to be attained elsewhere. This is, I take it, what the Germans would call a form of *Kultur*. There is, these people say, *Kultur* in war. I am not yet qualified to speak from experience; but I should not say there was any more of this kind of *Kultur* in war than in any other crisis when the chances of life and death have to be faced. And whether it is necessary, or even entirely good, to have been through such a crisis, I do not know. Personally I have had the experience of being well and in full possession of my senses, and at the same time of being practically certain that I should be dead within an hour. I do not think that the experience had any particular moral or spiritual effect on me. It was a powerful and ever-remembered sensation; but I doubt if it were a sensation in an entirely different class to any other. The sum of several other sensations would probably equal it.

Eliot Crawshay-Williams, *Leaves from an Officer's Notebook*

Youth and the Art of War

The day was fine, and the sky clear of clouds. An aeroplane buzzed high up above us, with little white flecks appearing from nowhere and disappearing again. This was our first seeing of war and of the intent of one man to kill another. It was difficult to translate this decorating of a blue background with white puff-balls into terms of killing. Had we ever truly believed that our military training was a perfecting of our power to kill, that we were of no value to the world unless we were skilled to hurt? I do not think so. However soldierly our muscles might be, however willingly the body accepted war, the mind was still a neutral. Through all the routine of training we were treading a path planned by others, looking to the right and to the left, sometimes looking backwards with longing, but never staring honestly into the face of the future. This is the damnable device of soldiering: confronted with an unending series of new tasks, trivial in themselves and harmless, full of the interest associated with any fresh test of skill and endurance, tempting even in their novel difficulties, the young soldier is so concerned to triumph over each passing obstacle that he does not see the goal at the end of the race. No one persuades him that drill is an exercise, that marksmanship is but a weapon; to him they are not means, but an end. If he perceived from the start that skill in the fulfilling of these daily tasks was destined only to help him to kill his fellow man, there would be fewer soldiers. The antiquity of arms is nowhere shown more clearly than in this evidence of its long practice in the art of war and its close understanding of youth.

Llewelyn Wyn Griffith, *Up to Mametz*

Barbaric and Useless Folly

I am engaged in a perilous trade, and at any moment my life may be cut short. I have a son and a daughter who will, I hope, live long after me; besides many dear friends. Should I die, I do not want any of them to misunderstand me and imagine I was a man who, full of glowing and somewhat theatrical patriotism, went to his death in a happy assurance of his own virtue, his country's and mankind's righteousness and the general fitness of things at large. If I die it will be the silly waste of a life, added to the silly waste of thousands of other lives which have been sacrificed owing to the stupid mismanagement of human affairs by the modern world. A war is like a slum; there can be no real justification for its existence at all. War is not glorious or noble, or a tonic, or an opportunity for national 'uplift', or anything else good or grand. It is a barbaric and useless folly due, of course, in part to a general human stupidity and ignorance, but chiefly to the incompetent statesmanship of mankind at large. If the members of all the Foreign Offices and Chancelleries were to be made to fight in the forefront of the first battle in every war, there would almost certainly be no war. But since the actual fighting is done by honest professional fighters, who are naturally keen on putting into practice their arts, aided by masses of recruits who are often humanly eager for a row and always told (with truth) that when there is a war they ought to fight, wars still occur. Moreover, the Press (which does not fight, but extracts money from the death and destruction of others) is always glad of a war; and this materially assists the blunders of the diplomatists. No doubt the Press ought to join the Foreign Office and the Chancelleries in the forefront of the first battle. No wars, if that could be.

Eliot Crawshay-Williams, *Leaves from an Officer's Notebook*

A Mind at War

One thinks of the hundreds of miles of trenches just a few yards away from them, lined with Germans. One thinks of each side alert, eager, ready to shoot. One thinks of the flares, the flashes, the sniping, all along this sinuous, far-stretching front. One thinks of this going on night after night, night after night, men killing, killing, killing, sometimes in driblets, sometimes, when there is an attack, in masses. One thinks.

Eliot Crawshay-Williams, *Leaves from an Officer's Notebook*

Dehumanisation

One of the strongest things in warfare is the way in which the individual soldiers of the enemy become a series of tiny ant-like figures, absolutely lacking in individuality and indistinguishable one from another. At close quarters a soldier is a man, even if an unfamiliar man; he is tall or short, fat or thin, he has a moustache or is clean-shaven, he is pleasant-looking or the reverse. At a thousand yards he has become a unit, a little black moving midget. He may be a Field-Marshal or a private, that tiny figure whose legs and arms are only just definable; he may be a hero or a coward, a strong man or a weakling. To the man who is trying to kill him he is only an enemy, a Turk, an Englishman. War, the war of today, mostly eliminates the personal element at all events for the gunner; he does not shoot at a man, but at a foe. He does not kill a human being with features and qualities; he hits a target. That is more pleasant for him.

Eliot Crawshay-Williams, *Leaves from an Officer's Notebook*

This is no case of petty right or wrong

This is no case of petty right or wrong
That politicians or philosophers
Can judge. I hate not Germans, nor grow hot
With love of Englishmen, to please newspapers.
Beside my hate for one fat patriot
My hatred of the Kaiser is love true –
A kind of god he is, banging a gong.
But I have not to choose between the two,
Or between justice and injustice. Dinned
With war and argument I read no more
Than in the storm smoking along the wind
Athwart the wood. Two witches' cauldrons roar.
From one the weather shall rise clear and gay;
Out of the other an England beautiful
And like her mother that died yesterday.
Little I know or care if, being dull,
I shall miss something that historians
Can rake out of the ashes when perchance
The phoenix broods serene above their ken.
But with the best and meanest Englishmen
I am one in crying, God save England, lest
We lose what never slaves and cattle blessed.
The ages made her that made us from dust:
She is all we know and live by, and we trust
She is good and must endure, loving her so:
And as we love ourselves we hate her foe.

Edward Thomas

Music's Remonstrance

' "Musician?" he asked, divining by certain words in the pocket-book that the Bavarian was a musician in civil life. A sad look crept into the prisoner's eyes. He raised his hands and held them a little distance from his lips, and moved his fingers rapidly; then he curved his left arm and drew his right slowly backwards and forwards across in front of his body. We understood; he played the flute and violin . . . I dressed his wound in silence . . . The bullet had blown away part of the man's jaw, and he could not speak.'

Patrick MacGill

Have you turned your music down
   That you waste the living blood
Heaven gave High Germany
   To quicken Mozart's mood
And hearten Bach's renown?

For the music in a man
   That war thinks nothing worth
Can bring High Germany
   More majesty and mirth
Than many warships can.

And the craft in one right hand
   That can with flute or strings
Make lovely melody
   And the voice that hymns and sings,
Can save the fatherland.

But what of them, made old
   With war – condemned to death –
Those sons of harmony
   That you have laid beneath
The suffocating mould?

And what will you reply
   When the song-lovers turn
Hating High Germany,
   That made the cities burn,
And broke with minstrelsy?

Ernest Rhys

The Folly of Mankind

March 11, 1916

I have just come into my tent after standing out in the still night. The crescent moon hung aloft, not sideways, as at home, but horns upward. The immeasurable blackness was pricked through with a million starry points. As one looked up, at the dead ages, dead moon, at the infinite, incomprehensible stars, whose vast and unknown fortunes work themselves out alongside ours – yet how far removed! – as one just began to edge into an understanding of a fraction of what it all meant, one was filled with an intense pity for our absurd little earth, writhing in the travail of things so great to it, so little to the universe. One felt a huge wonder at the folly of mankind, which, in the face of all mystery and beauty and awe, could fall to such mean and miserable tasks. One wept to find a world, so poised in the midst of strange and great things, given over to such small stupidity.

Eliot Crawshay-Williams, Leaves from an Officer's Notebook

Socialist
(Any Nation)

'Leave me alone; I do not want your war:
War that means fools cutting each others' throats
While smug sleek diplomats in dulcet notes
Prate on of God (does it not ever jar?).
Yes, you may call me coward if you please,
Bellow that "we" are battling for the Right,
"We!" – you must seek some subtler sophistries,
There'd be no wars if *you* had but to fight.
Oh! that the world were not so darkly blind,
That men would see the poor fooled things they are,
And making that fawning dog Democracy
Turn on its master 'stead of on its kind.
Sirs, I've no quarrel – save with Some on High;
Leave me alone; to Hell with you, and War!'

Eliot Crawshay-Williams

This Deflowering of Europe

The war affects me less than it ought. But I can do no service to anybody by agitating for news or making dole over the slaughter . . . I feel my own life all the more precious and more dear in the presence of this deflowering of Europe. While it is true that the guns will effect a little useful weeding, I am furious with chagrin to think that the Minds which were to have excelled the civilisation of ten thousand years, are being annihilated – and bodies, the product of aeons of Natural Selection, melted down to pay for political statues . . .

Wilfred Owen, letter to his mother, Susan Owen, August 28, 1914;
Wilfred Owen: Collected Letters

Like Dead Leaves in the Wind

Some of the evil of my tale may have been inherent in our circumstances. For years we lived anyhow with one another in the naked desert, under the indifferent heaven. By day the hot sun fermented us; and we were dizzied by the beating wind. At night we were stained by dew, and shamed into pettiness by the innumerable silences of stars. We were a self-centred army without parade or gesture, devoted to freedom, the second of man's creeds, a purpose so ravenous that it devoured all our strength, a hope so transcendent that our earlier ambitions faded in its glare.

As time went by our need to fight for the ideal increased to an unquestioning possession, riding with spur and rein over our doubts. Willy-nilly it became a faith. We had sold ourselves into its slavery, manacled ourselves together in its chain gang, bowed ourselves to serve its holiness with all our good and ill content. The mentality of ordinary human slaves is terrible – they have lost the world – and we had surrendered, not body alone, but soul to the overmastering greed of victory. By our own act we were drained of morality, of volition, of responsibility, like dead leaves in the wind.

The everlasting battle stripped from us care of our own lives or of others'. We had ropes about our necks, and on our heads prices which showed that the enemy intended hideous tortures for us if we were caught. Each day some of us passed; and the living knew themselves just sentient puppets on God's stage: indeed, our taskmaster was merciless, merciless, so long as our bruised feet could stagger forward on the road. The weak envied those tired enough to die; for success looked so remote, and failure a near and certain, if sharp, release from toil. We lived always in the stretch or sag of nerves, either on the crest or in the trough of waves of feeling. This impotency was bitter to us, and made us live only for the seen horizon, reckless what spite we inflicted or endured, since physical sensation showed itself meanly transient. Gusts of cruelty, perversions, lusts ran lightly over the surface without troubling us; for the moral laws which had seemed to hedge about these silly accidents must be yet fainter words. We had learned that there were pangs too sharp, griefs too deep, ecstasies too high for our finite selves to register. When emotion reached this pitch the mind choked; and memory went white till the circumstances were humdrum once more.

Such exaltation of thought, while it let adrift the spirit, and gave it licence in strange airs, lost it the old patient rule over the body. The body was too coarse to feel the utmost of our sorrows and of our joys. Therefore, we abandoned it as rubbish: we left it below us to march forward, a breathing simulacrum, on its own unaided level, subject to influences from which in normal times our instincts would have shrunk. The men were young and sturdy; and hot flesh and blood unconsciously claimed a right in them and tormented their bellies with strange longings. Our privations and dangers fanned this virile heat, in a climate as racking as can be conceived. We had no shut places to be alone in, no thick clothes to hide our nature. Man in all things lived candidly with man.

T. E. Lawrence, *Seven Pillars of Wisdom*

Sowing the Seeds of Another War

We left Poperinghe in a terrible storm. We reached Gwent Farm and moved on the following day to St Julien. We had to work extremely hard from dawn till dusk, under a relentless German bombardment. I watched a group of soldiers in the thick of battle nearby, and a few seconds later they were all dead . . .

Captain Fisher, the gentlest and meekest of men, was killed, as was Sergeant Ireland from Exeter. The Captain was an unassuming, unpretentious man, a gentleman through and through, whose great heart had not been hardened by military authority. It was he who asked me if I would push forward with him and the sergeant to look for a refuge for the numerous wounded. The three of us stood at the entrance of a dugout, and I went in to inspect it on his command. I had barely reached the floor of the dugout when a shell fell immediately outside the entrance, killing both of them there and then. It was only through the skin of my teeth that I avoided the same destiny. The Captain was a Canadian, and had told me that very morning that his military service was due to end in a month's time, and that he would be returning to Canada to his elderly mother, whom he adored.

It is Sunday once again, and we have moved to Minty Farm, where we were previously based. Several German aeroplanes came over to destroy the place, causing great havoc. O mothers of Europe, why can't you put an end to this barbarity? It would be a mercy to destroy the infants at your breasts, rather than nurture them to be a part of such a devilry as this. I feel bitter, bitter, when I consider that many of the church leaders in Wales had proclaimed this war to be a crusade on behalf of Christianity and civilisation . . .

We had to flee from our precarious refuge and look for another refuge in a safer place, and then we also had to escape from there. We had developed an instinct to enable us to sense danger, and our trust in that instinct saved us on many occasions. There are no signs that this ferocity will ease, and we are afraid to whisper to one another, unless it is absolutely necessary, because we are all on edge. We haven't received a word from back home in quite a while, nor have we been able to send a word to our families. The press back home is full of predictions that the enemy is weakening and is about to surrender. Here there are no indications of that, but day and night beautiful young men are being hurled into the great ravenous jaws of war. Why doesn't peace come? What mysterious hand prevents the end from coming? None of us is normal, we are all half-mad, and we generally believe that many back home are glad of this war, especially those who have used this great evil to make themselves rich, and that it is villains such as these who are forcing the Government to be obstinate and unyielding.

The soldiers here are not in the least jingoistic, and the general opinion is that such an ingenious, innovative nation as Germany will never be defeated. As for me, like Onias of antiquity, I do not wish for either side to emerge victorious, because victory in one war only sows the seeds of another. If England wins the war, or if Germany emerges victorious from the conflict, all hope for peace in Europe will be completely shattered.

Lewis Valentine, *Dyddiadur Milwr a Gweithiau Eraill* ('A Soldier's Diary and Other Works'), edited by John Emyr, entry for October 8-18, 1917 (1988) (Translated from the Welsh)

The End of All Things

Not from the breath of God
Will the world catch fire and burn,
But we who have sought in the sod,
With empty hands we will turn
And pluck down the moon and the sun,
We shall trample the stars every one,
And where Beauty alone can be,
Where nothing can be but she,
We shall find her whence she came,
Flame unto flame.

Saunders Lewis

Interludes
and
Intermissions

Christmas Day, 1914

On Christmas morning we stuck up a board with 'A Merry Christmas' on it. The enemy had stuck up a similar one. Platoons would sometimes go out for twenty-four hours rest – it was a day at least out of the trench and relieved the monotony a bit – and my platoon had gone out in this way the night before, but a few of us stayed behind to see what would happen. Two of our men then threw their equipment off and jumped on the parapet with their hands above their heads. Two of the Germans done the same and commenced to walk up the river bank, our two men going to meet them. They met and shook hands and then we all got out of the trench. Buffalo Bill rushed into the trench and endeavoured to prevent it, but he was too late: the whole of the Company were now out, and so were the Germans. He had to accept the situation, so soon he and the other company officers climbed out too. We and the Germans met in the middle of No Man's Land. Their officers were also now out. Our officers exchanged greetings with them. One of the German officers said that he wished he had a camera to take a snapshot, but they were not allowed to carry cameras. Neither were our officers.

We mucked in all day with one another. They were Saxons and some of them could speak English. By the look of them their trenches were in as bad a state as our own. One of their men, speaking in English, mentioned that he had worked in Brighton for some years and that he was fed up to the neck with this damned war and would be glad when it was all over. We told him that he wasn't the only one that was fed up with it. We did not allow them in our trench and they did not allow us in theirs. The German Company-Commander asked Buffalo Bill if he would accept a couple of barrels of beer and assured him that they would not make his men drunk. They had plenty of it in the brewery. He accepted the offer with thanks and a couple of their men rolled the barrels over and we took them into our trench. The German officer sent one of his men back to the trench, who appeared shortly after carrying a tray with bottles and glasses on it. Officers of both sides clinked glasses and drunk one another's health. Buffalo Bill had presented them with a plum pudding just before. The officers came to an understanding that the unofficial truce would end at midnight. At dusk we went back to our respective trenches.

Frank Richards, *Old Soldiers Never Die*

Christmas Day, 1915

Another day of inactivity faded into a dull evening, and shortly after dusk we paraded on the road. We were to go to the front line, there to spend our Christmas. Last year there had been much fraternising with the enemy, but this year strict orders had been issued that we must confine our goodwill not only to our fellow Christians, but to Christians of allied nationality. We were to remain throughout possessed by the spirit of hate, answering any advances with lead. This was the substance of the message read out to us on parade on Christmas Eve; it created no stir, nor did it seem in any way unreasonable at the time. Not one of us, standing on that road, had any desire to show cordiality to an enemy unseen and unknown, whose presence was manifested only in sudden moments of a great uprising of fear. Why should we cherish any thought of sharing with this impersonal cause of our degradation even one arbitrary day of peace? I do not say that we marched up the Rue Tilleloy inspired with a fresh determination to kill at every opportunity on Christmas Day, nor that we meditated a secret overthrowing of the orders that we had received. We reached the front line in a neutral mood, hoping rather for a quiet and uneventful spell of trench duty.

The night was fine and starry, with little wind. The front-line trench was wet and poor, flimsier even than Fort Erith – technically speaking it was a breastwork, not a trench. If Fort Erith seemed unfinished, this could not be rated higher than half-begun, with its evil-smelling wet walls, undrained sump-pits and ramshackle dugouts. There were five officers to share the watch, and when the company commander allotted to me a two-hour period, from one in the morning till three, I felt proud to command a stretch of the front line on my first visit. At dinner that evening a bottle of champagne gave a spurious glow to an ordinary meal, if a first meal in the front line can ever be called ordinary. Towards midnight we heard voices from the German trenches and some snatches of song: they were making merry. The night was still, and its quiet was unbroken by rifle or machine-gun fire. The artillery on both sides sent over a few shells towards the rear of the lines. The firing could rightly be described as desultory, for there was little desire on either side to create trouble; some rounds must of course be fired, otherwise questions would follow.

The battalion on our right was shouting to the enemy, and he was responding. Gradually the shouts became more deliberate, and we could hear 'Merry Christmas Tommy' and 'Merry Christmas Fritz'. As soon as it became light, we saw hands and bottles being waved at us, with encouraging shouts that we could neither understand nor misunderstand. A drunken German stumbled over his parapet and advanced through the barbed wire, followed by several others, and in a few moments there was a rush of men from both sides, carrying tins of meat, biscuits, and other odd commodities for barter. This was the first time I had seen No Man's Land, and it was now Every Man's Land, or nearly so. Some of our men would not go, and they gave terse and bitter reasons for their refusal. The officers called our men back to the line, and in a few minutes No Man's Land was once more empty and desolate. There had been a feverish exchange of 'souvenirs', a suggestion for peace all day and a football match in the afternoon, and a promise of no rifle fire at night. All this came to naught. An irate Brigadier came spluttering up to the line, thundering hard, throwing a 'court martial' into every other sentence, ordering an extra dose of militant action that night, and breathing fury everywhere. We had evidently jeopardised the safety of the Allied cause. I suspect that across No Man's Land a similar scene was being played, for later in the day the guns became active. The artillery was stimulating the infantry to resume the war. Despite the fulminations of the Generals, the infantry was in no mood for offensive measures, and it was obvious that, on both sides, rifles and machine guns were aimed high.

A few days later we read in the papers that on Christmas Day, 1915, there was no fraternising with the enemy – hate was too bitter to permit of such a yielding. Our men were wary enough to press as close as they might to the German wire in the hope of concealing from sight the weakness of our own defence. I could find no residue of tenderness towards the enemy as a result of this encounter, nor can I think now that any harm was done. The infantry hated the enemy artillery, and extended an impersonal hate to the opposing infantry if it interfered with the routine of trench life, but the infantry of one side never saw its opponents under the conditions of our soldiering except at times of battle or raiding. What was there of an enemy in an unarmed man clad in a different uniform, eager to secure something of ours in return for some little possession of his own? Let that man be armed, and intent to kill – all would be different, and lead and iron the only commodities for barter.

Llewelyn Wyn Griffith, *Up to Mametz*

Interlude
Dee Valley, 1916
(From 'The Song is Theirs')

No wilderness but there is beauty waiting
and life moves not from its hidden course
though all our strivings fill the days
with noise of purpose and paraded aim,
plot and pursuit enmesh the mind
but there are older hungers . . .
    A voice unstilled and with it Love
threading an ancient way within,
eyes yielding not, strong in their tenderness,
child-tender, beckoning me across the pit.
   No other trust than this, no burning bush:
beacon enough to lead me out of dark
if I be true, throw all upon the turn of love.

This cannot be . . . to touch lips
waking to find I dream not.
There is wizardry here and I the child of maze.
Some devilment concealed.

Green bravery upon the mountainside
rising falling with the rounded slopes,
a fleece of trees thrust o'er the shoulder of a hill
and all is beauty, silence.
    Let not that lamb cry out again,
  I have heard men in their pain . . .
   this world-old cry. There is no answer.
And all is beauty, silence.

Drink deep to love: I am but half-aware of sorrow.
This birch waving her tresses in the wind,
moonsilver bark in shower of feathered green,
a fairy caught in earth's mortality
and named a tree.
Noon is a silence, dusk a candlelight
on rough walls slanting.
Heap wood upon the fire: no evil in this flame.

264

Would I were done with all but love
and in the morning grey smoke curling
above the chimney and a voice singing.

Farewell my love . . . live with thy hope.
Look not on Time . . . farewell my love.
Brief song long silence and a new desire.

Farewell my love

Llewelyn Wyn Griffith

Release
(Found in his note-book when his kit came home)

There is a healing magic in the night,
The breeze blows cleaner than it did by day,
Forgot the fever of the fuller light,
And sorrow sinks insensibly away
As if some saint a cool white hand did lay
Upon the brow, and calm the restless brain.
The moon looks down with pale unpassioned ray –
Sufficient for the hour is its pain.
Be still and feel the night that hides away earth's stain.
Be still and loose the sense of God in you,
Be still and send your soul into the all,
The vasty distance where the stars shine blue,
No longer ant-like on the earth to crawl.
Released from time and sense of great or small,
Float on the pinions of the Night-Queen's wings;
Soar till the swift inevitable fall
Will drag you back into all the world's small things;
Yet for an hour be one with all escaped things.

Colwyn Philipps

Colwyn Philipps
Striking Work by Young Welsh Officer

Captain Colwyn Philipps was killed in battle last spring, and a tasteful volume now before us . . . is a memorial of this young and most gallant and brilliant officer, of whom two beautiful portraits are given. We may quote the title of the book in full:– 'Colwyn Erasmus Arnold Philipps, captain, Royal Horse Guards, elder son of John Wynford Philipps, 1st Baron St David's, and 13th Baronet of Picton, and Leonora his wife. Born December 11, 1888, killed in action near Ypres, May 13, 1915.' We confess to being much moved on turning the pages of this memorial, and we venture to say that no Welshman will rise from its perusal without a feeling of sorrow for the noble young life so suddenly cut short, coupled with a stern resolve that the losses of which this is one shall be amply and sternly avenged.

The book is made up almost entirely of the young captain's own writings, a good deal in poetry, and the rest in prose. The introduction modestly says, 'There may be differences of opinion as to the literary merits of these little verses; there can be none as to their sincerity.' No indeed there cannot, and, what is more, a study of the same will convince those capable of judging that by the death of young Philipps Wales has lost not only a Warrior and a Man, but a Poet. Let us quote just two specimens, as a test of the quality of his muse. Here is one that enshrines a whole world of truth in lines that are in every way worthy of their theme:–

FINALITY

You would unmake the thing that you have wrought,
You did not understand, you had no thought,
But you in truth have youth – go strive again,
With cleaner page, so cover o'er the stain,
But never catch the hour that is gone.

Letters of adamant shall dim and pass,
As also will the long-enduring brass,
Not all the fears, or tears that may be shed
By multitudes to come or millions dead,
Can e'er efface a deed that has been done.

Since life began no deed or thought or word,
Howe'er it seemed unknown, unguessed, unheard,
However light or slight to human seeming,
But has a consequence beyond our dreaming –
In all the world, there's nothing stands alone.

The serious thought here crystallised runs through many of the other pieces. The young nobleman and officer looked out upon life and found it a thing of solemn import. Duty to him was ever to the forefront; yet he was as gay as he was fearless. He never knew what fear was, he was devoted to his profession as a soldier, and he died as he would have wished – at the head of his men.

Here is just one more of the poems:–

A FACT

Down in a street of white-grey brick,
Where the sun ne'er shines and the air is thick,
With a hundred horrible haunting smells
From gutter and garbage and drinking hells.

Here is the home of the very poor:
Each house is the same as the house next door.
It is there they exist because they must,
Where winter means mud and summer means dust.

Here in a pitiful way they strive
At the awful business of being alive.
Where never there shineth a ray of hope
And there seldom is seen a bar of soap.

They are fouler than aught of the world within;
They are lost to virtue, but found to sin.
Think for a moment, I ask your grace:
Babies are born in this awful place.

Captain Philipps was passionately fond of children, as brave men always are, and they returned his love with interest. He was also most deeply devoted to his mother, and some of the most beautiful and touching things in this book were written or dedicated to her.

The second part of the memorial contains extracts from letters written at the front by the gallant young officer. The descriptive parts are almost brilliant in their touch, and whilst there is not the faintest trace of an effort at fine writing, abundant evidence is present of a rare literary gift. Pathos and humour are here, and through it all runs a practical vein; and the strong, clear, ringing note of Duty. A book like this is more than a memorial to the gallant dead. It is an inspiration to those who remain, and will come straight home as such to the hearts of thousands in Wales.

'A.M.', *Western Mail,* January 8, 1916

Running Waters

In Flanders there are pleasant sounds to which at times I 'arks:
I've 'eard big clouds go over 'ead with singing crews of larks,
I've 'eard a trumpet beautiful be'ind old Fritz's lines,
An' a blackbird singing careless right behind St Eloi's mines.

I've been out doing sentry-go beside the river Lys,
And 'igh above, I've 'eard the sound of flocks and flying geese
Wot called to us in No Man's Land below, as plain as plain,
An' we stood an' listened spellbound till the bullets come again.

On Christmas night there was a band played somewhere in our rear,
It may 'ave been at Romarin or p'rhaps at Armenteer,
But still it played those good old blighty tunes we used to sing,
I couldn't 'ardly 'eed the rats for listening to the thing.

An' back in rest I've 'eard the Jocks a-piping in Balloo,
An' Frenchy girls who sang our songs as good as me an' you;
The Guards went through to Wipers once, Lord! how them fifers blowed,
Oh, it was bon (you compree, 'bon'?) upon the 'Azebrook road.

But though old Flanders 'as its points, it's naught but ditch and mud,
For there's one sound I miss there always seems to stir my blood,
But we met it in the Springtime marching Southward through the snow
When at Armettes and Nedonchel we 'eard the waters flow!

Oscar Lloyd

On once more. Shuffle, shuffle through the silver sea of sand. The desert is a new and strange place by night. One is always the centre of a circle of sandy nothingness, which one never crosses, because it always advances with one. Shapeless black heaps diversify this nightmare-like circle of monotony, and pass by like things in a dream. One never gets anywhere. The horse in front is always there, kicking up a silver trail of sand; the circle of desert is always there; the shadowy mounds are always there. One falls into a kind of trance. One is voyaging through eternity.

At last we come to the anxiously awaited rise in the ground where we are to turn off on bearing 266. There is a wait while the C.O. takes bearings to Ballah light and various stars. Then more whispered orders, and our column turns away to the right. More marching, more monotony, more eternity, then a sharp, husky 'Halt!'

'Nearly in a bog that time,' I murmur to myself. But we skirt it. And now to the west looms up a dim belt of trees. And in the east, slowly, surely, there springs a pale greenish-pink radiance. Half-past three; it is the dawn. No use to us yet though, and we still steer by the stars. But just as we reach our destination the day is there. Lumps of darkness become human forms; there is the Sergeant-Major, the Senior Subaltern, the C.O.; we have completed our night march, and are 'ready for the attack' at the psychological moment.

The C.O. is pleased. 'You may talk.' We do . . .

Egypt can be very un-Egyptian. The spot in which we found ourselves in the cool of that June morning, just as the orange and purple radiance to the east grew brilliant enough to disclose it to us, might have been Le Touquet or Cromer.

A little thicket of pine-like trees thinned out into a long triple belt, which ran for a quarter of a mile down the banks of the freshwater canal. The ground beneath the trees was floored three inches deep with pine needles which smelt like Paradise. Looking out from the scented shade of the thicket on to the sand-dunes, there came to me a sudden passionate longing, what the Welsh call a *hiraeth**, for 'home'. I could almost imagine I was looking out over West Runton. Here were the woods of Roman Camp; there, where Ballah lay, would be Cromer itself; and beyond the canal over there, instead of that unending, nightmare sea of sand, would stretch the real sea, the cold, splendid sea that laves the coast of Norfolk. Cromer! West Runton! Sheringham! Oh, the sweet places! Oh, the sweet, sweet places! Roman Camp in June! The scent of the pines I could smell it. The joy of an English June!

But then the burning sun arose, and the sand-dunes quivered with heat, and the mirage danced over Ballah, and I was back in Egypt, a tiny cog in a killing machine.

Eliot Crawshay-Williams, *Leaves from an Officer's Notebook*

* 'Longing'

A Thrush in Flanders

Above the trenches all the sky is fair,
    Where anti-aircraft shells go shrieking by,
To burst in violet sparks against the blue –
    Bubbles of smoke drift slow across the sky.

To South the big guns peal the morning through
    And never give the ear a moment's pause,
While North some broken parapet calls forth
    Our Maxims grinding on like spiteful saws.

And, dulled by use, we do not heed such sounds,
    But plod regardless round the muddy bays,
Skirting the parts that rain has sapped with care,
    And think of naught but planks and struts and stays.

Till from the silent wood, behind the line,
    Where lie the dead who fought to make it ours,
There came a song that lit the soldier's eye
    And gilt the sun, and filled the heart with flowers.

From shell-torn boughs that crown the suffering trees,
    A thrush's song came pouring out so clear
We felt within our veins run fast and sweet
    The Spring that holds our England all the year.

The amber Severn ran beyond the trees;
    The daffodils played in the orchard fields;
And all the cloudy apple bloom was pink,
    And crocuses marched out with yellow shields.

And all our dew-washed England seemed around;
    Earth's fragrance leapt to meet us after rain –
The acrid smell of powder! – We return,
    Handle the gun, and tread the trench again.

Oscar Lloyd

Hearing the Welshmen Sing
Just Past Galita Island
February 20, 1916.

Our Welshmen have just been singing. I am always a bit afraid of making a fool of myself when I hear Welshmen sing, and more so than ever when it is far from home. Today it was quite something of a struggle not to. After luncheon the Welsh singers mustered in the fore part of the ship, just under the bridge deck. We officers hung over the bridge and listened. The rest of the ship's company who wanted to hear thronged round underneath. It was a glorious sunny afternoon, a stiff breeze, half a gale blowing from astern; great blue seas crested with white manes tearing past, the ship heaving and riding over them like a water-bird. The Welshmen sat in a little group in the sunshine, the sergeant who was conducting them in their midst. For a moment there was silence while they watched him. Then he motioned with his hand, and there arose the wailing minor strains of 'Aberystwyth'. It was a strange effect, that little group of men out on the sea, far from home, singing the music of their native land with those wonderful rich voices that are their natural right. I heard song after song full of the mournful beauty of my lovely land, and, despite myself, my eyes filled with tears. How many of those men in a little would sing no more, would see no more the land of which they sang? Oh, war is folly, insensate, cruel folly, and if there be a God anywhere He must weep these days. One touch from an engine of man, and all those breathing beings, capable of beauty, full of the power to enjoy, are useless carrion drifting with the tides. One would call any God to turn in vengeance on those who would do such a deed.

Eliot Crawshay-Williams, *Leaves from an Officer's Notebook*

Ivor Gurney with the Welsh

But O what luck! Here am I in a signal dugout with some of the nicest and most handsome young men I have ever met. And would you believe it? My luck I mean; they talk their native language and sing their own folksongs with sweet natural voices. I did not sleep at all for the first day in my dugout – there was too much to be said, asked, and experienced: the pleasure in watching their quick expressions, for oblivion. It was one of the most notable evenings of my life . . .

As I was in a Signallers' dugout, a bombardment means little else but noise and apprehension – as yet. But a whizz-bang missed me and a tin of Machonachie (my dinner) by ten yards; a shower of dirt, no more. Good luck to

271

us all. I have been told that I may say that we are with the Welsh. They sang 'David of the White Rock' and the 'Slumber Song', both of which Somerville has arranged. And O their voices! I thank God for the experience.

Ivor Gurney, letter to Marion Scott, 7 June, 1917;
quoted from *The Ordeal of Ivor Gurney*, Michael Hurd (1978)

Well, we landed at one of the noblest – what do I say, the noblest town it has been my good fortune to see; I hope to speak to you of it some day. But we had not long to stay there or anywhere till we were marched here and put in trenches with another battalion for instruction. They were Welsh, mostly, and personally I feared a rather rough type. But, oh the joy, I crawled into a dugout, not high but fairly large, lit by a candle, and so met four of the most delightful young men that could be met anywhere. Thin faced and bright eyed, their faces showed beautifully against the soft glow of the candlelight, and their musical voices delightful after the long march at attention in silence. There was no sleep for me that night. I made up next day a little, but what then? We talked of Welsh folksong, of George Borrow, of Burns, of the RCM; of – yes – of Oscar Wilde, Omar Khayyam, Shakespeare, and of the war: distant from us by 300 yards. Snipers were continually firing, and rockets – fairy lights they call them: fired from a pistol – lit up the night outside. Every now and again a distant rumble of guns to remind us of the reason we were foregathered. They spoke of their friends dead or maimed in the bombardment, a bad one, of the night before, and in the face of their grief I sat there and for once self-forgetful, more or less, gave them all my love, for their tenderness, their steadfastness and kindness to raw fighters and *very* raw signallers. Well, we had two days like that, and played Auction Bridge, talked, read, smoked, and went through a trench-mortar strafe together.

Once we were standing outside our dugout cleaning mess-tins, when a cuckoo sounded its call from the shattered wood at the back. What could I think of but Framilode, Minsterworth, Cranham, and the old haunts of home.

This Welshman turned to me passionately. 'Listen to that damned bird,' he said. 'All through that bombardment in the pauses I could hear that infernal silly "Cuckoo, Cuckoo" sounding while Owen was lying in my arms covered with blood. How shall I ever listen again . . .!' He broke off, and I became aware of shame at the unholy joy that filled my artist's mind. And what a fine thin keen face he had, and what a voice . . .

Ivor Gurney, letter to Catherine Abercrombie, [7 June, 1917?];
quoted from *The Ordeal of Ivor Gurney*

First Time In

After the dread tales and red yarns of the Line
Anything might have come to us; but the divine
Afterglow brought us up to a Welsh colony
Hiding in sandbag ditches, whispering consolatory
Soft foreign things. Then we were taken in
To low huts candle-lit, shaded close by slitten
Oilsheets, and there the boys gave us kind welcome,
So that we looked out as from the edge of home;
Sang us Welsh things, and changed all former notions
To human hopeful things. And the next day's guns
Nor any line-pangs ever quite could blot out
That strangely beautiful entry to war's rout;
Candles they gave us, precious and shared over-rations –
Ulysses found little more in his wanderings without doubt.
'David of the White Rock', the 'Slumber Song' so soft, and that
Beautiful tune to which roguish words by Welsh pit boys
Are sung – but never more beautiful than there under the guns' noise.

Ivor Gurney

A Concert in Flanders

On our last evening in Riez Bailleul, the Sergeant-Major came to the Company Headquarters to say that the men were anxious to give a concert. A piano had been found, and for a small fee the owner was willing to allow us to take it to the orchard for the evening, provided we kept a tarpaulin over it to 'keep out the damp'. Would the officers come, and would I persuade the Adjutant to play the piano?

A man of undoubted administrative ability, with a knowledge of one half of the world of the day that made backwoodsmen of us all, added to a large acquaintance with its more prominent citizens, he had sauntered through many occupations before attaining a large measure of success as a journalist. Through all his varying moods there ran one thread that gave a continuity to his changeful personality, and that was his love of music. He was an attractive pianist, not of the highest order of technique, but endowed with a capacity to make others share in his own delight in playing. Yes, he would play, and he would accompany the songs.

We assembled in the orchard in the dusk, a hundred-and-fifty men lying about on the trodden grass, talking and smoking. A thin haze of tobacco smoke hung as a pale blue shadow against the darkening sky, and two candles in the piano sconces gave a round blur of yellow light. The air was still, and in the distance a rumble of far-off shellfire served as an echo to the thunder of a limbered wagon passing along the road. We sang a chorus or two to unstiffen the minds of all, to weld us into a unity of mood.

Some forms had been lashed together to make a precarious platform, and on this the Sergeant-Major, by virtue of his office, president and prime mover of such an enterprise, stood to announce that Corporal Jackson 'would oblige', following the time-honoured formula, by singing a song.

Corporal Jackson was greeted enthusiastically by all as he stepped up. At some time or another he had been on the stage, according to the best informed of the company – 'made a lot of money in 'is day, 'e 'as, an' 'e carn't 'arf dance.' He walked across to the piano.

'Music?' said the Adjutant, with a smile.

'No sir, got no music.'

'What are you going to sing?'

'"Don't Stop Me", sir.'

'I don't know it – what's the tune?'

Jackson bent down and hummed into the Adjutant's ear.

'Right you are, Corporal . . . Carry on.'

'Will you play a few bars of introduction first, sir, and then play the tune for the dance after each chorus?'

Corporal Jackson walked to the centre of the stage and gave an expert shuffle with his feet to test its stability. 'Mind them boots, Corporal, the Quarter's looking,' shouted some irrepressible member of the company.

It was a third-rate song, sung by a fourth-rate singer, followed by a second-rate clog dance, but in the remoteness of that green orchard in Flanders, far from any standard of comparison, it claimed and held approval for its own sake. The words of the chorus still remain, wedded to a jerky tune, both trailing an air of days long passed away:

> Don't stop me, don't stop me,
> I've got a little job to go to,
> 'Twas advertised in ninety-eight,
> If I'm not there I'll be too late.

Another corporal, fat and tenorish, sang 'Thora', hanging precariously on its sentimental slopes, curving his mouth into a wonderful vowel fantasy over the:

> Noightin-gales in the brenches,
> Stawrs in the mej-jic skoy.

A good hard-working corporal, though his belt was a perpetual worry to him in his convexity.

But the evening grew to its grand climax when the stern-faced Sergeant-Major stood grimly on the stage, thin-lipped and hawk-eyed, to sing a ballad of Northern Lands. Every line in his face, and every contour in his spare body, gave the lie to his opening words:

> Oh, Oh, Oh, I'm an Eskimo,
> And I live in the Land of Snow . . .

The rest of the song has faded, but that sense of contradiction is still vivid. He had to sing it twice because he could remember no other.

Private Walton hunched his shoulders and adjusted the weight of his body carefully from one leg to another until he found a position of stable equilibrium, mental as well as physical. From his pocket he pulled out a mouth-organ, wiped it carefully on the underside of his sleeve, shook it and tapped it gently against his palm, presumably to remove any crumbs of tobacco or biscuit, and suddenly burst into a wild harmonic frenzy. From the welter of common chord and seventh there rose a recognisable tune, emphasised by the tapping of his foot, and he stimulated the whole company to song. When the audience had gathered sufficient momentum, he stopped to wipe his mouth-organ.

The next performer was Signaller Downs, who roused the community to a long-drawn-out sequence of 'Nev-vah Mind' in Gertie Gitana's undying song, a song that declined in speed as it grew in sentiment. The moon rose in the blue-grey sky, mellowing the darkness and deepening the shadows under the trees, turning the orchard into a fine setting for a nobler stirring of the spirit. Over the subdued chatter of many voices and the noise of an occasional lighting of a match came the silvery spray of notes from the piano. The Adjutant was playing quietly to himself, meditating in music. The talking ceased, and men turned away from their comrades to listen, until there was dead silence under the trees to make a background for the ripple of the piano.

The silence broke in upon the player and he removed his hands from the keyboard for an instant. The world seemed to plunge into a deep pool of silence, rising again to hear a supple cascade of showering notes as he played one of Debussy's *Arabesques*. When he finished there was a second or two of silence before the applause began, enough of a gap to show that his listeners had been travelling with him into another land. He played it again, and as he turned away from the piano he whispered to me, 'I told you that they could appreciate good music if they got the chance.' A summer night in an orchard, with a moon low in the sky, and in the heart of each man a longing – if music could not speak in such a setting it were not music.

Llewelyn Wyn Griffith, *Up to Mametz*

The Mail Has Come

'Intermission'
March 5, 1916

I have been writing about past events; but I must write about something that has happened right here and now. The mail has come; I can't help writing about it. No one who has been without letters for four weeks can quite realise what that means; but I want to try to make it realisable. So I write about it straight away, out of turn, anyhow. Every day for the last ten days the post orderly has gone down hopeful, and returned disconsolate. Every day glum faces have expressed what voices have refrained from saying. Now and then some bolder spirit has tackled the Post-Office authorities, and pointed out to them that if letters were posted three weeks ago, and have not yet reached here, something must be wrong. All to no effect. Desperate wires to Cairo and other parts of Egypt produced nothing. We settled down to a resigned gloom, and included scathing remarks upon the postal arrangements in our letters home, in the hope that they would be censored.

Then today the mail came. We had given up inquiring optimistically of the returning post orderly. It was on casually dropping in at the office tent to give an order against the present lavish distribution of orange peel in camp that I first became aware of a large brown sack, the contents of which were being avidly sorted.

'Letters?'

'Yes, sir.'

'Any for me?'

'Yes, sir.'

Then they were handed over to me. I had to go on to stables at once, and didn't like to stop to read anything; but I held the bundle as I would hold a parcel of jewels all through that unusually lengthy parade.

Now to open them!

Food has reached the starving men!

The mail has come!

Eliot Crawshay-Williams, Leaves from an Officer's Notebook

Playing Quoits on Deck

We officers have not much to do. Of course, we go now and then (like the men) to stables; but there is plenty of time to idle in. I fill up mine by writing, reading, getting a little preliminary instruction in Arabic from one of our sergeants, and playing various 'bumble-puppy' games. I laid out a little nine-hole golf links on the bridge deck the other day. Some might say the game had a suspicious resemblance to the extemporised shuffle-board, since it was based on sardine tins, chalk, and a piece of stick . . .

At deck quoits Wales played the World yesterday. After an exciting tie the replay was won by Wales (team: two infantry subalterns and self). The M.O. captained the World, and put the team off by adverse comments on their methods. The M.O.'s voice being something between the noise made by a hand-saw and that of a locomotive letting off steam, we begged him to be quiet, as there might be a submarine about. Anyhow, Wales won. (Net profit, 6d. per head to the Welsh team.)

Eliot Crawshay-Williams, Leaves from an Officer's Notebook

A.E. Jones (Cynan)

After the Battle
(From 'Mab y Bwthyn' – 'The Cottage Lad')

Between the hour of one and two
We writhed and wriggled our way through
The wires, struggling and crawling back
To our own trench, across the cracked,
Slippery, wet ground, through strand upon strand
Of wire where once stood No Man's Land;
Under the wires we pushed ahead,
And over heaps of piled-up dead.
Must I remember, God, the stench
Of that vile rat-infested trench,
And those *mute things* whose bluish fingers
Still on their rifles' triggers lingered?

At last, bent under my heavy load,
Wearily I reached the sunken road.

As we trudged our way through clinging mud,
Through constant rain and a heavy flood,
I said to my heart, 'I'll be far away
From the Somme long before break of day.
Farewell, I bid this hell farewell,
And make my way towards Flesselles,
Where there are wines, both white and red,
To drown the memory of the dead;
Where there are wines, both red and white,
To numb my pain and bring respite,
And Mimi there to serve me well
And fill my wineglass in Flesselles.

And yet my mind was still unclear,
Something oppressed me, some deep fear,
Something obscure clouding my mind,
Something I could not leave behind.
'I'll trample underfoot,' I said,
'These blood-soaked images in my head.
All these I'll trample as I trudge
My way through heavy rain and sludge.'

A. E. Jones (Cynan) (Translated from the Welsh)

279

Working in a Harvest Camp

When we were on the verge of going back to the trenches, I was summoned by my superiors and was asked how much farming experience I had, so I have been quite lucky to have been sent to a Harvest Camp to help gather the corn harvest. The British have taken possession of all the crops that are near the trenches. The French have had to flee, leaving everything behind them, because it is too dangerous for them to try to gather the harvest, and that is why we are here, to gather the crops before they are destroyed. We haven't been there yet, as there are not enough scythes for us. There are 200 men here, and many Welshmen, and we are situated far from the enemy lines, near a little village, and there are some French people living here, so we are quite far from the reach of the enemy. And we are to be carried to the fields and back, and will be working five hours a day. There are over a thousand acres here to be cut, and they say that there's enough work for us to last two months. And, indeed, it's much better here than in the Battalion with the others. We have been resting for a week because we have been waiting for the necessary implements to reap the corn. I am writing this on the fourth anniversary of the outbreak of the war on Sunday morning, August 4. I'm very glad to have been given this work; but it would be much better if I could go back to Anglesey. But I am grateful to have been spared from going to the trenches and from participating in the great battles, and having to endure hardships like many of our lads, although I often think to myself that I have been in the trenches and that I have done my part with the fighting and other matters necessary to this war. I am going to stop writing now for a while, but I will go back to recording events as they unfold. We were reaping wheat yesterday, on August 5.

Last entry in the Great War diary of Thomas Richard Owen, Anglesey
(Translated from the Welsh)

Holocaust
of
Youth

Sonnet of a Son

Because I am young, therefore I must be killed;
Because I am strong, so must by strength be maimed;
Because I love this life (thus it is willed)
The joy of life from me a forfeit's claimed.
If I were old or weak, if foul disease
Had robbed me of all love of living – then
Life would be mine to use as I might please;
Such the all-wise arbitraments of men!
Poor mad mankind, that like some Herod calls
For one wide holocaust of youth and strength!
Bitter your wakening when the curtain falls
Upon your drunken drama, and at length
With vision uninflamed you then behold
A world of sick and halt and weak and old.

Eliot Crawshay-Williams

Anthem for Doomed Youth

What passing-bells for these who die as cattle?
    – Only the monstrous anger of the guns.
    Only the stuttering rifles' rapid rattle
Can patter out their hasty orisons.
No mockeries now for them; no prayers nor bells;
    Nor any voice of mourning save the choirs, –
    The shrill, demented choirs of wailing shells;
And bugles calling for them from sad shires.

What candles may be held to speed them all?
    Not in the hands of boys, but in their eyes
Shall shine the holy glimmers of goodbyes.
    The pallor of girls' brows shall be their pall;
Their flowers the tenderness of patient minds,
And each slow dusk a drawing-down of blinds.

Wilfred Owen

283

A Simple Soldier

So simple and quiet a fellow,
  He wouldn't say boo to a goose;
Some of the lads thought him yellow,
  Some that he had a screw loose.

But when the place was a shambles,
  And the runners had all been killed,
Up to the Colonel he ambles,
  And all the jokes are stilled.

How he made that hell-fire passage
  No one can ever guess.
Gasping and choking – 'The message,
  Sorry it's got in a mess.'

His body was bloody and battered,
  His left arm hung by a shred,
His right held the message that mattered.
  When the hand let it go he was dead.

Charles Pritchard Clayton

. . . It is a bad day for the signallers and orderlies. The line of our forward communications is heavily shelled, the wires are continually being cut and men of the signals have to go out every time to search for the break and mend it under heavy fire. One after another is killed or wounded, and the runners, extra busy owing to the failure of the telephone wires, are suffering equally heavy. We get short of runners at Battalion Headquarters and I have to get the Sergeant-Major to get more men from the companies. About half a dozen come along. They do not seem to me a very promising lot. We want the toughest kind of fellow for the work of runner here. One of the runners, in particular, strikes me as a man of rather weak physique, and with the appearance of timidity. The Sergeant-Major confesses that when he first saw him he had the same impression but that he thinks the man – Evans, by name – will be reliable. In the afternoon the Sergeant-Major's judgment is proved sound, and I learn once more that external appearances are not to be trusted. Evans is sent up to the line and is given an important message from one of the companies for the colonel. After several close calls, a shell drops behind him and he is hit in several places. He comes back to consciousness in the dressing station. He has lost one eye and one arm is just hanging by a shred. The doctor is just about to operate, when Evans stops him to ask whether his message has been taken from his pocket and given to the Colonel. Duty first with Evans.

Charles Pritchard Clayton, *The Hungry One*

Greater Love

Red lips are not so red
    As the stained stones kissed by the English dead.
Kindness of wooed and wooer
Seems shame to their love pure.
O Love, your eyes lose lure
    When I behold eyes blinded in my stead!

Your slender attitude
    Trembles not exquisite like limbs knife-skewed,
Rolling and rolling there
Where God seems not to care;
Till the fierce love they bear
    Cramps them in death's extreme decrepitude.

Your voice sings not so soft –
    Though even as wind murmuring through raftered loft –
Your dear voice is not dear,
Gentle, and evening clear,
As theirs whom none now hear,
    Now earth has stopped their piteous mouths that coughed.

Heart, you were never hot,
    Nor large, nor full like hearts made great with shot;
And though your hand be pale,
Paler are all which trail
Your cross through flame and hail:
    Weep, you may weep, for you may touch them not.

Wilfred Owen

Strange Meeting

It seemed that out of battle I escaped
Down some profound dull tunnel, long since scooped
Through granites which titanic wars had groined.

Yet also there encumbered sleepers groaned,
Too fast in thought or death to be bestirred.
Then, as I probed them, one sprang up, and stared
With piteous recognition in fixed eyes,
Lifting distressful hands, as if to bless.
And by his smile, I knew that sullen hall –
By his dead smile I knew we stood in Hell.

With a thousand pains that vision's face was grained;
Yet no blood reached there from the upper ground,
And no guns thumped, or down the flues made moan.
'Strange, friend,' I said, 'here is no cause to mourn.'
'None,' said the other, 'save the undone years,
The hopelessness. Whatever hope is yours,
Was my life also; I went hunting wild
After the wildest beauty in the world,
Which lies not calm in eyes, or braided hair,
But mocks the steady running of the hour,
And if it grieves, grieves richlier than here.
For by my glee might many men have laughed.
And of my weeping something had been left,
Which must die now. I mean the truth untold,
The pity of war, the pity war distilled.
Now men will go content with what we spoiled,
Or, discontent, boil bloody, and be spilled.
They will be swift with swiftness of the tigress.
None will break ranks, though nations trek from progress.
Courage was mine, and I had mystery,
Wisdom was mine, and I had mastery:
To miss the march of this retreating world
Into vain citadels that are not walled.
Then, when much blood had clogged their chariot-wheels,
I would go up and wash them from sweet wells,
Even with truths that lie too deep for taint.

I would have poured my spirit without stint
But not through wounds; not on the cess of war.
Foreheads of men have bled where no wounds were.

'I am the enemy you killed, my friend.
I knew you in this dark; for so you frowned
Yesterday through me as you jabbed and killed.
I parried; but my hands were loath and cold.
Let us sleep now . . .'

Wilfred Owen

A Desert Grave

I thank my comrades that have laid me here
With a few feet of sand above my face
So that, almost, the blood that with my life
Welled from this shattered body, marks my grave.
I thank my comrades, for no otherwhere
Would I be laid. Not in the charnel-ground
Of some far city, where the crowded dead
Row upon row, row upon trim-set row,
Rot and become corrupt, each stately corpse
Boxed in his narrow cell, cramped and constrained,
One of a multitude – and yet foredoomed
To everlasting loneliness. But here
No walls of wood or leaden lining stand
Between me and my ancient mother, earth;
No fellow-corpses hem me; my companions
Are but the quail and foxes of the desert;
I have attained inviolable peace;
Peace, the good end of all . . .
        High youth I held,
Great-hearted youth, unconquerable youth,
Youth, with its fount of hope and joy and health;
Youth, that is careless of the years to come;
Youth, that is certain of eternity.
And in that youth I fell, my harvest passed
Untimely 'neath the sudden scythe of fate,
Green and unripe. The life that might have been,
The love that might have flamed, the unwon wife,
The children unconceived, the unbuilt home,
The unlived days of age, all these were torn
Quick from the womb of time. And yet, and yet
I grudge them not; I have been granted peace;
Peace, the good end of all, that some day comes
To teach the final truth to every man . . .

The world's small strivings are all one to me
Secure in my strong citadel of peace.
To me all days and years shall be the same;
The same strong sun shot up from out the East,
The same white clouds that follow up the day;

The same black shadow creeping o'er my grave;
The same still night and unperturbèd stars . . .

Thus would I lie in this unageing land
Where yet the silent sands that Abram trod
Unsullied spread; where yet the dim blue hills
Dream in the misty dawn, drowse through the noon
And die, red-black, each ridge a silhouette,
Into the Orient night; and ever there
To the far north, a line of blue, the sea,
My lovely sea, my dark and darling sea,
Rolls its unwearying waves on virgin shores . . .

So, where none comes to stir the scanty dust
That covers me, but throned in solitude,
Nature my sentinel, day after day,
Day after endless day, I sleep serene.

Eliot Crawshay-Williams

Gone, Gone Again

Gone, gone again,
May, June, July,
And August gone,
Again gone by,

Not memorable
Save that I saw them go,
As past the empty quays
The rivers flow.

And now again,
In the harvest rain,
The Blenheim oranges
Fall grubby from the trees

As when I was young –
And when the lost one was here –
And when the war began
To turn young men to dung.

Look at the old house,
Outmoded, dignified,
Dark and untenanted,
With grass growing instead

Of the footsteps of life,
The friendliness, the strife;
In its beds have lain
Youth, love, age, and pain:

I am something like that;
Only I am not dead,
Still breathing and interested
In the house that is not dark –

I am something like that:
Not one pane to reflect the sun,
For the schoolboys to throw at –
They have broken every one.

Edward Thomas

Mental Cases

Who are these? Why sit they here in twilight?
Wherefore rock they, purgatorial shadows,
Drooping tongues from jaws that slob their relish,
Baring teeth that leer like skulls' teeth wicked?
Stroke on stroke of pain – but what slow panic,
Gouged these chasms round their fretted sockets?
Ever from their hair and through their hands' palms
Misery swelters. Surely we have perished
Sleeping, and walk hell; but who these hellish?

– There are men whose minds the Dead have ravished.
Memory fingers in their hair of murders,
Multitudinous murders they once witnessed.
Wading sloughs of flesh these helpless wander,
Treading blood from lungs that had loved laughter.
Always they must see these things and hear them,
Batter of guns and shatter of flying muscles,
Carnage incomparable, and human squander
Rucked too thick for these men's extrication.

Therefore still their eyeballs shrink tormented
Back into their brains, because on their sense
Sunlight seems a blood-smear; night comes blood-black;
Dawn breaks open like a wound that bleeds afresh.
– Thus their heads wear this hilarious, hideous,
Awful falseness of set-smiling corpses.
– Thus their hands are plucking at each other;
Picking at the rope-knouts of their scourging;
Snatching after us who smote them, brother,
Pawing us who dealt them war and madness.

Wilfred Owen

291

The Parable of the Old Man and the Young

So Abram rose, and clave the wood, and went,
And took the fire with him, and a knife.
And as they sojourned both of them together,
Isaac the first-born spake and said, My Father,
Behold the preparations, fire and iron,
But where the lamb for this burnt-offering?
Then Abram bound the youth with belts and straps,
And builded parapets and trenches there,
And stretchèd forth the knife to slay his son.
When lo! an angel called him out of heaven,
Saying, Lay not thy hand upon the lad,
Neither do anything to him, thy son.
Behold! Caught in a thicket by its horns,
A ram. Offer the Ram of Pride instead.

But the old man would not so, but slew his son
And half the seed of Europe, one by one.

Wilfred Owen

The Green Roads

The green roads that end in the forest
Are strewn with white goose feathers this June,

Like marks left behind by someone gone to the forest
To show his track. But he has never come back.

Down each green road a cottage looks at the forest.
Round one the nettle towers; two are bathed in flowers.

An old man along the green road to the forest
Strays from one, from another a child alone.

In the thicket bordering the forest,
All day long a thrush twiddles his song.

It is old, but the trees are young in the forest,
All but one like a castle keep, in the middle deep.

That oak saw the ages pass in the forest:
They were a host, but their memories are lost,

For the tree is dead: all things forget the forest
Excepting perhaps me, when now I see

The old man, the child, the goose feathers at the edge of the forest,
And hear all day long the thrush repeat his song.

Edward Thomas

Futility

Move him into the sun –
Gently its touch awoke him once,
At home, whispering of fields half-sown.
Always it woke him, even in France,
Until this morning and this snow.
If anything might rouse him now
The kind old sun will know.

Think how it wakes the seeds –
Woke once the clays of a cold star.
Are limbs, so dear-achieved, are sides
Full-nerved, still warm, too hard to stir?
Was it for this the clay grew tall?
– O what made fatuous sunbeams toil
To break earth's sleep at all?

Wilfred Owen

Insensibility

I

Happy are men who yet before they are killed
Can let their veins run cold.
Whom no compassion fleers
Or makes their feet
Sore on the alleys cobbled with their brothers.
The front line withers.
But they are troops who fade, not flowers
For poets' tearful fooling:
Men, gaps for filling
Losses, who might have fought
Longer; but no one bothers.

II

And some cease feeling
Even themselves or for themselves.
Dullness best solves
The tease and doubt of shelling,
And Chance's strange arithmetic
Comes simpler than the reckoning of their shilling.
They keep no check on Armies' decimation.

III

Happy are these who lose imagination:
They have enough to carry with ammunition.
Their spirit drags no pack.
Their old wounds, save with cold, can not more ache.
Having seen all things red,
Their eyes are rid
Of the hurt of the colour of blood for ever.
And terror's first constriction over,
Their hearts remain small-drawn.
Their senses in some scorching cautery of battle
Now long since ironed,
Can laugh among the dying, unconcerned.

IV

Happy the soldier home, with not a notion
How somewhere, every dawn, some men attack,
And many sighs are drained.
Happy the lad whose mind was never trained:
His days are worth forgetting more than not.
He sings along the march
Which we march taciturn, because of dusk,
The long, forlorn, relentless trend
From larger day to huger night.

V

We wise, who with a thought besmirch
Blood over all our soul,
How should we see our task
But through his blunt and lashless eyes?
Alive, he is not vital overmuch;
Dying, not mortal overmuch;
Nor sad, nor proud,
Nor curious at all.
He cannot tell
Old men's placidity from his.

VI

But cursed are dullards whom no cannon stuns,
That they should be as stones;
Wretched are they, and mean
With paucity that never was simplicity.
By choice they made themselves immune
To pity and whatever mourns in man
Before the last sea and the hapless stars;
Whatever mourns when many leave these shores;
Whatever shares
The eternal reciprocity of tears.

Wilfred Owen

Dulce et Decorum est

Bent double, like old beggars under sacks,
Knock-kneed, coughing like hags, we cursed through sludge,
Till on the haunting flares we turned our backs,
And towards our distant rest began to trudge.
Men marched asleep. Many had lost their boots
But limped on, blood-shod. All went lame; all blind;
Drunk with fatigue; deaf even to the hoots
Of tired, outstripped Five-Nines that dropped behind.

Gas! GAS! Quick, boys! – An ecstasy of fumbling,
Fitting the clumsy helmets just in time;
But someone still was yelling out and stumbling
And flound'ring like a man in fire or lime . . .
Dim, through the misty panes and thick green light,
As under a green sea, I saw him drowning.

In all my dreams, before my helpless sight,
He plunges at me, guttering, choking, drowning.

If in some smothering dreams you too could pace
Behind the wagon that we flung him in,
And watch the white eyes writhing in his face,
His hanging face, like a devil's sick of sin;
If you could hear, at every jolt, the blood
Come gargling from the froth-corrupted lungs,
Obscene as cancer, bitter as the cud
Of vile, incurable sores on innocent tongues –
My friend, you would not tell with such high zest
To children ardent for some desperate glory,
The old Lie: Dulce et decorum est
Pro patria mori.

Wilfred Owen

The Sentry

We'd found an old Bosche dugout, and he knew,
And gave us hell; for shell on frantic shell
Lit full on top, but never quite burst through.
Rain, guttering down in waterfalls of slime,
Kept slush waist-high and rising hour by hour,
And choked the steps too thick with clay to climb.
What murk of air remained stank old, and sour
With fumes of whizz-bangs, and the smell of men
Who'd lived there years, and left their curse in the den,
If not their corpses . . .

                    There we herded from the blast
Of whizz-bangs; but one found our door at last –
Buffeting eyes and breath, snuffing the candles.
And thud! flump! thud! down the steep steps thumping
And sploshing in the flood, deluging muck –
The sentry's body; then his rifle, handles
Of old Bosche bombs, and mud in ruck on ruck.
We dredged it up, for dead, until he whined
'O sir – my eyes, – I'm blind, – I'm blind, – I'm blind!'
Coaxing, I held a flame against his lids
And said if he could see the least blurred light
He was not blind; in time they'd get all-right.
'I can't,' he sobbed. Eyeballs, huge-bulged like squids',
Watch my dreams still – yet I forgot him there
In posting Next for duty, and sending a scout
To beg a stretcher somewhere, and flound'ring about
To other posts under the shrieking air.

Those other wretches, how they bled and spewed,
And one who would have drowned himself for good –
I try not to remember these things now.
Let Dread hark back for one word only: how,
Half-listening to that sentry's moans and jumps,
And the wild chattering of his shivered teeth,
Renewed most horribly whenever crumps
Pummelled the roof and slogged the air beneath –
Through the dense din, I say, we heard him shout
'I see your lights!' – But ours had long gone out.

Wilfred Owen

Exposure

Our brains ache, in the merciless iced east winds that knive us . . .
Wearied we keep awake because the night is silent . . .
Low, drooping flares confuse our memory of the salient . . .
Worried by silence, sentries whisper, curious, nervous,
    But nothing happens.

Watching, we hear the mad gusts tugging on the wire,
Like twitching agonies of men among its brambles.
Northward, incessantly, the flickering gunnery rumbles,
Far off, like a dull rumour of some other war.
    What are we doing here?

The poignant misery of dawn begins to grow . . .
We only know war lasts, rain soaks, and clouds sag stormy.
Dawn massing in the east her melancholy army
Attacks once more in ranks on shivering ranks of gray,
    But nothing happens.

Sudden successive flights of bullets streak the silence.
Less deadly than the air that shudders black with snow,
With sidelong flowing flakes that flock, pause, and renew;
We watch them wandering up and down the wind's nonchalance,
    But nothing happens.

Pale flakes with fingering stealth come feeling for our faces –
We cringe in holes, back on forgotten dreams, and stare, snow-dazed,
Deep into grassier ditches. So we drowse, sun-dozed,
Littered with blossoms trickling where the blackbird fusses,
    – Is it that we are dying?

Slowly our ghosts drag home: glimpsing the sunk fires, glozed
With crusted dark-red jewels; crickets jingle there;
For hours the innocent mice rejoice: the house is theirs;
Shutters and doors, all closed: on us the doors are closed –
    We turn back to our dying.

Since we believe not otherwise can kind fires burn;
Now ever suns smile true on child, or field, or fruit.
For God's invincible spring our love is made afraid;
Therefore, not loath, we lie out here; therefore were born,
    For love of God seems dying.

To-night, this frost will fasten on this mud and us,
Shrivelling many hands, puckering foreheads crisp.
The burying-party, picks and shovels in shaking grasp,
Pause over half-known faces. All their eyes are ice,
    But nothing happens.

Wilfred Owen

Wilfred Owen

Waiting
and
Longing

Waiting and Longing

Through the long and weary night,
   I'm waiting, ever waiting;
For the harbinger of light
   I'm waiting:
Across the stormy heavens the clouds
Drift and sway like shivering shrouds;
Of clinging gloom my eyes are weary,
But through the night so dark and dreary,
   I'm waiting, ever waiting.

For the sunshine and the day
   I'm longing, ever longing;
For the tempest to allay
   I'm longing.
Reveal, O God!, one gleam of light,
And rift the storm-clouds, end the night;
O! roll away this gloom and sorrow,
Let dawn at last the bright tomorrow
   For which I'm longing, longing!

Harry W. Jones

E Tenebris

Another day! and yet another day!
They pass like lagging felons to their doom,
And still the murk and mist, and still the gloom,
And of the eventual dawn no faintest ray.
Can it then be that still the nightingale
In some far forest hymns the nights of June?
That still the pipes of Pan shrill out their tune,
And sound of tinkling water fills the vale?
Is there a world still left for our return,
The world we knew, the sweet and shaggy world?
Or is all man and nature hellward hurled?
Does all but memory in the furnace burn?
To us who live in one long treadmill round
The world we knew has shrunk to some far thing,
Remembered as a song we used to sing.
Dim as our youth; and with lust as profound
We long for it as for our sweet spent youth –
And with as little surety to attain.
For never can life be the same again –
Why should we seek to hide the staring truth? –
With comrades lying in many a foreign soil
And those we love misused by Time's rough hand,
With all the ancient fabric of our land
Twisted and tortured. Victory nor spoil
Can give us back our world . . .
    And yet the tune
Of Pan still riots in the woods, and, sure,
I'll hear the nightingale, if I endure,
In some far forest hymn the nights of June.

Eliot Crawshay-Williams

A Dream in the Desert

Blue seas
And a far horizon,
Foam-capped waves
That sink astern;
Jutting athwart
The unflecked dome,
Slim spars
And a cloud of sails.
After long days,
Days of peace,
Days of joy
On summer seas,
Faint and far
In the lonely distance,
White cliffs
And the green of hills.
White cliffs
And the green of hills
That come like a song
To the listening heart;
White cliffs
And the green of hills
That bring the tears
To happy eyes . . .

It is all a dream,
A dream in the desert,
A jewel fashioned
From barren sand,
From toil and strife
And the heat of the sun;
A dream in the desert,
All a dream.

Eliot Crawshay-Williams

A Prayer: Autumn, 1917

The birds are gathering in their flocks,
    They sweep across the grain;
Rehearsing for their Autumn flight,
    For home again.

The gleaners old, and husbandmen,
    Plod weary from the plain
And sigh, content, that they may rest
    When home again.

The fox has lair, the bird has nest:
    They know not of the pain
That aches within each soldier's breast
    For home again.

For us the stench, the sweat, the blood!
    O God, let us attain
A rule of Love, and bring us back
    Safe home again.

Oh Lord! grant of Thy balm to heal
    The chafing of the chain
That binds us in this Hell. Oh, bring
    Us home again.

Let not ambition, greed for power,
    O Lord, our honour stain,
But shield us; guard with loving care
    Our home again.

Fred Ambrose

September in Egypt

Far in my own land the curlew are crying,
  And there is light laughing of water on the shore;
The green of the bracken to golden is dying,
  Dying with the summer, lovelier than before.
Over the desert sand's stark yellow ridges
  Blue waters break in an alien foam;
Lit by the half-light that night with day bridges,
  Fancy weaves round them the magic of home.
Wild in my heart are the home sounds calling,
  The cry of the curlew, the lap of the waves;
As a sweet dream on tired eyes falling
  I see the grey headlands my lovèd sea laves.
Ever in my ears are the home names ringing:
  Kenfig, Llysworney, Tresilian, Tondu;
In my deep heart are my Welsh folk singing,
  Rich as the sunset, strong as the sea.
Brown sands of Kenfig, have you a greeting for me?
  Waves of Tresilian, do I long alone?
Moor of the mountain, home of them that bore me,
  Can your broad bosom thrill to my own?
Soft vales and hills, of all beauty begotten,
  Songs of my own land that pierce my soul through,
Let not your lover be lost and forgotten,
  Call him and lure him and bring him to you.

Eliot Crawshay-Williams

A Letter from Macedonia

My dear Megan,

I was overjoyed when I received your letter about a week ago. You have no idea how a word from old friends cheers a man up in a place like this, especially if they are joyful and comforting words. And do you know what? I believe that you have a very exceptional gift for writing in a light-hearted vein. This is not empty flattery. I mean what I say.

And you honestly believe that we will all be allowed to go home before the end of this year. Let's hope so. There is a good chance of that happening if we respond reasonably to Germany's next peace offer. I think that every country has had more than enough of the trouble and the strife, but a stubborn sense of pride prevents them from resolving matters. What difference does it make how much gold or land will be won by continuing this war? The important thing is that Prussia has realised the futility of its militarism, and that Germany has realised that a nation which tries to quash justice and one's right to one's own opinion can only incite the fury of the rest of the world. If Germany has already learnt this lesson, then one of the most important objectives of this war has been achieved, and its high time we reached a reasonable conclusion to the whole matter.

If we were to win Alsace and Lorraine by continuing to fight for another year, what good would that do us? Are gold and lands on one side of the scales sufficient to outweigh the lives of the best young men of the nation on the other side?

No, we have to believe that the world will come to its senses this year, Megan, that is, if it will ever come back to its senses.

Don't be surprised if you see me back at the Traphwll again before long, causing havoc among the fish and the rabbits. Perhaps, indeed, we will meet much sooner than any of us expects. The tale you heard from that little bird who whispered in your ear that someone you know is soon to be appointed a chaplain did have some truth in it. It's strange how these little birds can carry such tales, isn't it? I can here one singing now. I wonder if he'll carry a message for me back to Glandwr? I'll give it a try.

> Will you go, my little goldfinch,
>   On an errand overseas
> From the land of blood and carnage
>   To the land of song and peace?
> Though the Struma in the moonlight
>   Glitters under every beam,
> You won't yearn for Macedonia
>   Once you've seen the Menai's gleam.

308

How will you know when your journey
    To my homeland is complete?
Look for hills above the shoreline,
    Where the white waves wash their feet,
Where the summer lingers longest,
    Where the fairies live and roam,
Where the sea and sky are bluest,
    Where my heart is – that is home.

Search my homeland for a region
    Where the earliest cuckoo's heard;
Do not fear a heartfelt welcome,
    Fly to Mona, undeterred.
Fly much further than Brynsiencyn,
    Do not tarry by the Tŵr,
Make your nest, when you reach Traphwll,
    In the garden at Glandŵr.

That's a garden full of flowers
    (I can smell their fragrance now),
But there's Someone who is prettier
    Than the roses there, I vow.
Sing to her, my cousin Megan,
    Sing your utmost, on my part,
Sing until she feels the longing
    That is burning in my heart.

When her spirit's sad and weary,
    May your sweet song be her psalm;
When her troubled heart is aching,
    May your music be her balm.
Once you've seen that fragrant garden
    You will not return, I'm sure.
Who could yearn for Macedonia
    After having seen Glandŵr?

Your cousin and your friend,
Albert xx

A. E. Jones (Cynan), letter to his cousin Megan; original letter kept at the
Archives and Welsh Library at the University of Wales, Bangor
(Translated from the Welsh)

1918, Forward
(by a wounded soldier in a Cardiff hospital)

Another day has dawned – 1917,
With all its mysteries of joys and sorrow,
Has slipped away. Forget what might have been,
And fix your aim on what shall be tomorrow.
With steadfast heart to strive, and not to sigh,
Face the dark flag of strife that, still unfurled,
Hangs like a storm cloud, black against the sky,
And casts dread shadows on the troubled world.
Remember that brave smiles will help to cheer
The troubled road that waits for us beyond
The threshold of this dawn; let the New Year
Bind us still closer in a national bond.

'P. E.G.'

'It seems so very
long ago'

Five Years Ago
(Ploegsteert, 1915)

I look across the channel in the haze,
  And muse upon the lanes of Somerset,
  The hedges here and there are very wet,
And wet leaves fall upon the muddy bays;
So, seeing them, I think of winter days
  In woods and months I never shall forget –
  I feel the crash of 'eighteen-pounders' yet,
And see the crosses by the slippery ways.

Strangely I pine for these remembered things:
The spade and shell-turned earth, the acrid smoke
Of wet wood burning, and the troubled skies,
The smell of bacon that the morning brings,
The splintered branches of the shell-struck oak,
The life of toil, of danger, of surprise.

Oscar Lloyd

The Salient

It seems so very long ago.
Along the Menin Road – and hard by Gheluvelt
The shrapnel raves the night out 'neath a thousand stars:
And past the church, the gunners' ponies pelt
Their way to Hooge: and over Zillebeke
I see in dream, the gloating frenzy in the eyes of Mars;
'Tis in the night again, the fire and the blood
Meet in a horrid flame . . . 'tis fire still.

It burns me, sears my soul, and makes dissolve
My brain . . . my heart . . . my nerves as the shaken read:
And staring at the fiery skies, the Silent Past
Starts up and greets me from two sightless eyes;
And tells me what may be . . . and yet . . . and yet . . . and yet
I'm home . . . I'm home.
But, God, it seems so very long ago.

D. T. Jones

313

Ballade by the War Memorial
(A speech that would not be heard on Armistice Day)

From ghostly realms I come, a shade,
  On your dead sons' behalf, to see
What honour, praise or accolade
  We would return to, not that we
  Would wish for your false eulogy.
But what is this? – the old, old lie
  On stones, to shame our memory:
For one's own land, it's sweet to die.

When the wild heart of youth was made
  Tame by the clumsy artistry
Of some rough blacksmith's bayonet blade,
  Or the hot bullet's ecstasy,
  Or when the shells whined endlessly,
And then became a colder cry,
  Would you still sing so joyously:
For one's own land, it's sweet to die?

But is it sweet to be dismayed
  On seeing those whom we made free,
Through war grown wealthy, while, betrayed,
  My friends who fought for victory
  Now starve: I'd break these stones to be
Bread for old comrades of days gone by
  While you still sing with so much such glee –
For one's own land, it's sweet to die.

L'Envoi

Friend, in the colours of the O.T.C.,
  One day you will remember why
I challenged such hypocrisy:
  For one's own land, it's sweet to die.

A. E. Jones (Cynan)
(Translated from the Welsh)

314

To Comrades of the Great War

Sometimes when spring is in blossom,
   Or sometimes on a summer night,
When the feverish, sick earth is covered
   By God's flowers, colourful and bright;
Or perhaps when the moon's climbing over
   The slope in the twilight calm,
And the infinite stars are pouring
   Their peacefulness like a balm
On the wounds of a world full of violence,
   And the breeze under willow trees
Accompanies the sound of the river
   As it murmurs its soft melodies,
And a breeze gently blows in the moonlight
   Above cornfields that shimmer and gleam . . .
Do you ask: Was it only a nightmare,
   Was it nothing more than a dream?

A. E. Jones (Cynan)
(Translated from the Welsh)

Sospan Fach
(The Little Saucepan)

Four collier lads from Ebbw Vale
Took shelter from a shower of hail,
And there beneath a spreading tree
Attuned their mouths to harmony.

With smiling joy on every face
Two warbled tenor, two sang bass,
And while the leaves above them hissed with
Rough hail, they started 'Aberystwyth'.

Old Parry's hymn, triumphant, rich,
They changed through with even pitch,
Till at the end of their grand noise
I called: 'Give us the "Sospan" boys!'

Who knows a tune so soft, so strong,
So pitiful as that 'Saucepan' song
For exiled hope, despaired desire
Of lost souls for their cottage fire?

Then low at first with gathering sound
Rose their four voices, smooth and round,
Till back went Time: once more I stood
With Fusiliers in Mametz Wood.

Fierce burned the sun, yet cheeks were pale,
For ice hail they had leaden hail;
In that fine forest, green and big,
There stayed unbroken not a twig.

They sang, they swore, they plunged in haste,
Stumbling and shouting through the waste;
The little 'Saucepan' flamed on high,
Emblem of hope and ease gone by.

Rough pit-boys from the coaly South,
They sang, even in the cannon's mouth;
Like Sunday's chapel, Monday's inn,
The death-trap sounded with their din.

*   *   *

The storm blows over, Sun comes out,
The choir breaks up with jest and shout,
With what relief I watch them part –
Another note would break my heart!

Robert Graves

Silver Jubilee
1939

Faint now in the evening pallor
answering nothing but old cries,
a troop of men shouldering their way
with a new tune I recognize

as something near to Flanders, but far
from the dragon years we killed
to no purpose, scattered seed
on land none but the devil tilled.

That a poet sings as his heart beats
is no new word, but an ancient tale.
Grey shadows on the pavement
and Europe sick of its own bale.

I have no answer, no rising song
to the young in years who are old
with our arrogance, our failure.
Let it be silence: the world is cold.

Llewelyn Wyn Griffith

Glossary and Abbreviations

A.D.M.S.:	Assistant Director Medical Services
A.P.:	(First-) Aid Post
A.S.C.:	Army Service Corps
B.E.F.:	British Expeditionary Force
Black Marias:	the 1914-15 name for the 1916-18 *coal-box*: generally, for any big German high-explosive howitzer shell which gave off large quantities of black smoke when they burst
Blighty:	Britain or home, or a wound that was bad enough to send a soldier back home
B.T.:	Battery Training
C.B.:	Confinement to Barracks (punishment)
C.O.:	Commanding Officer; *OC* (Officer Commanding) also used
Coal-box:	high-explosive howitzer shell, which gave off large quantities of black smoke on bursting
C.Q.M.S.:	Company Quartermaster Sergeant
D.A.Q.M.G.:	Deputy Assistant Quartermaster General
Draft:	the form *draught* also in use during the Great War: part of larger body of troops drawn off for special assignment
Enfilade fire:	gunfire directed along the length of a trench
F.A.:	Field Artillery
Fire-step:	step built on the rear of the front wall of the trench from which the men could observe No Man's Land
H.A.:	Heavy Artillery
Hate:	enemy attack
Howitzers:	short-barrelled cannon designed for high-angle fire, firing shells in an almost horizontal trajectory, making it very effective at close range
Jack Johnsons:	heavy German shells that discharged a dense black smoke on exploding; named after the famous black American boxer
Lewis guns:	light machine guns
Maxims:	a type of machine gun
Mills bomb:	a type of grenade
M.O.:	Medical Officer
N.C.O.:	Non-commissioned Officer
O.P.:	Observation Post
O.T.C.:	Officer Training Corps
Pavé:	the shiny, cobbled roads of Belgium and northern France
Quick-firers:	Field Service Postcards
Q.W.R.:	Queen's Westminster Rifles
R.E.:	Royal Engineers
R.F.A.:	Royal Field Artillery
R.H.A.:	Royal Horse Artillery
R.N.D.:	Royal Naval Division
Sapper:	Royal Engineer private
S.B.:	Siege Battery
Sentry-go:	the duty of serving as a sentry, sentry duty

Stand-to: the act of manning and activating all weapons and equipment before dawn to prepare for any possible enemy action

Star shells: shells designed to burst in the air and light up enemy's position

Strafe: to 'strafe' means to attack ground troops with a machine gun or cannon fire from a low-flying aircraft; from German '*Gott strafe England*', 'God chastise or punish England'; also, in general, enemy attack

Traverse: a defensive barrier across a trench, as a bank of earth thrown up to protect against enfilade fire

Trench mortar bomb: a projectile fired from a short, stumpy tube (mortar) at a steep angle so that it falls straight down on the enemy

Uhlans: a body of horse cavalry that formed part of the German and Austria armies

Very light: a flare fired from a Very pistol for signalling or temporarily illuminating No Man's Land or part of battlefield, to watch enemy activity, named after the inventor, S. W. Very.

Vickers: a type of machine gun

Whizz-bangs: a type of German small-calibre, high-velocity (77-mm. [3-inch]) field gun shell, named after the sound it made as it approached and exploded

Wipers: Ypres

Y.M.C.A.: Young Men's Christian Association, which organised rest rooms for soldiers behind the lines

List of Authors, Index and References

FRED AMBROSE

Little is known of Fred Ambrose, and he seems to have disappeared without a trace. It was suggested in wartime issues of *The Welsh Outlook* that 'Fred Ambrose' was a pseudonym. *With the Welsh* was published by the *Western Mail* in 1917.

'The Aid Post Mametz' (from *With the Welsh*)
'The Grouser' (from *With the Welsh*)
'The Salient'
'Trench-French'
'A Prayer: Autumn, 1917'
'A Prayer: Autumn, 1917' appeared in *The Welsh Outlook*, vol. v, May 1918.

ANONYMOUS

'The Battle of Mametz Wood'
'Brwydr y Coed' was published in three Welsh weekly newspapers. It was published under the pseudonym 'Un o'r Ffosydd' ('One from the Trenches') in *Y Cymro*, August 7, 1918, and it is the *Cymro* version which has been translated here. Two other versions, corresponding to each other and differentiating slightly from the *Cymro* version, appeared in *Y Clorianydd*, January 24, 1917, and in *Y Dinesydd Cymreig*, September 25, 1918. In *Y Clorianydd* the original poem is attributed to 'D. C. Herbert C. F, Park Hall Camp, Oswestry', with this introductory note: 'After listening to my friend, Private O. T. Jones, Llanerchymedd [in Anglesey] relating the story of the Battle of Mametz Wood'.

SAPPER LLEW BASSETT

'To the Trench Again'

W. G. BOWDEN

Wilfred George Bowden was born in 1898 at Gwendoline Terrace, Abercynon, South Wales. He left school at the age of thirteen, and after a Co-op milk delivery job he became a junior clerk at Abercynon railway station. He enlisted at the Drill Hall, Pontypridd, on February 15, 1915, and the following day proceeded to Haverfordwest to join the 5th Battalion of the Welsh (or Welch) Regiment billeted there. He was eventually transferred to a Cheshire battalion quartered in Bedford, and in January 1916, to the Royal Welsh Fusiliers reinforcing unit at Oswestry. In March 1916 he was sent to France, and joined the 4th Battalion of the Royal Welsh Fusiliers on the way to the Somme. In March 1918, he was wounded in the Hindenberg Line area and taken prisoner. After the war he worked for British Railways as a passed fireman, a regular fireman, and eventually as an engine driver. He was quick to condemn 'the cruelty and the futility of war'.

Extract from *Abercynon to Flanders – and Back* (1984)

CHARLES PRITCHARD CLAYTON

Charles Pritchard Clayton was born in Garthmyl, a small village in Montgomeryshire. In 1914 he was appointed an officer in the Special Reserve of Officers and awarded the rank of 2nd Lieutenant. In March 1915 he went to the Western Front to join the 1st

Battalion of the Welsh Regiment. He was wounded at Ypres, and after a period of recuperation in Britain he returned to the Western Front in September 1915 to join the 2nd Battalion of his regiment at Loos. He also participated in the Battle of the Somme. During November-December 1916 he became Acting Lieutenant-Colonel, commanding the 2nd Battalion of the Welsh Regiment. He saw four years of active service. Later in the war he attended a Senior Officers' School at Aldershot.

Charles Pritchard Clayton took his M.A. degree at the University of Wales College, Aberystwyth, became a lecturer there and then entered the Welsh Inspectorate of Schools. He was also an excellent gymnast.

Extracts from *The Hungry One* (1978)

'A Simple Soldier'
'Dedication Before Battle'
'Died on Active Service'

Poems from *The Hungry One*.

ELIOT CRAWSHAY-WILLIAMS

Leonard Eliot Crawshay-Williams was born in 1879. His father was the Welsh barrister and politician A. J. Williams. Eliot Crawshay-Williams's great-great-grandfather was the industrialist Richard Crawshay (1739-1810), owner of the great ironworks at Cyfarthfa, Merthyr Tydfil, in Glamorgan. Crawshay-Williams was educated at Eton and Trinity College, Oxford. He stood as a Liberal candidate for Chorley, Lancashire, in 1906. He had been employed by Winston Churchill as Assistant Private Secretary in the Colonial Office from 1906 to 1908, and from 1910 to 1913 he was MP for Leicester, serving as a parliamentary secretary to Lloyd George. A scandal in 1913 ended his political career. He was cited in a divorce action brought by Hubert Carr-Gomm, the Liberal M.P. for Rotherhithe. Crawshay-Williams divorced his wife Alice in 1915, and married Kathleen Isabella Carr-Gomm.

He joined the army in 1900, and served in India. He was appointed Lieutenant-Colonel in the Royal Horse Artillery and commanded the 1st Leicestershire Royal Horse Artillery in Egypt and Sinai between 1915 and 1917.

After the war, Crawshay-Williams returned to the family home, Coedymwstwr, in Bridgend, and remained in Wales. He married for the third time in 1924, and devoted his time to writing and to Welsh affairs. He wrote poetry, short stories, novels, plays, film scripts and political texts. Several of his novels have a Welsh background, such as *Speckled Virtue* (1940), *The Wolf from the West* (1947) and *Rough Passage* (1950). His war poems were published in *Songs on Service* (1917), *The Gutter and the Stars* (1918), and *Clouds and the Sun* (1919). He also wrote two autobiographies, *Leaves from an Officer's Notebook* (1918) and *Simple Story* (1935). He died in 1962.

Extracts from *Leaves from an Officer's Notebook* (1918)

'A Desert Grave'
'A Soldier's Testament'
'By the Old Caravan Road'
'June in Egypt, 1916'
'Marching Song in Flanders'
'The Conqueror'
'The Pity of It'

'The Sandbag'
'To a Fly'
'To the Nations'
'Socialist'
'Sonnet of a Son'
'E Tenebris'
'A Dream in the Desert'
'September in Egypt'

'A Soldier's Testament', 'To the Nations', 'Sonnet of a Son' from *The Gutter and the Stars*; 'June in Egypt, 1916' and 'Socialist' from *Clouds and the Sun*; 'The Pity of It' from *Punch*, vol. 149, September 8, 1915; all other poems from *Songs on Service*.

DAVID JOHN DAVIES
Extracts from the War Diary of David John Davies

E. BEYNON DAVIES
E. Beynon Davies was a native of New Quay, Cardiganshire. He began working for the War Office, then situated in Pall Mall, London, in 1900. He served as a 2nd lieutenant with the 19th Bantam Battalion of the Royal Welsh Fusiliers, and saw action at the Battle of the Somme. He lost a brother in the Third Battle of Ypres.
Extract from *Ar Orwel Pell: Atgofion am y Rhyfel-Byd Cyntaf 1914-1918* ('On a Far Horizon: Reminiscences of the First World War 1914-1918') (1965)

EMLYN DAVIES
Emlyn Davies was brought up on a farm near Oswestry. On his nineteenth birthday, on July 27, 1915, he volunteered for active service and joined the 17th (Service) Battalion of the Royal Welsh Fusiliers. He was at Laventie, Neuve Chapelle, Festubert, Givenchy and the Somme. He was later transferred to the Brigade Signal Company, and served with 'F' Wireless Section (8th Army Corps) at Flamertinghe near Ypres, and at several listening posts in the Ypres Salient. He took part in the Battle of Pilkem Ridge with the 38th Welsh Division in July 1917. He was invalided home with trench fever in February 1918.
Extract from *Taffy Went to War* (1976)

HYWEL DAVIES
Hywel Davies, who was educated at the University College of Wales, Aberystwyth, served with different battalions. In May 1915, he was a member of the 4th Battalion of the Royal Welsh Fusiliers. He was promoted to Lance Corporal in July 1915, and in September he had joined the School of Musketry at Havant. By December 1915 he was a sergeant with the British Expeditionary Force in France. By April 1917 he was serving with the Northumberland Fusiliers, and was soon afterwards wounded. After the war he became a journalist. Hywel Davies was a Welsh-speaker. He translated Edward Prosser Rhys's controversial crown-winning poem at the 1924 Pontypool National Eisteddfod, published as *Memory: English Translation of Crown Poem by E. Prosser Rhys*.
'Dead Man's Joy'
'My Captain'
'My Captain' appeared in *The Welsh Outlook*, vol. v, March 1918.

W. H. Davies

W. H. Davies was born in Newport, Monmouthshire, in 1871. His father died when Davies was a child, and he was adopted by his father's parents after his mother remarried.

In 1893 he set out for America to seek employment, but failed and became a vagabond. He returned to Newport in 1898, and then set out for the Klondyke in search of gold. In Ontario in March 1899, he shattered his right foot trying to board a moving train, and his leg was amputated. His most famous work, *The Autobiography of a Supertramp* (1908), documents his experiences in America and Canada.

W. H. Davies was a very popular Georgian poet, and a close friend of Edward Thomas. It was Edward Thomas who prompted Davies to write *The Autobiography of a Supertramp*. W. H. Davies died in 1940.

'In Time of War'
'Killed in Action (Edward Thomas)'
'The Birds of Steel'

Poems from *Forty New Poems* (1918).

'E.C.H.'

'The Attack'

Ellis Humphrey Evans (Hedd Wyn)

Ellis Humphrey Evans was born near Trawsfynydd, North Wales, on January 13, 1887. He left school at the age of fourteen to help on his father's smallholding. He mastered the strict rules of *cynghanedd* at an early age and won several chairs in local eisteddfodau. He was conscripted into the 15th Battalion of the Royal Welsh Fusiliers in January 1917, and by January 29 he was at Litherland, the Royal Welsh Fusiliers' training camp near Liverpool. He was sent to France in June of that year. Before he was conscripted into the army, he had started working on his *awdl* (long poem in strict-metre), 'Yr Arwr' ('The Hero'), for the chair competition at the 1917 National Eisteddfod; he completed the poem on his way to the Front, and sent it from France to the Secretary of the National Eisteddfod of Wales, which was held that year in Birkenhead. He was struck by a shell at the Battle of Pilkem Ridge, on July 31, 1917, and later died of wounds. During the chairing ceremony at the Birkenhead Eisteddfod, on September 6, it was announced that the winner of the chair was Ellis Humphrey Evans or Hedd Wyn, who had recently fallen in Belgium. The chair was draped in black, and the Eisteddfod became known as 'the Eisteddfod of the Black Chair'. A volume of his verse, *Cerddi'r Bugail* ('The Shepherd's Poems') was published posthumously in 1918, and became an immediate best-seller.

A Letter from 'Somewhere in France'

'In Memoriam'
'The Black Spot'
'War'
'Written in an Album'

Poems from *Cerddi'r Bugail* (1918).

William Evans (Wil Ifan)

William Evans, popularly known as Wil Ifan, was born in Llanwinio, Carmarthenshire, in 1883, and educated at the University College of Wales, Bangor, and Mansfield College, Oxford, before becoming an Independent minister. He wrote both in Welsh and English, and published numerous volumes of verse. He won the crown at the National Eisteddfod of Wales on three occasions, in 1913, 1917 (when Hedd Wyn won the chair) and 1925, and presided as Archdruid at the National Eisteddfod from 1947 to 1950. He died in 1968.

'The Messenger'

'The Messenger' appeared in the *Western Mail*, May 6, 1915.

EYE-WITNESS ACCOUNTS
   The Somme and Mametz Wood

D. LLOYD GEORGE
   David Lloyd George was born in Manchester of Welsh parentage in 1863. At the age of two, after the death of his father, the family moved to Llanystumdwy, near Cricieth, North Wales, the home of Richard Lloyd, his uncle. In 1890 he was elected as an advanced Liberal for Caernarfon Boroughs. He was president of the Board of Trade from 1905 to 1908. As Chancellor of the Exchequer from 1908 to 1915, he was responsible for the Old Age Pensions Act (1908) and the National Insurance Act (1911). In 1915 he was appointed Minister of Munitions, in 1916 he became War Secretary, and superseded Herbert Asquith as coalition Prime Minister (1916-22). He became known as 'the man who won the war'. Later in life he denounced the war. He died in 1945.

Extract from *War Memoirs of David Lloyd George*, volume I (1938; originally published in six volumes, 1933-6)

HENRY ALFRED GIBSON
   'From Ypres to Loos'

'G.J.',
   Extract from 'Some of the Royal Welsh'

ROBERT GRAVES
   Robert von Ranke Graves was born in London and educated at Charterhouse. His father, Alfred Perceval Graves, owned a house in Harlech, North Wales, and Robert Graves was residing at his father's house when the war broke out. Alfred Perceval Graves had a profound interest in all things Welsh, and he was a member of the Gorsedd of Bards, a cultural body attached to the National Eisteddfod of Wales. In 1912 Alfred Perceval Graves published *Welsh Poetry Old and New in English Verse*, and in its eight-page appendix, 'A Note on Welsh Metres', the example given of an *englyn*, a four-line verse written in strict *cynghanedd* rules, is 'an englyn in English wrought after the Welsh pattern by my son Robert'. Robert Graves detected traces of *cynghanedd* in Wilfred Owen's poetry, and wrote to him in December 1917: 'Owen, you are a damned fine poet already & are going to be more so – I won't have the impertinence to criticize – you have found a new method and must work it yourself – those assonances instead of rhymes are fine – Did you know it was a trick of Welsh poetry or was it instinct?'
   Robert Graves was commissioned in August 1914 as a 2nd Lieutenant in the 3rd Battalion of the Royal Welsh Fusiliers. He served in France with the 2nd Battalion of the Welsh Regiment from April 1915 to July 1915, with the 2nd Battalion of the Royal

Welsh Fusiliers from July to November 1915, and with the 1st Battalion of the Royal Welsh Fusiliers from November 1915 to July 1916. He was promoted to Lieutenant in May 1915 and to Captain in October 1915. He was wounded in July 1916 and was invalided to England. He returned to France at the beginning of 1917 but ill-health prevented further active service and he was posted for home duties.

After the war, Robert Graves became a poet, novelist, scholar and critic. He married in 1918, and went to St John's College, Oxford, to read English the following year. He lived in Majorca with his second wife, Beryl Hodge, from 1946 onwards. He died in 1985.

His war poems are to be found in *Over the Brazier* (1916), *Goliath and David* (1917), *Fairies and Fusiliers* (1917), *Country Sentiment* (1920) and *Poems about War* (1988).

Extracts from *Goodbye to All That* (1929)

'Goliath and David'
'Sospan Fach'

Poems from *Poems About War* (1988).

LLEWELYN WYN GRIFFITH

Born in 1890, Llewelyn Wyn Griffith was educated at Blaenau Ffestiniog County School and Dolgellau Grammar School, in North Wales. He joined the Civil Service in 1909, working for the Inland Revenue. On the outbreak of the War he enlisted as a private soldier in the 7th Battalion of the Royal Welsh Fusiliers. In January 1915 he was commissioned into the 15th Battalion of the Royal Welsh Fusiliers, and served in France. He was mentioned in dispatches for his leadership and courage at the Battle of Mametz Wood, where his younger brother, Watcyn, was killed. He dedicated *Up to Mametz* to the memory of his brother. He was awarded the *Croix de Guerre* and the O.B.E. (military). He returned to work for the Inland Revenue after leaving the army and retired in 1952.

Llewelyn Wyn Griffith wrote several books. In *Spring of Youth* (1935) he pays homage to his Welsh upbringing. In *The Welsh* (1950) he describes Welsh culture and the Welsh way of life. He also wrote two novels, *The Wooden Spoon* (1937) and *The Way Lies West* (1945), and also a volume of verse, *The Barren Tree* (1945). He translated two works by Kate Roberts into English, *Tea in the Heather* (1968) and *The Living Sleep* (1976). Wyn Griffith was a popular broadcaster and a member of the Welsh team of the *Round Britain Quiz*, and also a prominent member of the Honourable Society of Cymmrodorion, a society dedicated to promoting Welsh culture. He died in 1977.

Extracts from *Up to Mametz* (1931)

'France, 1915'
'Interlude: Dee Valley, 1916'
'Mametz Wood, 1916'
'Silver Jubilee', 1939

Poems from *The Barren Tree* (1945).

IVOR GURNEY

Ivor (Bertie) Gurney was born in Gloucester in 1890, the son of a tailor, and was educated at King's School, Gloucester. He was awarded a scholarship in composition at the Royal College of Music, which he attended from 1911. He volunteered for active service at the outbreak of the war, but was rejected due to poor eyesight. In February

1915 he succeeded in enlisting in the 2/5th Battalion of the Gloucestershire Regiment, and served on the Western Front as a private from 1915 to 1917. He was wounded in the arm in April 1917, and after recuperating in a hospital at Rouen, he was transferred to the Machine-Gun Corp. In September 1917 he was severely gassed at St Julien, in the Ypres sector, and saw no more active service. He was discharged from the army in October 1918 with 'deferred shell-shock'. After the war he worked at various jobs, but was unable to settle, and he became increasingly unstable and disorientated. He was committed to a mental institution in 1922, and remained institutionalised until his death in 1937 in the City of London Mental Hospital. He published two volumes of verse, *Severn and Somme* (1917) and *War's Embers* (1919). He was a great admirer of Edward Thomas, and set six of his songs to music.

Extracts from *The Ordeal of Ivor Gurney* (1978)

'First Time In'

'First Time In' from *Collected Poems of Ivor Gurney*, edited by P. J. Kavanagh (1982).

ALFRED JENKINS

Private Alfred Jenkins served with the 100th Field Ambulance of the British Expeditionary Force.

'Behind the Trenches at Festubert'

'Behind the Trenches at Festubert' appeared in *The Welsh Outlook*, vol. v, June 1918.

ARTHUR LEWIS JENKINS

Arthur Lewis Jenkins was the son of Sir John Lewis Jenkins, at one time vice-president of the Indian Viceroy's Council. Arthur Lewis Jenkins's grandfather was County Councillor James Jenkins, of Llangadog, Carmarthenshire. Arthur Jenkins won a scholarship at Marlborough College, and later took an open classical scholarship at Balliol College, Oxford. It was his intention to enter the Indian Civil Service, following in his father's footsteps, before the war intervened. Obtaining a commission in September 1914, his regiment was posted to India, and afterwards to Aden. From Aden he proceeded to Egypt, where he joined the Flying Corps. He was killed in a flying accident at Ripon, in Yorkshire, aged 25.

'Happy Warriors'

'Happy Warriors' appeared in the *Western Mail*, January 3, 1918.

ELINOR JENKINS

Born in 1893, daughter of Sir John Lewis Jenkins and sister of Arthur Lewis Jenkins. She died in 1920.

'A Legend of Ypres'
'The House by the Highway'
'The Last Evening'

Poems from *Poems* (1915).

'J. L. P.'
'To R. J. Ford'

'To R. J. Ford' appeared in the *Western Mail*, May 18, 1915.

A. E. Jones (Cynan)

Albert Evans Jones, more popularly known as Cynan, was born in Pwllheli, North Wales, in 1895, and educated at the University College of Wales, Bangor. He joined the Welsh unit of the R.A.M.C. and served as a stretcher-bearer in France and Macedonia, and, later, as a chaplain. In 1921 he won the crown at the National Eisteddfod of Wales, held at Caernarfon that year, for his long narrative poem, *'Mab y Bwthyn'* ('The Cottage Lad'), which was based on his war experiences. His graphic and realistic descriptions of trench warfare enthralled and shocked the Welsh public. Most of his war poems were published in his first volume of poetry, *Telyn y Nos* (*'The Harp of the Night'*), also published in 1921. Cynan, who was a very popular poet in twentieth-century Wales, was also a dramatist. He did much to reform the National Eisteddfod of Wales, and served the Eisteddfod as its Archdruid twice (1950-54 and 1963-66). He also won the National Eisteddfod crown in 1923 and 1931, and the chair in 1924. He died in 1970.

A Letter from Macedonia
Extract from 'Cynan's Memoirs: On the Battlefield'

'After the Battle'
'Ballade by the War Memorial'
'Longing'
'The Funeral'
'The Unknown Grave'
'To Comrades of the Great War'

Poems from *Cerddi Cynan* (1959).

David Jones

David Michael Jones was born in Brockley, Kent, in 1895. His father moved to London from Holywell, Flintshire, to work as a printer. From 1909 to 1914 David Jones was a student at the Camberwell School of Art. He enlisted in 1915 as a private in the 15th Battalion of the Royal Welsh Fusiliers, and served in France until 1918 when he was wounded and invalided home. In 1921 he became a Roman Catholic. After the war he enrolled at the Westminster School of Art, and in 1922 began his long association with Eric Gill, and became a prominent illustrator and watercolourist. He was very conscious of his Welsh roots and his work is embedded in Welsh mythology and literature. He lived in Wales from 1924 to 1927. He wrote *In Parenthesis* after a nervous breakdown. As Jones says in the preface to *In Parenthesis*, 'The period covered begins early in December 1915 and ends early in July 1916,' that is, after the Battle of Mametz Wood, in which he participated. He also says in his preface to *In Parenthesis*: 'To any Welsh reader, I would say, what Michael Drayton, in a foreword to his *Poly-olbion*, says, speaking of Wales: "if I have not done her right, the want is in my ability, not in my love".' He died in 1974.

Extracts from *In Parenthesis* (1937)

D. T. Jones

'Before Battle: Ypres, July 1917'
'The Salient'

'Before Battle: Ypres, July 1917' appeared in *The Welsh Outlook*, vol. v, October 1918, and 'The Salient' in *The Welsh Outlook*, vol. vii, January 1920.

EDWIN EVAN JONES

Edwin Evan Jones was born in 1879. He enlisted in Chelsea as a private with the 2nd London Sanitary Company R.A.M.C.T. (Royal Army Medical Corps Transport) in March 1915. He was in France with the British Expeditionary Force by mid-March 1915, and remained in France until December of the same year, and was then posted to India. His last two years of service were spent in Egypt, acting as 2nd Lieutenant of the Egyptian Labour Corps. He took part in the drive towards Damascus under General Allenby, before being demobilised in 1919.

He was sent home in a troop ship in the clothes that he wore in the desert. On the way home he and a number of others caught pneumonia and died shortly after landing in Britain. Edwin Jones himself died at his father's home in Aberdyfi, on September 25, 1919, of dysentery and acute hepatitis.

Extracts from the War Diary of Lieutenant Edwin Evan Jones

NURSE M. JONES

'In a City of Mystery: Welsh Nurse's Story of the Salonika Air Raids'

HARRY W. JONES

Harry W. Jones served with the British Expeditionary Force.

'The Fallen'
'Waiting and Longing'

'The Fallen' appeared in *The Welsh Outlook*, vol. vi, April 1919, and 'Waiting and Longing' in *The Welsh Outlook*, vol. v, July 1918.

T. E. LAWRENCE

Thomas Edward Lawrence was born in Tremadog, near Porthmadog, in North Wales, in 1888. He was educated at Jesus College, Oxford, where he became interested in archaeology and the Middle East. He studied Arabic and from 1910 to 1914 worked on the excavation of Carchemish, on the banks of the Euphrates. During the Great War he worked for army intelligence in North Africa (1914-16), and in 1916 he was British liaison officer to the Arab revolt against the Turks, led by Faisal I, and became known as Lawrence of Arabia. He entered Damascus in October 18 with the Arab forces, as part of General Allenby's triumphal march after the defeat of the Turks. *Seven Pillars of Wisdom*, his account of the Arab Revolt, was completed in 1922 and printed in a limited edition for private circulation in 1926 and for the general public in 1935. An abridged version, *Revolt in the Desert*, was published by Lawrence in 1926. After the war, Lawrence enlisted in the ranks of the R.A.F., twice, and in the Royal Tank Corps. He died of wounds sustained in a motor-cycling accident in 1935.

Extracts from *Lawrence of Arabia: The Selected Letters* (2007)
Extracts from *Seven Pillars of Wisdom* (1935)

'To S. A'

'To S. A' from *Seven Pillars of Wisdom*.

SAUNDERS LEWIS

John Saunders Lewis was born in Liverpool of Welsh parents in 1893. He was a student at Liverpool University, reading English and French, when the war broke out. In November 1914 he volunteered for the 19th (Service) Battalion of the King's Liverpool Regiment (3rd City Battalion), formed in Liverpool on August 29, 1914, by Lord Derby. In May 1915 he was commissioned into the 12th (3rd Gwent) South Wales Borderers, a 'Bantam' battalion. He went to France in June 1916. His brother Ludwig was killed in France on July 7, 1917. Saunders Lewis was wounded in April 1917, and after a period of convalescence, he was posted to Athens to work for the War Office, where he remained until the end of the war.

He met Margaret Gilcriest at Liverpool University, where they were both students, before the outbreak of the War. They were married in 1924. He completed his studies at Liverpool University after the war, and in 1922 became a lecturer in Welsh at the University College of Wales, Swansea. He was one of the founder members of *Plaid Genedlaethol Cymru* ('The National Party of Wales'), later known as Plaid Cymru, in 1925. In 1936, with two other nationalists, D. J. Williams and Lewis Valentine, he set part of the Bombing School at Penyberth in the Llŷn peninsula on fire, and was imprisoned for nine months. Saunders Lewis became a major force and figure in Welsh political and literary life. He wrote poetry, plays, novels, literary criticism and political essays, and was an eminent writer and scholar. He died in 1985.

Extracts from *Letters to Margaret Gilcriest* (1993)
'The Experience of a Welshman in the Army: On French Soil'

'In the Trenches'
'The End of All Things'

'In the Trenches' and 'The End of All Things' from *Letters to Margaret Gilcriest*.

OSCAR LLOYD

Little is known of Oscar Lloyd. He contributed reviews and poems to *The Welsh Outlook*. He lived in Newnham-on-Severn, Gloucestershire, after the war.

'A Thrush in Flanders'
'Five Years Ago'
'Going West'
'K.G.H.F. Killed in Action'
'Running Waters'
'The Last Peal'

'A Thrush in Flanders' appeared in *The Welsh Outlook*, vol. vi., May 1919; 'Five Years Ago' in *The Welsh Outlook*, vol. vii, May 1920; 'Going West' in *The Welsh Outlook*, vol. vi, January 1919; 'K.G.H.F. Killed in Action' in *The Welsh Outlook*, vol. v, July 1918; 'Running Waters' in *The Welsh Outlook*, vol. vi., July 1919; 'The Last Peal' in *The Welsh Outlook*, vol. v, June 1918.

'M. J. L.'
'To One Who Fell in Early Youth'

'To One Who Fell in Early Youth' appeared in *The Welsh Outlook*, vol. ii, September 1915.

J. DYFNALLT OWEN

John Dyfnallt Owen was born in the parish of Llan-giwg in Glamorgan in 1873. He was educated at the University College of North Wales, Bangor, and at Bala-Bangor theological college. and became an Independent minister. He won the crown at the 1907 National Eisteddfod at Swansea, and was Archdruid at the National Eisteddfod of Wales from 1954 to 1957.

He enlisted as a chaplain with the Y.M.C.A., and spent three months in the La Béthune region and near La Bassée canal in the summer of 1916. He admired the Welsh soldiers for their unswerving courage and cheerfulness in the face of adversity. He died in 1956.

'No Man's Land'

'The Hour of Terror'

Poems from *Myfyrion a Chaneuon Maes y Tân* (1917).

THOMAS A. OWEN

Lance Corporal Thomas A. Owen was attested in November 1916 and was called up in February 1917. He served in France and Belgium, mainly on sections of the Ypres Salient. He served with the 1st Battalion of the South Wales Borderers, 1st Division. He was wounded and taken prisoner near Festubert, on April 18, 1918. He was then taken to Schleswig. He spent six months in hospital and was then discharged for labour at Munster Prisoner of War Camp, until Armistice. He was repatriated on December 2, 1918.

'Stand-to' on Givenchy Road

THOMAS RICHARD OWEN

Thomas Richard Owen was born in Coedana, Anglesey, in 1895. He enlisted in 1916 and served with 10th Battalion of the South Wales Borderers. He was killed in action near the village of Sailly-Saillisel in the Somme region of France on September 2, 1918, and was buried in Le Transloy on the Somme, in an unknown grave.

Extracts from the Great War Diary of Thomas Richard Owen

WILFRED OWEN

Wilfred Edward Salter Owen was born near Oswestry, Shropshire, in 1893. Both his parents were of Welsh ancestry, and Owen was proud of his Welsh background. The family moved from Oswestry to Birkenhead in 1897, and to Shrewsbury in 1907, and Owen was educated at Birkenhead Institute and Shrewsbury Technical School. In 1913 he went to Bordeaux, France, to teach at the Berlitz School of Languages. When war was declared, he was working as a tutor to a family at Bagnères-de-Bigorre in the High Pyrenees. He returned to England and enlisted in the Artists' Rifles in October 1915. He was commissioned in June 1915 as a 2nd Lieutenant in the 5th Battalion, Manchester Regiment. On December 30, 1916, he arrived at the Base Camp in Etaples, and two days later he joined the 2nd Battalion. He served on the Western Front until May 1916, when he was severely shell-shocked and invalided to Craiglockhart Hospital near Edinburgh. There he met Siegfried Sassoon, who had an enormous influence on him. He later met Robert Graves, Sassoon's friend, and other important literary figures. He was posted back to France in August 1916 and was killed by machine-gun fire on

November 4, at the Sambre Canal, a week before the Armistice was signed. Owen is generally recognised as the greatest poet of the First World War.

Extracts from *Wilfred Owen: Collected Letters* (1967)

'Anthem for Doomed Youth'
'Arms and the Boy'
'Dulce et Decorum est'
'Exposure'
'Futility'
'Greater Love'
'Insensibility'
'Mental Cases'
'1914'
'Spring Offensive'
'Strange Meeting'
'The Parable of the Old Man and the Young'
'The Send-off'
'The Sentry'

Poems from *The War Poems of Wilfred Owen*, edited by Jon Stallworthy (1994).

R. Williams Parry

Robert Williams Parry was born in Tal-y-sarn in Nantlle Valley, North Wales, in 1884. He was educated at the University College of Wales, Aberystwyth, and in 1910 won the chair at the National Eisteddfod of Wales. He taught at several schools in Wales and England before being appointed, partly as a lecturer and partly as a lecturer in night-classes providing adult education, in the Welsh Department at the University College of Wales, Bangor. He married in 1923 and settled in Bethesda, North Wales. R. Williams Parry was one of the most important Welsh-language poets of the twentieth century. He died in 1956.

He volunteered for active service in November 1915, but was rejected due to defective eyesight. He was eventually accepted for general service, Class A. By February 1917 he was at the Hetherfield Cadet School, Berkhamstead, Hertfordshire, and in April 1917 he was transferred to the Royal Garrison Artillery camp at Mornhill, Winchester.

'Hedd Wyn'
'Mater Mea'
'The Draft'

Poems from *Yr Haf a Cherddi Eraill* (1924).

'P. E. G.'

'1918, Forward'

'1918, Forward' appeared in the *Western Mail*, January 1, 1918.

Colwyn Philipps

Captain Colwyn Erasmus Arnold Philipps was the elder son of John Wynford Philipps, 1st Baron St David's, and Leonora his wife. He was born on December 11, 1888, and educated at Eton College. Colwyn Philipps was commissioned into the Royal

Horse Guards in October 1908. At the beginning of November 1914 he was at the Ypres Salient, and after leave in England in December 1914 and in February 1915, he rejoined his battalion in the Ypres Salient. He was killed in action near Ypres, on May 13, 1915.

Extracts from *Verses: Prose Fragments: Letters from the Front* (1916)

'Release'
'To Mother'

Poems from *Verses: Prose Fragments: Letters from the Front.*

A. G. PRYS-JONES
Arthur Glyn Prys-Jones was born in Denbigh, North Wales, in 1888, but the family moved to Pontypridd, Glamorganshire, when he was nine years of age. He was educated at Llandovery College and Jesus College, Oxford. He taught History and English at grammar schools in Macclesfield and Walsall, and also at Dulwich, London, and then entered the Welsh Inspectorate of Schools.

He published several volumes of verse and books on Welsh history. He died in 1987.

'A Song of the Welsh'

'A Song of the Welsh' appeared in the *Western Mail,* March 1, 1916.

ERNEST RHYS
Ernest Percival Rhys was born in Islington in 1859. His father came from Carmarthen, and Ernest Rhys spent six of his childhood years in his father's home town. He trained as a mining engineer in the North of England, but decided in 1886 to become a journalist and writer. He was very much a part of London literary society, and in 1891 he established 'The Rhymers' Club' with W. B. Yeats and T. W. Rolleston.

Ernest Rhys was appointed to edit the 'Everyman Library' series by Dent in 1908, and he produced 983 titles in his capacity as editor. According to his friend Ezra Pound, he had sacrificed his talent to weave 'Welsh gold' because he had devoted so much of his time to editorial work and hackwork. He published six volumes of verse, and also wrote novels, two of which have a Welsh background, *The Whistling Maid* (1900) and *The Man at Odds* (1904). He published two autobiographies, *Everyman Remembers* (1931) and *Wales England Wed* (1940), also two school textbooks, *Readings in Welsh Literature* (1924) and *Readings in Welsh History* (1927). He translated poems from Welsh into English and contributed to *Welsh Poets*, edited by A. G. Prys-Jones (1917). He died in 1946.

'A. R. P.'
'Music's Remonstrance'
'Lost in France: Jo's Requiem'

Poems from *The Leaf Burners and Other Poems* (1918).

FRANK RICHARDS
Frank Richards, whose real name was Francis Philip Woodruff, was born in 1883 and brought up by his aunt and uncle in Monmouthshire. He joined the Royal Welsh Fusiliers in April 1901 and served in India and Burma from 1902 to 1909 when, having completed his seven years with the colours, he was transferred to the reserves. He extended his service for a further four years until 1912.

A reservist soldier when war broke out in August 1914, working as a timber assistant, Richards was reattached to the 2nd Battalion of the Royal Welsh Fusiliers, in which he remained for the duration of the war. He saw action in most of the major British campaigns on the Western Front without suffering any notable injury.

In 1933 he published *Old Soldiers Never Die*, his account of the war from the viewpoint of the regular soldier. It was written with the uncredited assistance of Robert Graves. He also published another memoir, *Old Soldier Sahib*, in 1936. He died in 1961.

Extracts from *Old Soldiers Never Die* (1933)

GLYN C. ROBERTS

Glyn C. Roberts was the son of the Reverend Peter Jones Roberts, Book Steward of the Wesleyan Bookroom at Bangor, North Wales. Glyn Roberts had been educated at Friars School, Bangor, and Kingswood School, Bath, before he entered the University College of Bangor, with a scholarship, and was reading for Honours in Latin and French when he accepted a commission as a 2nd Lieutenant in the 9th (Service) Battalion of the Royal Welsh Fusiliers in the second month of the war. He went to France in July 1915. He was killed at the Battle of the Somme, in July 1916, at La Boiselle, near Contalmaison, while rushing to the assistance of a fellow officer. He had three brothers who also served on the Western Front, but all three survived the war, although one brother, Aubrey, was taken prisoner of war in December 1916. Their father also served as a chaplain on the Western Front.

Extracts from *Witness These Letters: Letters from the Western Front 1915-18* (1983)

PATRICK SHAW-STEWART

Patrick Shaw-Stewart was born on August 17, 1888, the son of Major-General John Heron Maxwell Shaw-Stewart and Mary Catherine Bedingfield, at Llanenddwyn, on the Meirionydd coast. He was educated at Eton and Balliol College, Oxford, with Julian Grenfell, the poet who was killed on the Western Front in May 1915. Shaw-Stewart was a brilliant scholar who left Balliol with a First in Greats. He volunteered for the newly formed Royal Naval Division in September 1914. In December 1914 he was sent to Blandford Camp in Dorset to join the Hood Battalion, of which his friend, Rupert Brooke, was also a member. In February 1915 the Hood Battalion left for the Dardanelles and landed at Cape Helles on April 29, but the Gallipoli campaign was unsuccessful, and after heavy losses the remaining Allied troops were evacuated from Gallipoli during December 1916 and the beginning of January 1917. Shaw-Stewart was then posted to Salonika to work as a liaison officer with the French. He became Lieutenant-Commander in the Royal Naval Division a short while before he was killed in France on December 30, 1917. He was buried in Metz-en-Couture Communal Cemetery British Extension in France.

Extracts from *Patrick Shaw-Stewart* (1920)

'I Saw a Man this Morning' from *Patrick Shaw-Stewart*.

EDWARD THOMAS

Edward Thomas was born in Lambeth, London, of Welsh parents in 1878. His father was a civil servant with the Board of Trade. Edward Thomas was educated at St Paul's School and Lincoln College, Oxford. He married Helen Noble, the daughter of his mentor, James Ashcroft Noble, in 1899. He earned a meagre living as a reviewer and essayist, and a writer of biographies and topographical works. He gave his three children Welsh names – Merfyn, Bronwen and Myfanwy. He was a friend of Rupert Brooke, Gordon Bottomley, W. H. Davies and other well-known Georgian poets. In 1914 he met Robert Frost, the American poet who was at the time renting a cottage near the village of Dymock in Gloucestershire, and it was Frost who encouraged and inspired Edward Thomas to write poetry. Edward Thomas wrote all his poetry during the war years, between December 1914 and January 1917. In July 1915 he enlisted in the Artists' Rifles, and was promoted to Corporal in March 1916. In August 1916 he was commissioned as a 2nd Lieutenant in 244th Siege Battery, Royal Garrison Artillery. He was killed at Arras on Easter Monday, April 9, 1917, by the blast of a shell, and was buried in Agny Military Cemetery, France.

Extract from 'Tipperary', *The Last Sheaf* (1928)
Extracts from *The Diary of Edward Thomas* (1971)
Extracts from *Edward Thomas: the Last Four Years* (Eleanor Farjeon, 1958)

'A Private'
'As the Team's Head-Brass'
'Gone, Gone Again'
'No One Cares Less Than I'
'The Cherry Trees'
'The Green Roads'
'The Trumpet'
'This is no case of petty right or wrong'

Poems from *Collected Poems* (1920).

MARGARET HAIG THOMAS

Margaret Haig Thomas was the only daughter of David Alfred Thomas, Lord Rhondda, and Sybil Haig. She was born in 1883 and was educated at Notting Hill High School and St Andrews and Somerville College, Oxford. She married Humphrey Mackworth in 1908. Four months later she joined the Women's Social and Political Union, and was sent to prison for attempting to destroy a post-box with a chemical bomb. A hunger-strike led to her early release. In May 1915 she was returning with her father from the United States on the *Lusitania* when it was torpedoed by a German submarine. Both father and daughter were rescued. Her father had been sent to the United States by D. Lloyd George to arrange the supply of munitions for the British armed forces. Margaret Haig Thomas died in 1958.

Extract from *This Was My World* (1933)

'T.O.M.'
'The Fallen Petal'

'The Fallen Petal' appeared in the *Western Mail*, July 18, 1916.

UNNAMED MEMBER OF THE WELSH CYCLIST SCOUTS
Letter to a friend in Cardiff

LEWIS VALENTINE

Lewis Valentine was born in Llanddulas, near Denbigh, in 1893. His studies at the University College of Wales, Bangor, were interrupted by the war, and, like A. E. Jones (Cynan) and several others, he joined the special Welsh unit of the R.A.M.C. He enlisted at Rhyl, North Wales, on January 8, 1916, and served in Belgium, France and Ireland. He initially supported the war, but soon became disillusioned. He returned from the war an ardent pacifist and nationalist, and became a Baptist minister. He was a member of the group of nationalists who founded *Plaid Genedlaethol Cymru* ('The National Party of Wales') in 1925, later to become known as Plaid Cymru. Lewis Valentine was elected the first president of the new political party, and he was also its first candidate, in 1929. In 1936, Lewis Valentine D. J. Williams and Saunders Lewis set part of the Bombing School at Penyberth, in the Llŷn peninsula in North Wales, on fire as a protest against the Air Ministry's plans to violate what was then a very strong Welsh-speaking area. All three participants served a prison sentence of nine months. Lewis Valentine died in 1986.

Extract from *Dyddiadur Milwr a Gweithiau Eraill* (A Soldier's Diary and Other Works).

MORGAN WATCYN-WILLIAMS

Morgan Watcyn-Williams was born in 1891 and brought up in Cardiff. He lost his mother at an early age and he and his brother were brought up by their father, a Calvinistic Methodist minister. The family moved from Cardiff to Pontypool, Monmouthshire, when Morgan Watcyn-Williams's father accepted an invitation to minister the St David's Hall church there. In 1909, Watcyn-Williams was accepted as a candidate for the ministry and entered the University College of South Wales at Cardiff. In September 1914 he joined the 21st (Public Schools) Battalion of the Royal Welsh Fusiliers. He served in France from November 1915 to March 1916, and was then sent for officer training to Cambridge. He was then posted to the Royal Welsh Fusiliers at Kinmel Park, Rhyl, North Wales, and returned to France in September 1916 with the 10th Battalion. He was wounded by a shell splinter in his left eye at Zonnebeke in 1917 and was invalided home

At the beginning of October 1918, he went to the University College of Wales, Aberystwyth, to pursue a year's course in Theology, and soon after commenced his ministerial career at Nolton Presbyterian Church, Bridgend, before moving to Merthyr Tydfil in 1923 'to take charge of two small struggling missions'. He died in 1938.

Extracts from *Khaki to Cloth* (1948)

E. WILLIAMS-DAVID

'In Memoriam (R. G. Popkin, killed in action, 27th September, 1918)'

'In Memoriam (R. G. Popkin, killed in action, 27th September, 1918)' appeared in *The Welsh Outlook*, vol. vi, December 1919.